BEYOND MANAGEMENT COMPLIANCE

Organizational Conformity for Business Legitimacy

BEYOND MANAGEMENT COMPLIANCE

Organizational Conformity for Business Legitimacy

Petter Gottschalk
BI Norwegian Business School, Norway

World Scientific

NEW JERSEY • LONDON • SINGAPORE • BEIJING • SHANGHAI • HONG KONG • TAIPEI • CHENNAI • TOKYO

Published by

World Scientific Publishing Europe Ltd.
57 Shelton Street, Covent Garden, London WC2H 9HE
Head office: 5 Toh Tuck Link, Singapore 596224
USA office: 27 Warren Street, Suite 401-402, Hackensack, NJ 07601

Library of Congress Cataloging-in-Publication Data
Names: Gottschalk, Petter, 1950– author
Title: Beyond management compliance : organizational conformity for business legitimacy / Petter Gottschalk.
Description: USA : WORLD SCIENTIFIC (EUROPE), 2026. | Includes bibliographical references and index.
Identifiers: LCCN 2026012496 | ISBN 9781800619500 hardcover | ISBN 9781800619517 ebook | ISBN 9781800619524 ebook other
Subjects: LCSH: Corporate governance--Law and legislation | Business ethics | Commercial crimes--Prevention | Sports--Corrupt practices
Classification: LCC K1327 .G66 2026
LC record available at https://lccn.loc.gov/2026012496

British Library Cataloguing-in-Publication Data
A catalogue record for this book is available from the British Library.

For any available supplementary material, please visit
https://www.worldscientific.com/worldscibooks/10.1142/Q0573#t=suppl

Desk Editors: Aanand Jayaraman/Cian Sacker Ooi

Typeset by Stallion Press
Email: enquiries@stallionpress.com

About the Author

Petter Gottschalk is a professor in the Department of Leadership and Organizational Behaviour at BI Norwegian Business School in Oslo, Norway. He has served as the president and chief executive officer at major corporate business enterprises and held several important chair positions on public boards. Dr Gottschalk received his education at Technische Universität Berlin, Henley Management College, Massachusetts Institute of Technology, and Dartmouth College. He has published extensively on convenience theory, knowledge management, corporate investigations, and economic crime.

Contents

About the Author v

Introduction xi

Chapter 1 Alignment with Laws and Norms **1**
1.1 Management Compliance Characteristics 2
1.2 Organizational Conformity Characteristics 10
1.3 Business Legitimacy Characteristics 21
References 24

Chapter 2 Corruption in Sport Perspectives **33**
2.1 Seven Causes of Corruption in Sport 33
2.2 Consequences of Corruption in Sport 39
2.3 Actions against Corruption in Sport 40
2.4 Issues in District Court Verdict 43
References 46

Chapter 3 The Prosecuted Sport President **51**
3.1 Replacing Defense Lawyers at Appeal 52
3.2 The International Biathlon Union 54
3.3 Court Verdict of Sixty-Seven Pages 56
3.4 The Rotten Apple Metaphor 58
References 63

Chapter 4 Case: BMW as Biathlon Sponsor **67**
4.1 Concern by Sponsors as Stakeholders 68
4.2 Notification to Compliance Officer 74

4.3 Compliance – Conformity – Transparency 81
4.4 Ice Communications as Biathlon Sponsor 84
References 90

Chapter 5 Facing Harassment Accusations 95
5.1 Top Academic Coming to Norway 97
5.2 CMS Kluge Report Accusation Findings 99
5.3 CMS Kluge Report Maturity Assessment 100
5.4 Maturity Assessment Outcome 111
5.5 Problematic Internal Investigation 116
5.6 Preparing for Oslo Court Trial 118
5.7 Reporting from Oslo Court Trial 120
References 126

Chapter 6 The Fraud Investigation Business 133
6.1 Deviance by Corporate Investigators 134
6.2 Investigation Compliance Characteristics 138
6.3 Investigation Conformity Characteristics 139
References 141

Chapter 7 Case: Sanctions against Russia 147
7.1 Boycotted versus Blacklisted Companies 148
7.2 Conformity Debate in the Media 151
7.3 State for Compliance Not Conformity 154
7.4 Some Conformity beyond Compliance 156
References 158

Chapter 8 Case: Sanctions against Myanmar 161
8.1 Challenging the Social License 163
8.2 Bestseller's Convenience Themes 164
8.3 The Fraud Investigation Report 167
8.4 Regaining the Social License 169
References 171

Chapter 9 Case: Member Revolt in Housing 173
9.1 Criminal Conformity Deviance 174
9.2 Obos Deviance Member Revolt 176
9.3 Social License Recovery Measures 181
9.4 Student Interviews with Stakeholders 187
9.5 Internal Investigation Outcome 192

9.6 Assessment of Offender Convenience 193
9.7 Assessment of Examination Maturity 200
References 202

Chapter 10 JFC Research Articles **209**
10.1 The Crime Convenience Triangle 210
10.2 Research Method for Reviewing Articles 213
10.3 Research Result: Crime Motives 214
10.4 Research Result: Crime Opportunities 216
10.5 Research Result: Willingness Attitudes 223
10.6 Future Research on Offender Perspectives 225
References 228

Chapter 11 Deviant Behavior Willingness **239**
11.1 Research Method for Reviewing Articles 241
11.2 Research Result: Attitudes in JEC Articles 242
11.3 Research Result: Attitudes in JWCCC Articles 243
11.4 Research Result: Attitudes in JFC Articles 246
11.5 Future Research on Crime Justification 248
References 251

Conclusion 257

Index 267

Introduction

While compliance is a matter of behaving in accordance with legal regulations by not violating laws, conformity is a matter of behaving in accordance with social expectations by not violating norms. Compliance secures the legal license to operate, while conformity secures the social license to operate. Legitimacy is then a matter of acceptance by society of organizational behavior. While scholars have long suggested that various entities move beyond management compliance into organizational conformity for business legitimacy, many public and private entities struggle with both compliance and conformity, as exemplified by case studies in this book. Violating legal and other formal obligations and violating societal and other informal norms and obligations often occur together in gray criminological zones. The gray zones exist because "crime" in criminology is defined as behavior constituting actions considered wrong and punishable, while crime in legal terms is defined as behavior that violates laws and other formal obligations. In legal terms, an action is not a crime if there is no law or formal obligation to behave otherwise.

This book begins in Chapter 1 by addressing alignment for both the legal license by compliance and the social license by conformity. The book continues in Chapters 2–4, exemplifying the challenge of moving beyond organizational compliance into conformity for business legitimacy, as illustrated by the case of the International Biathlon Union (IBU) and the BMW car company as its sponsor. At the IBU, rumors of corruption developed into criminal charges against IBU president Anders Besseberg, who is, at the time of writing, on trial. In nations with criminal justice systems, a defendant is considered innocent in legal terms until eventually receiving a final conviction verdict in court. At the BMW company, it did not withdraw from its sponsorship despite allegations of corrupt practices at the IBU.

The IBU is headquartered in Austria. Besseberg is a Norwegian citizen and served as president of the IBU from 1992 to 2018. In 2024, at the age of 77, he was prosecuted for corruption in a district court in Norway. The judges sentenced him to a prison term of three years and one month (Buskerud tingrett, 2024). Besseberg appealed the verdict, and the case was admitted for a complete retrial at the Borgarting Court of Appeal, scheduled for the following year (Christiansen, 2024):

> Three luxury watches, a free BMW, Russian prostitutes and a number of exclusive hunting trips in Europe will once again become topics. It is one of these watches that Besseberg is now said to have removed from the appeal, and pleaded guilty to, according to first state prosecutor Marianne Djupesland.
>
> We notice that the consequence of this does not seem to have been considered by the appeal committee. We are now taking a closer look at the significance of this for the further proceedings, she tells VG.

The watch in question was an Omega in gold that was worth approximately USD 19,000. It was in 2011, during board meeting number 100 of the IBU in Khanty-Mansiyk in Russia, that IBU president Besseberg received the watch as a gift from an official in the Russian Biathlon Federation. Besseberg did explain in the district court that watches were common presents on various occasions (Buskerud tingrett, 2024: 14):

> The defendant has explained more generally that watches have commonly been given as gifts on various occasions. According to the defendant, this applied on various occasions, such as if someone is to leave or it is a round year. The defendant has also personally received watches. The defendant saw it as a recognition for his efforts in biathlon. In his explanation, the defendant mentioned that he had made great and "unselfish effort" on his own part.

The watch was given to him by the Russian Sergey Kushchenko. Besseberg unwrapped it when he came home to Norway. According to his explanation in court, he had no interest in watches and therefore kept them lying around his home. Kushchenko had given Besseberg the Omega watch because Besseberg had just managed the 100th meeting and recently celebrated his 65th birthday. Besseberg said in district court that he thought he deserved the gift, or at least that it was not undeserved. He stated more generally that he believed everyone likes to be appreciated for what they do. Regarding the issue of transparency concerning the receipt of the gift, he explained that he perceived the gift to be from the wealthy Kushchenko and not from the Russian Biathlon Federation. The court disagreed and found him guilty of corruption for accepting the Omega gift since "here lies the possibility of influence in the direction of Russian biathlon" (Buskerud tingrett, 2024: 16).

The trial at the Borgarting Court of Appeal was scheduled for April and May 2025, and the sentence could be expected some months later. The losing party – whether defendant Besseberg or prosecutor Djupesland – was likely to appeal the verdict to the Norwegian Supreme Court. Since the criminal case has principal issues regarding both facts and laws, the case would probably be admitted at the Supreme Court. Then, a final verdict cannot be expected until 2026 or 2027.

The gray zone in the IBU case became visible when private investigators were hired to review the allegations of corruption. The Taylor (2021) report by the investigators claimed that wrongdoing and misconduct had occurred. The media quickly jumped to conclusions in the report by considering the IBU president Besseberg guilty (e.g., Panja, 2021, in *The New York Times*, United States). Media coverage continued to rely on the private investigation report (e.g., Dahlkamp and Latsch, 2024a, 2024b, in *Der Spiegel* in Germany; and MacInnes, 2024, in *The Guardian* in the UK) by considering Besseberg guilty of criminal charges.

The IBU case is interesting from this book's perspective on organizational conformity beyond mere management compliance for business legitimacy. Management compliance is currently being tested in Norwegian courts regarding the case involving the former president, with the district court case in 2024 moving to the court of appeal in 2025 and potentially to the Norwegian Supreme Court in 2026, which might return the case to a different court of appeal for a final verdict in 2027. The compliance issue is whether or not the former president can be convicted of corruption if the evidence meets requirements under Norwegian law. Organizational conformity at the IBU is somewhat independent of the legal issues. The IBU established an integrity unit and published ethical guidelines.

The new IBU president was more reasonably compensated financially. Conformity can now lead to legitimacy, referring to the acceptance of behavior by IBU executives.

The IBU case is also interesting from the perspective of corporate investigator Taylor (2021), who had already concluded on corruption long before the police charged the former IBU president. The biased report influenced perceptions of deviance at the IBU, prompting efforts to restore its social license, as described above. Scholars have long discussed the problematic role of private investigators paid by client organizations to conduct internal reviews (e.g., Button *et al.*, 2023; Meerts, 2021).

The next case study in Chapter 5 is concerned with an internal investigation by private reviewers in which the investigated individual at a university was unable to dispute the investigators' allegations against her. University management used the investigation report in a court trial to justify dismissal of the faculty member. Problems concerning compliance and conformity related to employment law and leadership style are important issues in the case study.

The gray zone of overlap between compliance and conformity is visible in transnational misconduct, where an act may be considered both a law violation and a norm violation in some countries but not in others. As mentioned above, crime, in legal terms, is present only when a formal law is violated, while in criminology, it is present when the wrongdoing is considered punishable. A typical example is corruption, which is considered a crime globally; however, some countries have no laws against it, some countries have only criminalized the briber, others have only criminalized the bribed, and still others have criminalized both the briber and the bribed. Another typical example is prostitution, which is considered harmful globally; however, some countries have no laws against it, some countries have only criminalized the sex worker, some countries have criminalized only the sex buyer, and others have criminalized both the sex worker and the sex buyer. Given this magnitude of differences in legal terms, there is a need to look beyond compliance into conformity, as discussed in this book.

A recent example illustrates the issue of compliance versus conformity. Beaching of ships is illegal in Norway but not in India. Therefore, a Norwegian shipowner was beaching two ships in India. The prosecutor in Norway charged the company with a criminal offense and fined it NOK 8 million (USD 800,000) to the Norwegian state. The company first decided to dispute the charge. A few days before the trial, the company accepted the fine but denied any wrongdoing. The acceptance seemed more to be a result of conformity rather than compliance. The prosecutor at the Norwegian national authority for investigation and prosecution of economic and environmental crime (Økokrim) nevertheless issued the following press release on December 9, 2024, with the heading "Norwegian company fined for beaching two ships" (www.okokrim.no):

> A Stavanger-based management company has accepted a fine of NOK 8 million for violating pollution regulations. The case concerns the export of two ships to India. Both ships have operated as loading buoys in the North Sea for a number of years. Oil companies do not allow buoy loaders older than 20 years to be used for storage and transport of oil, and the ships were therefore not allowed to renew their contracts. The two ships sailed from Norwegian waters towards Asia shortly before they turned 20 years and their class certificates expired. The sale for scrapping took place while the ships were in storage in Sri Lanka. Both ships were broken up on a beach in Alang, India, between 2018 and 2020.

This type of ship breaking is called beaching and is considered a serious environmental crime. The ships are driven onto the beach using their own power, and then they are broken up in the tidal zone. Beaching of decommissioned ships is considered a major international environmental problem, which seems to have significant negative environmental consequences, including for local ecosystems. The scrapping causes pollution, such as the release of heavy metals. Environmentalists question whether hazardous waste from scrapping activities is properly treated after ship dismantling. In addition, beaching activities also pose a high risk of occupational injuries for local workers. The prosecutor, Maria Bache Dahl, argued in the press release that an accepted fine has the same effect as a criminal conviction.

The company, though, clarified that they did not admit criminal liability, even though they accepted the fine. The shipping management company Altera, formerly known as Teekay Offshore, said the fine did not make sense (Malm and Ogre, 2024):

> — We are very surprised, and we do not agree with Økokrim's conclusion, says communications manager Steffen Rogne at Altera. He says this is not about waste, but fully functioning ships that had many years left.
> — They were therefore to be rebuilt in Asia. We are investing a lot of resources and time in this. We do not admit any guilt.

Many more examples exist where law violations are not obvious, yet accused entities accept changes in practice due to conformity issues rather than compliance issues. For example, the clothing firm Bestseller in Denmark did not violate legal sanctions against Myanmar, yet the public found it socially unacceptable that the Danish firm was manufacturing clothes in facilities run by the military junta. Bestseller decided to withdraw from Myanmar, leaving hundreds of employees without work and income to support their families (Meixler and Creery, 2022). Another example is Mondelez in Switzerland, which decided not to withdraw from Russia while blacklisted in Ukraine. Instead, in response to pressure to conform, the Swiss producer of sweets made the business in Russia more independent, stating that "products sold in Russia are now produced and distributed locally, with no imports of finished goods from Europe to Russia or exports from Russia to Europe" (Ostiller, 2024).

This book argues that management compliance is not sufficient for business legitimacy. Legitimacy stems from the alignment of values and actions with those of a company's stakeholders and society. Business activities are then considered legitimate in the eyes of society (Saenz, 2019). Alignment with laws and regulations is not sufficient for legitimacy. People do not trust companies simply because they do not violate laws. When trust is defined as "a willingness to be vulnerable and accept risk in relationships" that is typically motivated by an expectation of a positive outcome (Legood *et al.*, 2023: 1), an organization has to move beyond compliance into conformity.

An example is the corporate investigation industry itself, as discussed in Chapter 6. There are both compliance issues and conformity issues in the fraud investigation business. While corporate investigators are in the business of reviewing compliance and conformity issues within client organizations, their own compliance and conformity have been questioned by scholars. For example, many corporate investigators are suspected of illegally gathering information (Kapend *et al.*, 2024). In 2023, corporate investigators in the UK were accused of illegally bugging phones, intercepting communications, and "blagging" – impersonating someone else to gain access to restricted areas or systems and obtain information. Private investigators make "widespread use of illegal information-gathering", exemplified by private investigator Gavin Borrows, who said that "he and his team obtained information, hacked voicemails, tapped landline phones and bugged cars" (Waterson, 2023).

Organizational conformity for business legitimacy beyond management compliance is illustrated in three case studies in Chapters 7–9. The first case study addresses the differences between sanctions and blacklists during the war in Ukraine. While companies had to obey sanctions, it was voluntary whether they would obey the blacklist. Sanctions relate to compliance, while blacklists relate to conformity. Stakeholders reacted. Then, companies implemented conformity measures. The second case study presents a clothing store chain in Denmark that sourced its garments from factories controlled by the military junta in Myanmar. While the procurement of garments was not part of the sanctions against Myanmar, many stakeholders in Denmark reacted to the clothing firm's business there. Then, the company implemented conformity measures. The third and final case study in Chapter 9 presents a social housing company in Norway that was in the business of building simple homes for ordinary people. Suddenly, the new management began building luxury homes for wealthy individuals and selling complete apartment blocks to a commercial rental enterprise. Stakeholders did not like it. Then, the company implemented conformity measures.

Chapters 10 and 11 review research addressing compliance and conformance violations in relevant journals. Chapter 10 reviews recently published articles in the *Journal of Financial Crime* in 2024, where the journal published four issues containing 69 research articles during that year. While only 12 articles focused on the motives, possibilities, and threats, and only 6 articles focused on attitudes of deviant willingness, surprisingly many – 51 articles – focused on the opportunity structure of committing and concealing financial crime. The review is relevant, as it may illuminate both what seems important and unimportant in understanding management violations of compliance and conformance. It also explores propositions within convenience theory that warrant attention in future research, considering the convenience triangle's suggested motives, opportunities, and attitudes for financial criminals. The theory of convenience for financial crime suggests that offenders have motives of possibilities and threats, opportunities to commit and conceal crime, and attitudes of willingness for deviant behavior driven by choice and innocence. Convenience theory suggests 14 propositions regarding motives, opportunities, and attitudes. In this chapter, research articles from the *Journal of Financial Crime* are reviewed from the perspective of convenience theory. Specifically, the chapter addresses the following research questions: What propositions in convenience theory are supported by published articles in the journal? What aspects of criminal convenience seem to be missing so far in research articles published in the journal?

Finally, Chapter 11 combines research from three academic journals that primarily publish articles on crime for profit: the *Journal of Economic Criminology*, the *Journal of White Collar and Corporate Crime*, and the *Journal of Financial Crime*. Research articles in these journals are reviewed in this chapter to identify offender attitudes that contribute to a willingness for deviant behavior when committing and concealing economic crimes. The theory of convenience is applied, suggesting five willingness propositions addressing choice (personal identity, rational choice, and learning from others) and innocence (justification and neutralization). Deviant personal identity is exemplified by psychopathic and narcissistic traits, as well as Machiavellian personality traits. Rational choice is exemplified by the lack of perceived deterrence. Learning from others is exemplified by differential association. Justification is exemplified by a lack of crime seriousness, while neutralization is exemplified by romance fraudsters in Ghana who cause no perceived harm, as victims in Western countries have access to safety nets such as social welfare and other benefits.

References

Buskerud tingrett (2024). Court case number 23-03940MED-TBUS/THOK, *Buskerud tingrett* (Buskerud district court), professional judge Vidar Toftøy-Lohne, lay judges Kari Aasen Ingebo and Gunnar Sanden, Hokksund, Norway, verdict document, p. 67.

Button, M., Kapend, R. and Stiernsted, P. (2023). Investigative private policing beyond the police: An exploratory study, *Policing and Society*, 33(2), 150–169.

Christiansen, A.K. (2024). Aktor: Besseberg trekker klokke-anke (Prosecutor: Besseberg withdraws watch appeal), Norwegian daily newspaper *VG*, www.vg.no, published October 15.

Dahlkamp, J. and Latsch, G. (2024a). Prozess gegen ehemaligen Biathlon-Weltverbandchef: Uhren, Prostituierte, Trophäenjagden (Process against former biathlon union chief: Watches, prostitutes, trophy hunts), German magazine *Der Spiegel*, www.spiegel.de, published January 12.

Dahlkamp, J. and Latsch, G. (2024b). Blattschuss beim Pinkeln (Leaf shot while peeing), German magazine *Der Spiegel*, number 8, February 17, pp. 84–85.

Kapend, R., Button, M. and Stiernstedt, P. (2024). Private investigations and ethical orientations: A cause for concern? *Journal of Financial Crime*, published first online https://doi.org/10.108/JFC-02-2024-0066.

Legood, A., Werff, L., Lee, A. and Hartog, D.D. (2023). A meta-analysis of the role of trust in the leadership-performance relationship, *European Journal of Work and Organizational Psychology*, 30(1), 1–22.

MacInnes, P. (2024). Fifa ignores own report into Qatar World Cup over workers' compensation, *The Guardian*, www.theguardian.com, published November 30.

Malm, M. and Ogre, M. (2024). Stavanger-selskap får 8 millioner i bot for ulovlig skipseksport (Stavanger company fined 8 million for illegal ship export), web-based Norwegian newspaper *E24*, www.e24.no, published June 10.

Meerts, C.A. (2021). Struggles in cooperation: Public-private relations in the investigation of internal financial crime in the Netherlands, in: Lord, N., Inzelt, E., Huisman, W. and Faria, R. (editors), *European White-Collar Crime: Exploring the Nature of European Realities*, Bristol University Press, Bristol, UK.

Meixler, E. and Creery, J. (2022). EU targets Myanmar's lucrative energy sector in latest sanctions, *The Financial Times*, www.ft.com, published February 22.

Ostiller, N. (2024). Reuters: Oreos manufacturer Mondelez overhauls Russian operations amid boycott, protests, *The Kyiv Independent*, www.kyivindependent.com, published February 17.

Panja, T. (2021). Hunting trips, sex and cash: How grooming biathlon's leader paid off for Russia – An investigation accuses biathlon's longtime president of accepting gifts from Russians and then doing the country's bidding as a doping scandal swirled, *The New York Times*, www.nytimes.com, published January 28.

Saenz, C. (2019). Building legitimacy and trust between a mining company and a community to earn social license to operate: A Peruvian case study, *Corporate Social Responsibility and Environmental Management*, 26(2), 296–306.

Taylor, J. (2021). *Final Report of the IBU External Review Commission*, International Biathlon Union, Austria, www.biathlonintegrity.com, jonathan.taylor@twobirds.com, p. 220, January 28.

Waterson, J. (2023). Witness in Prince Harry's case against Daily Mail owner unreliable, says lawyers, *The Guardian*, www.theguardian.com, published March 29.

Chapter 1

Alignment with Laws and Norms

This chapter addresses management alignment for the legal license by compliance and organizational alignment for the social license by conformity. Compliance is alignment to avoid violations of legally binding statutes and is typically pursued through formal controls (Rooij and Fine, 2020). Conformity is alignment to avoid violations of norms and values among stakeholders and in society in general (Durand *et al.*, 2019). Legitimacy stems from the alignment of values and actions with those of a company's stakeholders and society. Business activities are then considered legitimate in the eyes of society (Saenz, 2019).

In recent years, conformity rather than compliance has gained attention in executive suites. While compliance with laws, regulations, statutes, and other formal legal frameworks for corporate activity has been on the agenda for decades (Andreisova, 2016; Majluf and Navarrete, 2011), conformity with norms, values, ethics, and guidelines expected by stakeholders and others in society is now a top priority for executive agendas (Durand *et al.*, 2019; Lewis and Carlos, 2022). An important reason for this shift in focus from compliance to conformity is the speed and severity of damage and harm resulting from breaches and violations of the social license to operate, as compared to violations of the legal license to operate. While a legal process in the criminal justice system addressing corporate wrongdoing tends to last for years before a final outcome is reached, a social process in society addressing corporate misconduct typically has serious consequences within a few days after disclosure, exposure, and condemnation. An example is boycotts of companies quickly mobilizing in social and traditional media as a reaction to corporate misconduct.

Several measures are taken to restore corporate conformity. One of them is termination of top executives by scapegoating them in scandals. For example, in the financial industry, a number of chief executives have been dismissed, including Birgitte Bonnesen at Swedbank in Sweden (Alabi, 2022), Thomas Borgen at Danske Bank in Denmark (Palma and Milne, 2022), Alison Rose at NatWest owning the bank Coutts in the United Kingdom (Makortoff, 2023), and Carrie Tolstedt at Wells Fargo in the United States (Cowley, 2023). As argued by Hersel *et al.* (2023: 642), "dismissing the CEO demonstrates that a firm is addressing a serious problem that requires top-down remediation". They found that executive dismissals are frequently deployed as a crisis management tactic.

1.1 Management Compliance Characteristics

Organizational compliance consists of meeting and potentially exceeding legal and other formal obligations (Teichmann and Wittmann, 2024). According to Durand *et al.* (2019: 300), "compliance relates to formal mandatory regulations that typically enact only minimal conditions of institutional acceptability". They argued that management's attention to compliance might be either symbolic or substantive. Symbolic responses imply management promises to engage in practice changes they have not yet implemented or may not implement, as well as nominal actions to produce impressions of more material change. Symbols are presented artifacts used to portray management in a better light by communicating and influencing support for their efforts and achievements. Symbols are used in impression management when managers release information to distort perceptions of accomplishments (Demaline, 2024). Perceptions refer to the ways in which something is regarded, understood, and interpreted. Impression management refers to the release of information regarding accomplishments to reduce the discrepancy between an organization's desired and perceived professional image (Lim and Jiang, 2021). Impression management aims to generate positive evaluations of the business (Bass *et al.*, 2023).

Symbolic responses differ from substantive responses, as the latter imply management engagement in practice changes (Durand *et al.*, 2019: 300):

> Substantive responses, on the other hand, refer to managers' implementation of significant changes that involve material costs and are not easily reversible, such as revamping deep-seated practices and inefficient distribution processes, or buying and selling divisions.

The term "compliance" can be defined as the act of adhering to a law, rule, guideline, code, demand, or request. In a business environment, legal adherence is referred to as corporate compliance. Corporate compliance involves keeping a watchful eye on an ever-changing legal, regulatory, and moral climate and implementing necessary changes to ensure the business operates in good standing within its industry, community, and customer base to the satisfaction of all stakeholders. Baer (2009: 949) referred to compliance as "the internal programs that organizations adopt in order to educate employees, improve ethical norms, and detect and prevent violations of law".

Corporate compliance is a matter of organizational ability to carry out business activities without violating formal laws, the spirit of the laws, regulations, rules, and other forms of legally guiding principles for the business. Corporate compliance is the ability to lead a group of people toward achieving certain standards of conduct while performing their activities. Corporate compliance programs require monitoring, auditing, corrective actions, and system modifications or redesigns to prevent future problem behavior (Andreisova, 2016; Majluf and Navarrete, 2011; Remisova *et al.*, 2019). A company's intolerance for wrongdoing is evidenced by corporate actions consistent with its corporate compliance efforts.

New legislative rules reshape corporate impacts on society and the natural environment. The new regulations often result from social movements. However, since the strength of legislation may vary in terms of restrictiveness and enforcement, some legislation can be ambiguous regarding both performance requirements and the related means for compliance. Legislation tends to consider all imaginable circumstances and therefore often remains flawed despite the social movements that might have triggered it. Legislative reform is therefore not necessarily the culmination of successful institutional change.

Adding to the challenges of compliance is regulatory complexity. As argued by Lehman *et al.* (2020), rule complexity can prevent compliance. Rule complexity can create a situation where no one is able to tell whether or not an action represents compliance. It is impossible to understand what is right or wrong. Some laws, rules, and regulations are so complex that compliance becomes random. The regulatory legal environment is supposed to define the boundaries of appropriate corporate conduct. However, legal complexity is often so extreme that even specialist compliance officers struggle to understand what to recommend to business executives within their organizations. Then, regulatory inspections do not ensure compliance (Braithwaite, 2020). Business executives can thus find the large gray zone in legal matters a convenient space for misconduct and wrongdoing.

This is particularly true when operating internationally and globally, where states may not agree on what constitutes legal or illegal activities (Boghossian and Marques, 2019; Pontell *et al*., 2020). Eberlein (2019) argued that globalization opens markets for corporations but outstrips the capacity of states to regulate and enforce laws related to cross-border business conduct for the public good. Similarly, Schneider and Scherer (2019: 1147) argued that "the extent to which state authorities can regulate the externalities and the behavior of multinational corporations is limited", and "gaps in governance abound in today's globalized world". There can be an erosion of state power and a shift toward private regulation. National governments are collectively taking limited initiatives through the OECD, European Union, United Nations, World Bank, and other multinational organizations.

Maher *et al*. (2019) found that governments, not only in global business but also in local business, are reluctant to intervene. They observed ambiguity regarding the state's involvement. This is in line with the observation by Pontell *et al*. (2014) that some companies are too big to fail, and some offenders among the elite in society are too powerful to jail.

A lack of compliance represents violations of laws and regulations. It can be a matter of issue salience and profitability in terms of benefits exceeding costs. However, "studies consistently demonstrate that regulations and sanctions directed against the firm can discourage offending" and result in compliance (Rorie *et al*., 2015: 587). In fact, sometimes overcompliance can occur (Rorie, 2015).

One characteristic of corporate compliance, as argued by Fotaki *et al*. (2020: 19), is that compliance can complement corporate governance:

> Compliance, although not sufficient in itself, serves as a complementary mechanism strengthening the effects of ethical values and creating the

> conditions by which instrumental values can act in favor of corporate governance. The results highlight that governance benefits can emanate from maintaining high ethical standards as well as from synergies between compliance and a focus on organizational values.

Many corporations have compliance functions that serve as advisors to management as a governance branch. People in such functions tend to cooperate with internal and external auditors as well as various controllers (Maher *et al.*, 2019; Schneider and Scherer, 2019). Sometimes, they have the task of investigating suspicions by reconstructing past events and sequences of events. If they find sufficient evidence of law violations, then the case stops, moves internally, or moves externally to the criminal justice system. If secrecy to protect corporate reputation is the main concern, then the case typically stops and remains internal. Sanctions can be implemented in complete secrecy.

In addition to the task of investigating suspicions, compliance functions need to conduct compliance audits to develop potential concerns. Compliance audits gauge how well organizations ensure adherence to various applicable laws and other regulatory matters (Thottoli, 2021: 137):

> It helps avoid risk of fines, penalties and closure of business. Compliance audit gives specific attention to assessing compliance by criteria derived from responsible authorities.

Organizations with inefficient or non-existent compliance functions or governance branches generally tend to suffer from disorganized institutional deterioration. An institution is a system of interrelated elements governing relationships between institutional members within which members pursue their mutual interests (Gyõry, 2020).

Compliance risk assessment is about the introduction of a systematic approach to "the entity's identification of relevant risks to achievement of its objectives, forming a basis for determining how risks should be managed" (Marchetti, 2012: 74). Risk assessment processes should consider potential deviant behaviors among board members and corporate executives to safeguard complaint decision-making. As Koller (2005: 28) noted, "fostering a risk assessment process upon an organization will not only change how opportunities or liabilities are assessed but will significantly alter the way an organization makes critical decisions".

Fotaki *et al.* (2020: 23) argued that "compliance with a given set of structural corporate governance regulatory requirements guarantees that the firm adopts the relevant practices to avoid legal liabilities":

> This means that compliance is primarily a quantitative issue, i.e., it denotes the number of corporate governance practices the firm reports that it adopts out of the set of best practices that it adheres to. We argue that compliance can affect the influence of enacted ethical and instrumental values on corporate governance for the following reasons. On one side, compliance with codes of best practices can also provide a compass to principals and agents, educating and guiding them on governance best practice. It defines roles and increases actors' participation in the governance-related issues, activating a process of learning and fostering a culture of corporate governance. (...) On the other hand, compliance safeguards the firm against legal liabilities resulting also in some levels of accountability over the long term. In this context, principals, being usually assigned the monitoring role, have the confidence that agents at least adhere to rules and regulations regarding corporate governance.

This quote reflects on principal–agent relationships and accountability. Agency problems arise when principals and agents have differing risk tolerances and preferences, as well as knowledge asymmetries regarding tasks to be completed. The agency perspective assumes narrow self-interest among both principals and agents. The interests of principals and agents tend to diverge, and each principal has imperfect information about each agent's contribution (Bosse and Phillips, 2016). The above quote suggests that compliance by governance can reduce agency problems. Accountability refers to liability, answerability, and blameworthiness. It is the acknowledgement and assumption of responsibility for actions and decisions. Accountability relates to situations in which someone is required or expected to both explain and justify their actions and decisions (Saifer and Zanoni, 2024). It is concerned with holding them responsible to someone for something (Smith, 2009). Ordonez (2025) discussed horizontal accountability in the public sector as internal state mechanisms of control, where horizontal accountability then refers to "the oversight and sanctions exercised by autonomous state agents over other state agents as a mechanism for combating corruption at the municipal level in Latin America".

Fotaki *et al.* (2020) studied 234 companies listed on the Athens Stock Exchange in Greece. The companies had issued their balance sheets and corporate governance statements. The findings suggest that interactions with compliance by corporate governance enhance the positive effects of ethical values, whereas compliance can also alter the role of instrumental values in favor of corporate governance. The study results suggest that compliance over a period of several years may increase the engagement of principals and agents with their learning of corporate governance issues.

Corporate compliance functions need internal and external intelligence to collect information on a continuous basis to prevent and detect deviant behaviors. Workplace deviance is voluntary behavior that violates significant organizational principles and legal obligations, and in doing so threatens the well-being of an organization, its members, or both. If a corporate compliance function never prevents or detects actual incidents of wrongdoing, then it is likely that incidents escape under the radar (Desai, 2016; Williams *et al.*, 2019), rather than there being a situation characterized by the absence of wrongdoing.

Actors in auditing and compliance functions within business and public enterprises seem to have a preference for formal rules and guidelines in the form of window dressing, rather than detecting potential offenses and offenders (Desai, 2016). Alon *et al.* (2019) argued that accounting and auditing functions have undergone a legitimacy crisis in recent years because of formal rather than substantive financial reviews.

Compliance emerged as an important management topic following a stream of corporate scandals in the United States and many other nations. Companies and their industries adopted internal policies and procedures for reporting and preventing misconduct (Chen and Soltes, 2018: 119):

> Those efforts helped legislators who had sought to more heavily regulate and penalize firms for dishonest practices. Self-policing appealed to business leaders as a way to avoid the cost and disruption of additional regulation. It also eased the investigative burden on regulators, and many people believed it would successfully deter wrongdoing.

But it apparently did not. Compliance programs did not deter wrongdoing. These programs often served primarily as window dressing, creating a clean and professional public image while concealing underlying organizational problems. Chen and Soltes (2018) argued that the solution to this problem is to link compliance initiatives to business objectives.

A distinction can be made between external and internal compliance (Kawasaki, 2020). External compliance is concerned with the laws, rules, and regulations established by a government that spell out how an organization should conduct itself. Internal compliance is concerned with the internal statutes, regulations, policies, and procedures implemented within the organizational structure and culture. Here, "structure" refers to the division of labor in task completion, while "culture" refers to the shared norms among organizational members when completing tasks. It is a matter of external and internal constraints and restraints from control that influence organizational members toward compliance (Abadinsky, 2007).

Engdahl (2013: 332) found that duality in terms of segregation of duties might ensure regulatory compliance in banking and finance:

> Today the segregation of duties is commonly used to ensure regulatory compliance in various industries. (...) The argument is made that an effective duality-based segregation-of-duties type control system presupposes social relations characterized by relative autonomy and third-party dependence, along with work task interdependence.

Corporations have a hierarchy where there is a duty to oblige others and comply with decisions. Hierarchy entails a form of organized power. Organizations can issue commands and can decide upon rules that their members are expected to follow in their actions. Organizations have the right to monitor compliance with commands and rules (Kawasaki, 2020; Rooij and Fine, 2020). They also have the right to impose sanctions, both positive and negative. They can decide to change a member's status using promotions, grading systems, awards, diplomas, and medals. Within this hierarchical perspective, compliance at the top is far more difficult to monitor than compliance at lower organizational levels. For example, chief executive officers (CEOs) typically enjoy substantial individual freedom in their professions with little or no control (Khanna *et al.*, 2004).

In fact, research on white-collar crime has consistently shown that deviance at the top of organizations is much more convenient than further down the hierarchy (Schoultz and Flyghed, 2021; Simpson, 2019; Simpson *et al.*, 2022; Sutherland, 1983; Taylor, 2018; White, 2019). Convenience is a concept primarily associated with efficiency in time and effort. Today, convenience is associated with a number of other characteristics, such as reduced effort and reduced pain. It is linked to terms such as "fast", "easy", and "safe". Convenience says something about attractiveness and accessibility. A convenient individual is not necessarily bad or lazy. On the contrary, the person can be seen as smart and rational (Sundström and Radon, 2015).

Cowen *et al.* (2016: 152) suggested that employment contracts for CEOs should include a clause related to misconduct and wrongdoing:

> For example, a claw back could be triggered by a financial restatement that happens after an executive's dismissal or by new evidence that surfaces indicating he or she engaged in misconduct while serving as CEO. Claw backs can also force terminated executives to repay benefits if there is evidence their actions have violated restrictive covenants.

The popular choice of strengthening the formalistic compliance function in organizations seems to be no substantive action (Eberl *et al.*, 2015: 1207):

> Internal rule adjustments have the potential to signal a voluntary willingness to change the moral standards of an organization, whereas simple compliance with external legal requirements may prove less effective.

Legal remedies generally have little effect on integrity when they are inconsistent with individual and cultural values. Integrity is the quality of acting in accordance with rules that are considered valid and relevant within the context in which the actor operates (Loyens *et al.*, 2021). Integrity is adherence to acceptable and accepted principles for attitudes, behaviors, and actions (Rawski *et al.*, 2024).

Compliance functions are sometimes introduced in companies after being hit by a scandal followed by a crisis. A scandal refers to "an unexpected, publicly known, and harmful event that has high levels of initial uncertainty, interferes with the normal operation of an organization, and generates widespread, intuitive, and negative perceptions" (Bundy and Pfarrer, 2015: 350). A scandal can develop into a crisis, where a crisis refers to a fundamental threat to the organization, which is often characterized by ambiguity of cause, effect, and means of resolution (König *et al.*, 2020). While a scandal is an event, a crisis is a process of "organizational weakening" (Karam *et al.*, 2024: 4). An example is the Icelandic seafood company Samherji, which was involved in corruption for fishing rights outside the coast of Namibia. The scandal developed into a crisis, which led Samherji (2020) to announce a compliance program:

> All operations in Namibia were stopped already in 2019. On 17 January 2020, Samherji announced that it was in the process of launching a modern state-of-the-art compliance program which is being implemented throughout our global organization this year. That work is already well underway. Samherji's ambition is to be a pioneer in compliance, governance and internal control within the global fisheries industries. Samherji will also proactively keep reaching out to relevant authorities that show dedication to mutual cooperation, offering assistance and cooperation during ongoing investigations into the Namibia-related allegations.

Antonsen and Madsen (2021) suggested a maturity model for the compliance function where the function matures from being reactive and inconsistent to becoming a proactive and integrated part of the company's business practices. They defined a number of key enablers of a compliance function in the areas of technology, coordination, policies and processes, resources, and business integrity.

1.2 Organizational Conformity Characteristics

Organizational conformity consists of meeting and potentially exceeding societal and other informal norms and obligations. According to Durand *et al.* (2019: 300), "conformity characterizes voluntary actions that constitute a response to social and normative expectations not (yet) codified in standards and law". Conformity entails organizational members' "modified belief, behavior, or cognition to align with that of salient others or with prevailing normative standards" where it is a matter of "matching attitudes, beliefs, and behaviors to group norms or politics" (Hollebeek *et al.*, 2022: 92).

Conformity characterizes voluntary actions that constitute a response to social and normative expectations (Durand *et al.*, 2019; Rorie, 2015; Rorie *et al.*, 2015). Conformity is the concept of delivering results within acceptable limits as defined by requirements (Pedersen *et al.*, 2013). The term "conformity" has the same meaning as "conformance" and is similar to "congruence", "agreement", and "harmony". Conformity is behavior in accordance with socially accepted conventions. It is keeping or changing beliefs, attitudes, actions, or perceptions to match those held by others whose approval is desired.

Organizational conformity may result from social and normative pressures. Similar to the issue of management attention to compliance, organizational attention to conformity could be either symbolic or substantive. A symbol is an object, artifact, or phrase to portray the company in a better light. Symbols can take the form of words, sounds, gestures, or visual images. Symbolic conformity aligns with window dressing, which refers to the act or instance of making something appear better than it actually is (Eberl *et al.*, 2015). Substance is the real thing with unique properties. Substantive actions require a greater extent of resource mobilization to close other avenues in response to normative pressures. Symbolic versus substantive conformance was discussed by Augustine *et al.* (2025) in terms of the impact of social movements on organizations, which the authors labeled "upstream" and "downstream" conformance. Upstream conformance refers to symbolic concessions by management when confronted with activist stakeholders, while downstream conformance refers to the institutionalization of activist demands within organizations. Institutionalization is the process of embedding activist requirements within an organization as a system of interrelated formal elements – rules, guidelines, norms, traditions, and beliefs – that govern relationships among institutional members and enable them to pursue their mutual interests (Ashforth and Humphrey, 2022; Gyõry, 2020), thereby altering the nature of the organization toward alignment with broader stakeholder values and norms. In contrast to upstream conformance, downstream conformance is thus a matter of institutionalization (Augustine *et al.*, 2025: 26):

> In contrast to this focus on upstream movement processes that involve the mobilization efforts that generate initial concessions, downstream movement processes refer to the implementation, operationalization, and scaling of movement demands, or the institutionalization of movement priorities.

Corporate business conformity is the ability of corporate processes to meet the desired and required specifications indicated by stakeholders.

The specifications represent an interpretation of what stakeholders expect. The term "stakeholder" refers to someone who has an interest or concern in something, especially in business (Gomulya and Mishina, 2017). A stakeholder is someone who can affect or be affected by the business, and a stakeholder is someone who associates with the business and does or does not derive utility from that association (Lange *et al.*, 2022).

Acceptance of business operations is a matter of corporate conformity (Lewis and Carlos, 2022). Durand *et al.* (2019: 314) argued that institutional conformity adaptation to normative pressures is stronger than "the more traditional list of strategic responses to institutional pressures". Normative institutional pressure is concerned with conformity, where deviance is disliked, disapproved, or even dismissed (Witt *et al.*, 2022). Deviance refers to deviant behaviors that violate social norms, values, obligations, and expectations. Corporate deviance is a form of organizational misconduct that represents a critical intersection of societal norms, corporate behavior, and public accountability. It is based on organizational practices that violate ethical expectations and standards in society. Conformity can represent a reaction to pressure that results from professionalization and socialization, implying a collective process of establishing a shared base of values and norms.

At this stage of discussing values for conformance, it is important to reflect on the term values itself as both desirable states and desirable processes (Espedal and Carlsen, 2024: 1077):

> With values, researchers typically discuss emotionally laden conceptions of the desirable that are worth having, doing, and being, and that seem relatively enduring and trans-situational. The last decade of research has brought nuance to such positions, particularly in exploring values as verbs rather than nouns, and values work as distributed, interactive and ongoing processes. Turning away from the dominance of cognitive and cultural perspectives allows for a focus on practice as the site where values are constituted and performed on an ongoing basis. This focus parallels a broader turn to embedded ethics and situated ethics in organization studies, including the performative emphasis in the sociology of valuation taken more broadly.

Social conformity pressures can occur in the form of rating systems, as discussed by Lewis and Carlos (2022: 1094):

> Private citizens, social activists, and non-governmental organizations have long attempted to motivate improvements in organizational performance, transparency, and accountability. To incentivize organizational change, these third parties often introduce evaluation metrics to harness the mechanism of reactivity, the idea that organizations will change their behavior in reaction to being evaluated, observed, or measured. One increasingly prevalent way these groups stimulate reactivity is by formally rating organizations based on their past performance.

While companies want to avoid bad ratings and strive for good ratings, it is not always obvious that they want to move beyond the requirements of social conformity pressure. If a company is perceived as conformant, Lewis and Carlos (2022) found that recognized firms may question the perceived value of achieving superior performance. For example, companies rated as generous and charitable organizations tended to decrease philanthropic contributions relative to firms that were not rated as generous.

Social conformity pressure can originate with social actors who "might decide to intervene because they feel that a shared norm has been violated – often in ways that threaten morality, health, safety, or the well-being of society – even if no laws are broken" (Piazza *et al.*, 2024: 253). Social control agents can exert social conformity pressure. Social control agents can have the legitimate authority to define specific conduct as right or wrong. In well-functioning organizations, "social control agents will often intervene so that the rule system is not upended" (Piazza *et al.*, 2024: 250). Criminal law plays a role as a social control mechanism, as do many norms and values generally agreed upon. Social control agents include nonprofits, neighborhood associations, interest groups, labor organizations, members, agencies, authorities, media, and social movement organizations. Social control agents "discipline organizations and draw the line between appropriate organizational behavior and misconduct" (Cattani *et al.*, 2024: 785). Increased social control reduces criminogenic behavior, which refers to the tendency to commit crime. Corporate deviant power can be countered by social control (Haines *et al.*, 2022). As argued by Uygur and Napier (2024: 569), "stakeholders are the agents or performers of social control". Cattani *et al.* (2024: 785) studied social control agents and found that violations of rule-based norms tended to generate greater engagement and agreement among agents compared to violations of value-based norms: "Violations of rule-based norms generate more agreement because such norms are less ambiguous and ascertaining when they are violated is easier to establish".

Mechanisms for social control of organizational deviance are relevant here to prevent and terminate organizational participation in cartel activities and other deviant acts. Piazza *et al.* (2024: 251) discussed the notion of social control:

> In its broadest sense, social control is the normative aspect of social life. As such, it encompasses a wide range of behaviors: law is social control, but so are etiquette, custom, ethics, bureaucracy (…) While it is understood by some as the totality of practices and arrangements that contribute to the maintenance of social order, social control is also used as an umbrella term for how deviant behavior within society is identified and addressed. As a result, the scope of social control as a phenomenon is remarkably broad – it includes not only legal, and highly formalized, types of sanctioning such as property seizures, prison sentences, and capital punishment but also peer pressure and informal ostracism. Importantly, theories of social control have also been concerned with how deviant behavior is channeled via various pathways through which deviant actors and social control agents can interact with the purpose of resolving conflict and adjudicating differences.

Social conformity pressure does not always work, however. Witt *et al.* (2022) studied nonconformity. Despite the prevalence of norms and conformity pressure, they found that dominant block holders, strong labor rights, and small organizational size are some of the reasons for potential under-conformity that sometimes occurs. Managerial discretion can also be a reason for executives' power and influence over board members.

It is important at this point to emphasize that nonconformity is generally not always a bad thing. In a civil society, heterogeneity rather than homogeneity is welcomed – some people have decided to be different. Jeong *et al.* (2024: 729) studied the interesting example of the Amish people and community who seek "to be not conformed to this world and maintain non-permeable boundaries from the non-Amish in order to resist the forces of modernity" However, in our context of compliance and conformity, where deviance implies sliding into misconduct and crime, nonconformity and thus a lack of homogeneity is a bad thing.

Adapting to the homogeneity pressure rather than creating response strategies seems to be a more successful path to achieving acceptance among stakeholders. Pedersen *et al.* (2013: 358) suggested that three types of pressures promote homogeneity within organizational fields: "coercive (from regulatory bodies or holders of critical resources), mimetic (imitating successful organizations as a standard reaction to uncertainty), and normative (resulting from a professionalization of a field)".

A lack of conformity often has immediate and serious consequences when revealed. People react when corporations pollute rivers, engage in business with authoritarian regimes, provide favors to government officials, turn a blind eye to money laundering, and commit other forms of wrongdoing that might never reach the criminal justice system. People express their reactions on social media, in the press, and in the form of street demonstrations. People stop buying goods and services from violators and avoid doing business with them in the role of vendors. They avoid employment at companies that lack conformity and remove themselves from being shareholders. The consequences include market value losses, executive dismissals, unemployment, and bankruptcy in the worst-case scenarios.

Even when incidents end up being prosecuted in the criminal justice system due to compliance violations, the immediate and serious reactions to conformity violations can be much more challenging for a company. Upon instances of conformity violations, the situation can quickly become unmanageable for the company, and the criminal justice system provides a well-established framework for understanding procedures and addressing potential contradictions in the defense of one's activities. As mentioned in the introduction, an important reason for the shift in focus from compliance to conformity is the speed and severity of damage and harm resulting from breaches and violations of conformity requirements compared to violations of compliance requirements. While a legal process in the criminal justice system addressing corporate wrongdoing tends to last for years before a final outcome is reached, a social process in society addressing corporate misconduct tends to have serious consequences in just a few days after disclosure, exposure, and condemnation. An example is boycotts of companies quickly mobilizing in social and traditional media as a reaction to corporate misconduct, where sometimes "news sources distort the reality of crime" (Horn, 2024: 204). Therefore, while it might seem intuitively more serious to violate laws than norms for corporations, the difference between the two in terms of seriousness can, in fact, be in the opposite direction in many cases when looking at the extent of damage and harm to business activities and the fate of executives. If the salience of an issue reflects the seriousness of non-compliance versus non-conformity, then corporations tend to suffer more from the latter than from the former.

Responding to pressure regarding norms, values, and ethical issues by adapting is very different from responding with a strategy. When responding with a strategy, executives believe they can handle the situation through various forms of actual and symbolic means. Window dressing is a typical example of symbolic action, where management claims adherence to pressures without really acting accordingly. In window dressing, there is no real substance. As mentioned previously, window dressing is the act or the instance of making something appear better than it actually is (Desai, 2016).

An example of symbolism in many business organizations is the ceremonial adoption of a code of ethics, potentially copied from other business organizations or implemented in the organization by external consultants. Symbolic conformity is very different from substantive conformity (Durand *et al.*, 2019: 300):

> Symbolic responses, on the one hand, describe managers' promises to engage in practice changes they have not yet implemented or may not implement, as well as nominal actions to produce impressions of more material change. Substantive responses, on the other hand, refer to managers' implementation of significant changes that involve material costs and are not easily reversible, such as revamping deep-seated practices and inefficient distribution processes, or buying and selling divisions. While such distinction in responses is well observed in practice and well established in the literature, bridging symbolic and substantive responses with conformity and compliance is a distinctive contribution of the model we propose.

When conformity results from professionalization and socialization in establishing a shared base of values and norms, professionalization refers to the standards that guide individuals in their work, while socialization refers to learning through the appraisal of specific events and incidents to determine acceptable behavior (Ashforth and Humphrey, 2022).

Socialization of employees starts when entering the organization, where new members learn the value system, norms, and required behavioral patterns (Orudzheva *et al.*, 2020). For example, some organizations primarily focus on cooperation among employees through extensive knowledge sharing, while other organizations find some forms of competition among employees beneficial to the organization. The homogenization of employees tends to occur over time based on both professional and social expectations. This seems fine as long as newcomers enter an organization that is recognized for conformity.

However, socialization when entering an organization characterized by institutional deterioration, misconduct, decay, and crime will have the opposite effect by leading to socialization into deviance, as exemplified by outlaw biker clubs (Barker, 2011: 208):

> The selection and socialization processes ensure the perpetuation of the deviant culture and values of crime and violence. Many clubs or club chapters only invite for membership prospects that demonstrate criminal propensities, some making the commission of crimes a prerequisite for membership. Given the selection and socialization processes, many clubs have evolved into social criminal organizations.

While outlaw biker clubs are extreme examples, some corporations suffer from institutional deterioration (Rodriguez *et al.*, 2005). Normative institutional pressure might in such cases work to restore conformity.

In their model of organizational responses to normative pressures, Durand *et al.* (2019) proposed that a corporation may choose to respond to some issues but not to other issues based on varying assessments of issue salience and resource mobilization. Some issues might be met with complete inaction, some might be met with symbolic action, and still others might be met with substantive action. In the model, assessment of an issue as salient is a necessary but not sufficient condition for initiating a response. In addition, the cost–benefit ratio should be less than one for taking action.

The concept of stakeholders is important in our understanding of corporate conformity. As mentioned earlier, the term "stakeholder" refers to someone with an interest or concern in something, especially in business (Gomulya and Mishina, 2017).

The rise of social media, nongovernmental organizations, and the increased knowledge level among citizens have led to the strengthening of stakeholder demands (Panda and Sangle, 2019: 1085):

> As a result, firms often find themselves in conflicts. The cost of these conflicts for the firm is the opportunity cost of future projects due to loss of reputation, and for the stakeholders, it is the loss of opportunities, both social and economic, that could be brought by the projects. The tension between firms and stakeholders creates a dynamic environment where following compliance is not enough and social acceptance is equally important as government licenses.

Generally, stakeholder theory is concerned with business performance and corporate management in the promotion of justifiable ways to perform and manage organizational matters in varying environmental situations. The theory supports business issues by assisting decisions in line with stakeholder expectations (Waheed and Zhang, 2022). Stakeholder theory argues in favor of cooperation, which refers to an actor's behavior that benefits another actor as a recipient.

Stakeholders self-identify with a company when they believe that they affect and are themselves affected by the actions of the company. Individuals come to self-identify as a company's stakeholders based on their own perceptions (Alvarez and Sachs, 2023).

In addition to stakeholder theory, institutional theory and convenience theory can provide insights into corporate conformity. Institutional theory suggests that opportunities are shaped by individuals, groups, and other organizations, as well as society at large. The theory argues that business enterprises are much more than simple tools and instruments for achieving financial goals and ambitions. It states that organizations are adaptable systems that seek conformity as they recognize and learn from the environment by mirroring values in society (Brammer *et al.*, 2012).

Convenience theory suggests that normative pressure to cause conformity will be successful among business organizations when conformity to the pressure seems more convenient than a lack of conformity: "The theory of convenience explains that people are driven not to engage in unethical behavior when they have a reason, a chance, and the determination to do so" (Ali, 2024: 97). The convenience triangle consists of motive, opportunity, and willingness (Gottschalk, 2025; Lee, 2025).

When the motive for conformity is strong, the opportunity for conformity is attractive, and the willingness for conformity is high, conformity is more convenient than non-conformity.

While compliance is mainly a matter of opportunity restrictions in the convenience triangle, conformity addresses motive and willingness as well. In the motive dimension, conformity is a matter of pursuing possibilities and avoiding threats by being consistent with norms and values. Similarly, the willingness based on choice and justification remains consistent with norms and values.

In addition to the theoretical perspectives of stakeholders, institutions, and convenience, conformity is also a matter of corporate social responsibility (CSR). CSR refers to the state or fact of having a duty and obligation to address issues and take actions that generate societal benefits for all stakeholders who are influenced by or influence corporate business (Sajko *et al.*, 2021; Sorour *et al.*, 2021). CSR consists of "actions on the part of firms that appear to advance, or acquiesce in the promotion of some social good beyond that which is required by law" (Bachrach *et al.*, 2022: 533). To take on CSR means to pay back to society. Payback is the opposite of causing costs to society. CSR is supposed to be a self-regulatory mechanism whereby a business monitors and ensures its active conformity with the spirit of national and international norms. It is a concept whereby companies integrate social and environmental concerns into their business operations and in their interactions with stakeholders on a voluntary basis.

A distinction is typically made between symbolic and substantive CSR. Symbolic CSR refers to the adoption of low-cost activities intended to signal social responsibility without effectively benefiting anyone in society (Nardi, 2022: 283):

> Drawing on research on decoupling and symbolic management, the literature generally defines symbolic CSR as any set of activities, practices, or initiatives intended to promote a firm as a socially responsible entity while lacking more tangible socioenvironmental action. Typically, symbolic CSR combines CSR communication efforts and low-cost activities with no relevant social benefits. As an example of a symbolic CSR initiative, a company may publicly announce the creation of an internal CSR committee that, although serving as a signal of social responsibility, never really acts to improve the firm's performance in

> social or environmental dimensions. Symbolic CSR is also often associated with greenwashing or social washing, a practice whereby firms claim to be more environmentally or socially responsible than they in fact are.

In contrast to symbolic CSR, substantive CSR includes resource-intensive initiatives with the potential to generate societal benefits. Substantive CSR requires the application of valuable resources with real potential to benefit society (Nardi, 2022). Resources refer to enablers of benefits. Substantive responses imply implementation of significant changes that involve material costs and are not easily reversible. "Substance" refers to the real thing and possesses unique properties. Substantive CSR can be characterized by giving, while symbolic CSR can be characterized by taking. Substantive CSR consists of sincere efforts, while symbolic CSR activities are scripted efforts. Conformity based on symbolism rather than substantive efforts can be a risky endeavor for companies, as detection and disclosure of window dressing can lead to a scandal, followed by a corporate crisis.

To be successful, corporate conformity should be characterized by substance rather than symbolism and by adaptation rather than strategy. The company should strive for legitimacy, credibility, and trust. While legitimacy and trust are defined below, credibility refers to the consistent provision of accurate information and fulfillment of commitments to the community. Credibility is achieved through morally defensible business relations that resemble implicit agreements or social contracts.

Weber and Stepien (2020) distinguished between passive conformity and proactive conformity in the case of sanctions against a country such as Russia, where the company is not on the sanction list. Passive conformity refers to reducing activities on the sanctioned market and using cash reserves to hibernate, while proactive conformity refers to establishing new markets and relocating activities. Case studies later in this book illustrate those two alternatives, where Mondelez did not withdraw from Russia, while Bestseller withdrew from Myanmar. None of them were violating sanctions, but Mondelez chose passive conformity, while Bestseller chose proactive conformity.

Corporate conformity does not need to be an obstacle for corporate differentiation, where the business attempts to distinguish itself from its competitors. Difference "is especially rewarded when it conforms to popular expectations about what constitutes novelty", and "organizations gain positive attention when they are moderately different from their competitors" (Gouvard *et al.*, 2023: 783):

> To gain legitimacy, organizations need to conform to fundamental audience expectations. Those that manage to do so while remaining distinct from their competitors are judged favorably by outside audiences.

When there is a gap between corporate opinion and stakeholder opinions, stakeholders are not always correct. Conformity is thus not necessarily a matter of closing the gap through corporate adaptation to stakeholder demands. Sometimes, stakeholders have to be challenged. However, CSR requires that the company successfully close the gap through an active clarification and communication process with key stakeholders to secure the social license to operate.

1.3 Business Legitimacy Characteristics

According to Oberhauser *et al.* (2024: 1), legitimacy refers to "a generalized perception or assumption that the actions of an entity are proper or appropriate within some socially constructed system of norms, values, beliefs, and definitions (…) that is widely accepted as necessary for a corporation's survival and success". "It is typically conceptualized as a form of social evaluation that is socially constructed and rooted in cognition" (Neuberger *et al.*, 2024: 3). As Meyer and Rowan (1991: 50) argued, "legitimacy is a currency that organizations must continually earn to maintain their standing in society". Fiss and Zajac (2006: 1174) argued that "legitimacy is a perception or assumption that the actions of an entity are desirable, proper, or appropriate within some socially constructed system of norms, values and beliefs".

Legitimacy is a characteristic of corporate conformity. Demuijnck and Fasterling (2016: 680) referred to legitimacy as "conformity to social norms, values or expectations". Neuberger *et al.* (2023: 68) referred to organizational legitimacy as "a general perception that an entity is appropriate in the context of a socially constructed system of norms, values, beliefs, and definitions" based on "a collective social evaluation – a shared perception of the organization – on the part of a specific audience or set of audiences". Legitimacy stems from the alignment of values and actions with those of a company's stakeholders and society. Business activities are then considered legitimate in the eyes of society.

Sometimes, three forms of legitimacy are discussed. First, pragmatic legitimacy is based on the self-interested calculations of a company's most immediate stakeholders (Saenz, 2019: 297):

> Pragmatic legitimacy is based on the self-interests of the public and is most often exchange or influential in nature. Under exchange legitimacy, society supports a company's policy based on the expected material benefits to the society, such as technological improvements or employment opportunities. Influential legitimacy is attained by being responsive to stakeholders and incorporating society's wider interests into the company's decision-making process.

Next, moral legitimacy is based on a positive normative evaluation of the company and its business activities (Saenz, 2019: 297):

> Moral legitimacy hinges on whether a particular action is viewed as acceptable by a company's powerful stakeholders. Moral legitimacy is comprised of four aspects: consequential, procedural, personal, and structural legitimacy. Consequential legitimacy is result-oriented and is based on visible achievements such as increased employment, reduced emissions, and fewer numbers of workplace injuries. With procedural legitimacy, the focal point is not merely results of an action; rather, emphasis is placed on the morality surrounding the means to achieve a particular outcome. (…) Structural legitimacy is based on the company's identity and whether or not it forms a part of a 'morally favored taxonomic category', whereas personal legitimacy is dependent on the character of the company's leaders.

Melé and Armengou (2016) emphasized the importance of moral legitimacy, which could be achieved if the intended ends of business operations contribute to the common good, the means of those operations are acceptable, stakeholder concerns are respected, and, where possible, the risk of harm is minimized.

The third and final form of legitimacy is cognitive legitimacy, which is based on a perception of the company as a natural phenomenon in the community that is conforming to established cultural norms (Saenz, 2019: 298):

> Cognitive legitimacy can be split into two elements: comprehensibility and being taken for granted. The former attempts to make society understand the company through providing logical and easily understandable explanations for its actions and plans whereas the latter relies on the very existence of the company being taken for granted as an integral part of the social fabric.

As mentioned above, corporate conformity should be characterized by substance rather than symbolism and by adaptation rather than strategy. The company should strive for legitimacy, credibility, and trust. Trust cannot be reestablished through formal, legalistic measures. Trust is the intention to accept (Sala and Pratt, 2023) or the actual acceptance of vulnerability to another's actions (Baer *et al.*, 2021). Trust is "a willingness to be vulnerable and accept risk in relationships" that is typically motivated by an expectation of a positive outcome (Legood *et al.*, 2023: 1). Mangold (2024: 10) stated that "Trust is oriented toward the future and reduces complexity" by referring to trust as an attitude rather than an action. However, Schilke *et al.* (2023) distinguished between attitudinal and behavioral trust. Trusting someone is a risk because you make yourself vulnerable. Trust is referred to as ranging from higher to lower levels of trust, or as a continuum from distrust to trust.

Schilke and Lumineau (2023) studied interorganizational trust, arguing that it represents a key social mechanism facilitating collaboration in interorganizational relationships. They defined trust as the decision to rely on another party under conditions of risk. They argued that trust can exist both at the individual and organizational levels. Trust in interorganizational relationships can be organizational or individual in nature, to varying degrees, as a function of the organizational character of the trustor (the source of trust) and the trustee (the target of trust).

Sala and Pratt (2023: 1263) studied interpersonal trust repair, "given that responses to trust violations can be highly consequential". They defined interpersonal trust repair as the process of restoring trust to a positive state following a transgression or violation that has harmed trust between the person whose trust is violated (the trustor) and the trust violator (the trustee). The researchers argued that an organizationally directed trust repair process, through communication of trust standards via selection and socialization, can positively influence interpersonal trust repair.

References

Abadinsky, H. (2007). *Organized Crime*, Eighth Edition, Thomson Wadsworth, Belmont, CA.

Alabi, L.O. (2022). What to watch in Europe today, *Financial Times*, www.ft.com, published July 19.

Ali, Z. (2024). White-collar crime investigating and prosecuting agencies in Pakistan: A review on structure and challenges of agencies, *Pakistan Journal of Social Issues*, XV, 97–104.

Alon, A., Mennicken, A. and Samsonova-Taddei, A. (2019). Dynamics and limits of regulatory privatization: Reorganizing audit oversight in Russia, *Organization Studies*, 40(8), 1217–1240.

Alvarez, S. and Sachs, S. (2023). Where do stakeholders come from? *Academy of Management Review*, 48(2), 187–202.

Andreisova, L. (2016). Building and maintaining an effective compliance program, *International Journal of Organizational Leadership*, 5(1), 24–39.

Antonsen, H.H. and Madsen, Ø. (2021). Developing a maturity model for the compliance function of investment firms: A preliminary case study from Norway, *Administrative Sciences*, 11, 109, published online https://doi.org/10.3390/admsci11040109.

Ashforth, B.E. and Humphrey, R.H. (2022). Institutionalized affect in organizations: Not an oxymoron, *Human Relations*, 75(8), 1483–1517.

Augustine, G., Hedberg, L., Choi, T.U. and Lounsbury, M. (2025). Wasted? The downstream effects of social movement-backed occupations, *Administrative Science Quarterly*, 70(1), 23–68.

Bachrach, D.G., Vlachos, P.A., Irwin, K. and Morgeson, F.P. (2022). Does "how" firms invest in corporate social responsibility matter? An attributional model of job seekers' reactions to configurational variation in corporate social responsibility, *Human Relations*, 75(3), 532–559.

Baer, M.H. (2009). Governing corporate compliance, *Boston College Law Review*, 50(4), 949–1019.

Baer, M.D., Frank, E.L., Matta, F.K., Luciano, M.M. and Wellman, N. (2021). Untrusted, overtrusted, or just, right? The fairness of (in)congruence between trust wanted and trust received, *Academy of Management Journal*, 64(1), 180–206.

Barker, T. (2011). American based biker gangs: International organized crime, *American Journal of Criminal Justice*, 36(3), 207–215.

Bass, A.E., Pfarrer, M.D., Milosevic, I. and Titus, V.K. (2023). Better to be loved by some? Firm flaunting as an impression management strategy, *Academy of Management Review*, 48(2), 292–312.

Boghossian, J. and Marques, J.C. (2019). Saving the Canadian fur industry's hide: Government's strategic use of private authority to constrain radical activism, *Organization Studies*, 40(8), 1241–1268.

Bosse, D.A. and Phillips, R.A. (2016). Agency theory and bounded self-interest, *Academy of Management Review*, 41(2), 276–297.

Braithwaite, J. (2020). Regulatory mix, collective efficacy, and crimes of the powerful, *Journal of White Collar and Corporate Crime*, 1(1), 62–71.

Brammer, S., Jackson, G. and Matten, D. (2012). Corporate social responsibility and institutional theory: New perspectives on private governance, *Socio-Economic Review*, 10(1), 3–28.

Bundy, J. and Pfarrer, M.D. (2015). A burden of responsibility: The role of social approval at the onset of a crisis, *Academy of Management Review*, 40(3), 345–369.

Cattani, G., Clemente, M., Durand, R. and Mai, K.M. (2024). Who controls the controller? People reaction to social control agent's decisions about organizational misconduct, *Journal of Management Studies*, 61(3), 785–819.

Chen, H. and Soltes, E. (2018). Why your compliance programs fail – and how to fix them, *Harvard Business Review*, March–April, 116–123.

Cowen, A.P., King, A.W. and Marcel, J.J. (2016). CEO severance agreements: A theoretical examination and research agenda, *Academy of Management Review*, 41(1), 151–169.

Cowley, S. (2023). Former Wells Fargo executive to plead guilty in sham accounts scandal, *The New York Times*, www.nytimes.com, published March 15.

Demaline, C.J. (2024). Financial disclosure manipulation: A virtue ethics perspective, *Journal of Financial Crime*, 31(5), 1208–1221.

Demuijnck, G. and Fasterling, B. (2016). The social license to operate, *Journal of Business Ethics*, 136, 675–685.

Desai, V.M. (2016). Under the radar: Regulatory collaborations and their selective use to facilitate organizational compliance, *Academy of Management Journal*, 59(2), 636–657.

Durand, R., Hawn, O. and Ioannou, I. (2019). Willing and able: A general model of organizational responses to normative pressures, *Academy of Management Review*, 44(2), 299–320.

Eberl, P., Geiger, D. and Assländer, M.S. (2015). Repairing trust in an organization after integrity violations. The ambivalence of organizational rule adjustments, *Organization Studies*, 36(9), 1205–1235.

Eberlein, B. (2019). Who fills the global governance gap? Rethinking the roles of business and government in global governance, *Organization Studies*, 40(8), 1125–1146.

Engdahl, O. (2013). Ensuring regulatory compliance in banking and finance through effective controls: The principle of duality in the segregation of duties, *Regulation & Governance*, 8(3), 332–349.

Espedal, G. and Carlsen, A. (2024). Value inquiry and constructing the good in organizations, *Organization Studies*, 45(8), 1075–1098.

Fiss, P.C. and Zajac, E.J. (2006). The symbolic management of strategic change: sensegiving via framing and decoupling, *Academy of Management Journal*, 49(6), 1173–1193.

Fotaki, M., Lioukas, S. and Voudouris, I. (2020). Ethos in destiny: Organizational values and compliance in corporate governance, *Journal of Business Ethics*, 166, 19–37.

Gomulya, D. and Mishina, Y. (2017). Signaler credibility, signal susceptibility, and relative reliance on signals: How stakeholders change their evaluative processes after violation of expectations and rehabilitative efforts, *Academy of Management Journal*, 60(2), 554–583.

Gottschalk, P. (2025). Trusted chief executives in convenient white-collar crime, *Crime & Delinquency*, 7(8), 2845–2873.

Gouvard, P., Goldberg, A. and Srivastava, S.B. (2023). Doing organizational identity: Earnings surprises and the performative atypicality premium, *Administrative Science Quarterly*, 68(3), 781–823.

Győry, C. (2020). The institutional context of financial fraud in a post-transition economy: The Quaestor scandal, *European Journal of Criminology*, 17(1), 31–49.

Haines, F., Bice, S., Einfeld, C. and Sullivan, H. (2022). Countering corporate power through social control: What does a social license offer? *The British Journal of Criminology*, 62, 184–199.

Hersel, M.C., Gangloff, K.A. and Shropshire, C. (2023). Mixed messages: Crisis communication – dismissal (in)coherence and shareholder trust following misconduct, *Academy of Management Journal*, 66(2), 638–666.

Hollebeek, L.D., Sprott, D.E., Sigurdsson, V. and Clark, M.K. (2022). Social influence and stakeholder engagement behavior conformity, compliance, and reactance, *Psychology & Marketing*, 39, 90–100.

Horn, J.M. (2024). Accident, scandal, disaster: The media framing of corporate crime, *Crime, Law and Social Change*, 81, 203–229.

Jeong, S., Sinnicks, M., Burton, N. and Vu, M.C. (2024). "Be not conformed to this world": MacIntyre's critique of modernity and Amish business ethics, *Journal of Business Ethics*, 195, 729–761.

Karam, C.M., DeJordy, R., Creed, W.E.D., Daouk-Öyry, L., Scott, S.P., Geha, C. and Daou, A. (2024). Resourcing agency for sustained collective action amid creeping crises, *Organization Studies*, published first online https://doi.org/10.1177/01708406241295485.

Kawasaki, T. (2020). Review of comparative studies on white-collar and corporate crime, in: Rorie, M.L. (editor), *The Handbook of White-Collar Crime*, Hoboken, NJ: Wiley & Sons, chapter 27, pp. 437–447.

Khanna, T., Palepu, K.G. and Srinivasan, S. (2004). Disclosure practices of foreign companies interacting with US markets, *Journal of Accounting Research*, 42(2), 475–508.

Koller, G. (2005). *Risk Assessment and Decision Making in Business and Industry: A Practical Guide*, Boca Raton, Florida: Chapman & Hall/CRC Press.

König, A., Graf-Vlachy, L., Bundy, J. and Little, L.M. (2020). A blessing and a curse: How CEOs' trait empathy affects their management of organizational crisis, *Academy of Management Review*, 45(1), 130–153.

Lange, D., Bundy, J. and Park, E. (2022). The social nature of stakeholder utility, *Academy of Management Review*, 47(19), 9–30.

Lee, J.Y. (2025). Unveiling insider threats in South Korean companies: Causes and countermeasures through convenience theory and perceived punishment, *Deviant Behavior*, published first online https://doi.org/10.1080/01639625.2025.2545442.

Legood, A., Werff, L., Lee, A. and Hartog, D.D. (2023). A meta-analysis of the role of trust in the leadership-performance relationship, *European Journal of Work and Organizational Psychology*, 30(1), 1–22.

Lehman, D.W., Cooil, B. and Ramanujam, R. (2020). The effects of rule complexity on organizational noncompliance and remediation: Evidence from restaurant health inspections, *Journal of Management*, 46(8), 1436–1468.

Lewis, B.W. and Carlos, W.C. (2022). Avoiding the appearance of virtue: Reactivity to corporate social responsibility ratings in an era of shareholder primacy, *Administrative Science Quarterly*, 67(4), 1093–1135.

Lim, J.S. and Jiang, H. (2021). Linking authenticity in CSR communication to organization-public relationship outcomes: Integrating theories of impression management and relationship management, *Journal of Public Relations Research*, 33(6), 464–486.

Loyens, K., Claringbould, I., Heres-van Rossem, L. and Eekeren, Frank van. (2021). The social construction of integrity: A qualitative case study in Dutch football, *Sports in Society*, published online https://doi.org/10.1080/17430437.2021.1877661.

Maher, R., Valenzuela, F. and Böhm, S. (2019). The enduring state: An analysis of governance-making in three mining conflicts, *Organization Studies*, 40(8), 1169–1192.

Majluf, N.S. and Navarrete, C.M. (2011). A two-component compliance and ethics program model: An empirical application to Chilean corporations, *Journal of Business Ethics*, 100(4), 567–579.

Makortoff, K. (2023). A role model in financial services: Who is Alison Rose, forced to quit NatWest top job? *The Guardian*, www.theguardian.com, published July 26.

Mangold, F. (2024). Improving media trust research through better measurement: An item response theory perspective, *Journal of Trust Research*, 14(1), 8–38.

Marchetti, A.M. (2012). *Enterprise Risk Management Best Practices: From Assessment to Ongoing Compliance*, Hoboken, NJ: John Wiley & Sons.

Melé, D. and Armengou, J. (2016). Moral legitimacy in controversial projects and its relationships with social license to operate: A case study, *Journal of Business Ethics*, 136, 729–742.

Meyer, J.W. and Rowan, B. (1991). Institutionalized organizations: formal structure as myth and ceremony, in: Powell, W.W. and DiMaggio, P.J. (editors), *The New Institutionalism in Organizational Analysis*, Chicago, Ohio: University of Chicago Press, pages 41–62.

Nardi, L. (2022). The corporate social responsibility price premium as an enabler of substantive CSR, *Academy of Management Review*, 47(2), 282–308.

Neuberger, I., Kroezen, J. and Tracey, P. (2023). Balancing "protective disguise" with "harmonious advocacy": Social venture legitimation in authoritarian contexts, *Academy of Management Journal*, 66(1), 67–101.

Neuberger, I., Mattioli, F., Richards, H., Nyilasy, G. and Tracey, P. (2024). Intermediated legitimation: How founders build new venture legitimacy among make-or-break audiences, *Academy of Management Journal*, published first online https://doi.org/10.5465/amj.2022.1258.

Oberhauser, M., Conrad, M. and Holtbrügge, D. (2024). Apologize or deny? How companies defend legitimacy of Wall Street, Main Street, and Market Street after corporate misconduct, *Corporate Social Responsibility and Environmental Management*, published first online https://doi.org/10.1002/csr.2951.

Ordonez, M. (2025). The checks of the council: Local horizontal accountability's effects on municipal corruption in Latin America, *Public Performance & Management Review*, published first online https://doi.org/10.1080/15309576.2025.2468980.

Orudzheva, L., Salimath, M.S. and Pavur, R. (2020). Vortex of corruption: Longitudinal analysis of normative pressures in top global companies, *Journal of Business Ethics*, 163, 529–551.

Panda, S.S. and Sangle, S. (2019). An exploratory study to investigate the relationship between social license to operate and sustainable development strategies, *Sustainable Development*, 27, 1085–1095.

Palma, S. and Milne, R. (2022). Danske Bank to pay $2bn penalty for defrauding US banks, *Financial Times*, www.ft.com, published December 13.

Pedersen, E.R.G., Neergaard, P., Pedersen, J.T. and Gwozdz, W. (2013). Conformity and deviance: Company responses to institutional pressures for corporate social responsibility reporting, *Business Strategy and the Environment*, 22, 357–373.

Piazza, A., Bergemann, P. and Helms, W. (2024). Getting away with it (or not): The social control of organizational deviance, *Academy of Management Review*, 49(2), 249–272.

Pontell, H.N., Black, W.K. and Geis, G. (2014). Too big to fail, too powerful to jail? On the absence of criminal prosecutions after the 2008 financial meltdown, *Crime, Law and Social Change*, 61(1), 1–13.

Pontell, H.N., Ghazi-Tehrani, A.K. and Burton, B. (2020). White-collar and corporate crime in China, in: Rorie, M.L. (editor), *The Handbook of White-Collar Crime*, Hoboken, NJ: Wiley & Sons, Chapter 22, pp. 347–362.

Rawski, S.L., Djurdjevic, E., Soderberg, A.T. and Foster, J.R. (2024). The devil is in the details: Sexual harassment e-training design choices and perceived messenger integrity, *Journal of Business Ethics*, 195, 879–898.

Remisova, A., Lasakova, A. and Kirchmayer, Z. (2019). Influence of formal ethics program components on managerial ethical behavior, *Journal of Business Ethics*, 160(1), 151–166.

Rodriguez, P., Uhlenbruck, K. and Eden, L. (2005). Government corruption and the entry strategies of multinationals, *Academy of Management Review*, 30(2), 383–396.

Rooij, B. and Fine, A. (2020). Preventing corporate crime from within: Compliance management, whistleblowing, and internal monitoring. Pages 229–245 in *The Handbook of White-Collar Crime*, Chapter 15, edited by Melissa L. Rorie, Hoboken, NJ: Wiley & Sons.

Rorie, M. (2015). An integrated theory of corporate environmental compliance and overcompliance, *Crime, Law and Social Change*, 64, 65–101.

Rorie, M., Rinfret, S. and Pautz, M. (2015). The thin green line: Examining environmental regulation and environmental offending from multiple perspectives, *International Journal of Law, Crime and Justice*, 43, 586–608.

Saenz, C. (2019). Building legitimacy and trust between a mining company and a community to earn social license to operate: A Peruvian case study, *Corporate Social Responsibility and Environmental Management*, 26(2), 296–306.

Saifer, A. and Zanoni, P. (2024). The political economy of accountability: Philanthropy's 'double dispossession' of racial justice organizations under racial capitalism, *Human Relations*, published first online https://doi.org/10.1177/00187267241303268.

Sajko, M., Boone, C. and Buyl, T. (2021). CEO greed, corporate social responsibility, and organizational resilience to systemic shocks, *Journal of Management*, 47(4), 957–992.

Sala, G.R. and Pratt, M.G. (2023). How organizations influence interpersonal trust repair: The case of a French antiterrorist unit, *Academy of Management Journal*, 66(4), 1263–1293.

Samherji (2020). *Samherji's Namibia investigation finalized*, Samherji ice fresh seafood, website https://www.samherji.is/en/moya/news/samherjis-namibia-investigation-finalized, Akureyri, Iceland, published by margret@samherji.is.

Schilke, O. and Lumineau, F. (2023). How organizational is interorganizational trust? *Academy of Management Review*, published online AMR.2022.0040.

Schilke, O., Powell, A. and Schweitzer, M.E. (2023). A review of experimental research on organizational trust, *Journal of Trust Research*, 13(2), 102–139.

Schneider, A. and Scherer, A.G. (2019). State governance beyond the 'shadow of hierarchy': A social mechanisms perspective on governmental CSR policies, *Organization Studies*, 40(8), 1147–1168.

Schoultz, I. and Flyghed, J. (2021). "We have been thrown under the bus": Corporate versus individual defense mechanisms against transnational corporate bribery charges, *Journal of White Collar and Corporate Crime*, 2(1), 24–35.

Simpson, S.S. (2019). Reimagining Sutherland 80 years after white-collar crime, *Criminology*, 57(2), 181–372.

Simpson, S.S., Galvin, M.A., Loughran, T.A. and Cohen, M.A. (2022). Perceptions of white-collar crime seriousness: Unpacking and translating attitudes into policy preferences, *Journal of Research in Crime and Delinquency*, published online.

Smith, G. (2009). Citizen oversight of independent police services: Bifurcated accountability, regulation creep, and lessons learning, *Regulation & Governance*, 3, 421–441.

Sorour, M.K., Boadu, M. and Soobaroyen, T. (2021). The role of corporate social responsibility in organizational identity communication, co-creation and orientation, *Journal of Business Ethics*, 173, 89–108.

Sundström, M. and Radon, A. (2015). Utilizing the concept of convenience as a business opportunity in emerging markets, *Organizations and Markets in Emerging Economies*, 6(2), 7–21.

Sutherland, E.H. (1983). *White Collar Crime – The Uncut Version*, New Haven, CT: Yale University Press.

Taylor, J. (2018). White-collar crime and the law in nineteenth-century Britain, *Business History*, 60(3), 343–360.

Teichmann, F.M.J. and Wittmann, C. (2024). Psychology and white-collar crime – Compliance recommendations based on the social and psychological reality dictating perception, *Journal of Financial Crime*, published online https://doi.org/10.1108/JFC-07-2022-0158.

Thottoli, M.M. (2021). The relevance of compliance audit on companies' compliance with disclosure guidelines of financial statements, *Journal of Investment Compliance*, 22(2), 137–150.

Uygur, S.A. and Napier, C.J. (2024). Understanding fraud in the not-for-profit sector: A stakeholder perspective for charities, *Journal of Business Ethics*, 190, 569–588.

Waheed, A. and Zhang, Q. (2022). Effect of CSR and ethical practices on sustainable competitive performance: A case of emerging markets from stakeholder theory perspective, *Journal of Business Ethics*, 175, 837–855.

Weber, P.M. and Stepien, B. (2020). Conform or challenge? Adjustment strategies of sanction-torn companies, *The World Economy*, 43, 3006–3024.

White, M.J. (2019). What I've learned about white-collar crime, *Harvard Business Review*, July–August, 58–59.

Williams, M.L., Levi, M., Burnap, P. and Gundur, R.V. (2019). Under the corporate radar: Examining insider business cybercrime victimization through an application of routine activities theory, *Deviant Behavior*, 40(9), 1119–1131.

Witt, M.A., Fainshmidt, S. and Aguilera, R.V. (2022). Our board, our rules: Nonconformity to global corporate governance norms, *Administrative Science Quarterly*, 67(1), 131–166.

Chapter 2

Corruption in Sport Perspectives

Corruption in sports is a research topic that has received increased attention and interest in recent years. One of the reasons is the rapidly growing amount of money involved in sports. Both public and commercial television stations, as well as advertising agencies with their sponsors, are willing to pay much more to broadcast and be visible at popular sporting events. The price to pay for such actors depends on the popularity of each sport based on television viewers and spectators. When popularity grows, so does the price to broadcast, as does the price to be visible at sporting events. With more money involved comes an increased temptation of corruption, both among potential actors seeking to bribe others to achieve what they want and among those potential actors seeking to be bribed to achieve their desires (Jennings and Sambrook, 2000; Kihl *et al.*, 2017; Kulczycki and Koenigstorfer, 2016; Philippou, 2022, 2023; Stathopoulou *et al.*, 2022).

2.1 Seven Causes of Corruption in Sport

There are many causes of corruption in sports. The selection in the following is based on a literature review examining sport corruption in general, seemingly reflecting the situation at the International Biathlon Union (IBU). Seven causes presented here are the rapidly increasing amounts of money involved in sports, the rapidly increasing prestige and fame in hosting major sporting events, the rapidly rising gambling and betting industry aligned with the modern sports industry, the lack of recognition and organizational inclusion of diversity, the lack of compensation for people in leadership positions, the potential for narcissistic leadership styles, and an organizational culture dominated by competition rather than cooperation and secrecy rather than transparency.

There are rapidly increasing amounts of money involved in sports, originating from the sale of broadcasting licenses for sporting events and the sale of advertising spaces at sporting events to sponsors. Broadcasting and advertising rights for biathlon events have become an important source of income for the IBU, with profits shared among member states despite the organization being not-for-profit (Gillespie *et al.*, 2024). Offenders are interested in achieving economic benefits from the rising monetary inflow for organizational and personal gain, and they are motivated to misuse available money for organizational and personal benefit. Both public and commercial television stations, as well as advertising agencies with their sponsors, are willing to pay much more to broadcast and be visible at popular sporting events. The price to pay for such actors depends on the popularity of each sport based on television viewers and spectators. When popularity grows, so does the price to broadcast, as does the price to be visible at sporting events. With more money involved comes an increased temptation of corruption, both among potential actors seeking to bribe others to achieve what they want and among potential actors seeking to be bribed to achieve what they desire (Jennings and Sambrook, 2000; Kihl *et al.*, 2017; Kulczycki and Koenigstorfer, 2016; Philippou, 2022, 2023; Stathopoulou *et al.*, 2022).

There is rapidly increasing national prestige and fame in hosting major sporting events such as world cups, world championships, and the Olympic Games. This was visible when Qatar became the host nation for the FIFA World Cup (Locatelli *et al.*, 2017) and when Russia became the host for the Olympic Winter Games, including biathlon (Panja, 2021). In both instances, corporate investigators suggested that Qatari officials (Garcia, 2014) and Russian officials (Taylor, 2021) had bribed decision-makers to secure the bids for the sporting events in their respective countries. Specifically, Taylor (2021: 153) also found that IBU officials were bribed by Russian officials to host three biathlon events in the country:

> Three IBU events were scheduled to be held in Russia in the 2017/18 season, namely the last two IBU Cup events (in Uvat on 9-11 March and Khanty-Mansiysk on 13-17 March) and the final IBU World Cup event, which was scheduled to be held in Tyumen on 22-25 March 2018.

> Following the Schmid Report and the IOC's decision to exclude the ROC from the 2018 Olympic Games, there was significant pressure from many different stakeholders, not least the biathletes for the IBU to move those events out of Russia.

In the competition for rapidly increasing national prestige and fame in hosting major sporting events, nations that violate human rights often face a problem that is compensated by corruption. Although bodies equipped with the task of assigning major events to host nations tend to be skeptical of human rights violations, nations violating human rights can bribe body officials to vote for them anyway (FIFA, 2023; Grafström, 2024a, 2024b). This has been documented in previous as well as current reports, such as the one regarding human rights violations in Qatar for the World Cup (MacInnes, 2024):

> A long-awaited Fifa report into the legacy of the Qatar World Cup has finally been published, but only after its key recommendation was rejected by the organization.
>
> Fifa's subcommittee on human rights and social responsibility has found that the game's world body "has a responsibility" to provide financial remedy to workers who suffered loss because of employment related to the 2022 World Cup. Its report argues that Fifa should use its Qatar legacy fund to remedy those workers. Two days before the report was published, however, Fifa announced that the $50m fund would be used on international development projects instead.

There has been a rise in the gambling and betting industry, aligned with the modern sports industry, where winning versus losing can be influenced by corruption (Gardiner *et al.*, 2017). Lee (2017: 50) described one of the match-fixing scandals that involved the Brother Elephants in the Chinese Professional Baseball League (CPBL):

> Chuang admitted that approximately 10 players on the Brother Elephants had received bribery money; 23 people were named as defendants, including the Brother Elephants player Chin-hui Tsao and coach Shin Nakagomi, the La New Bears player Chih-chia Chang, and the Sinon Bulls player Chia-sheng Hsieh. On 21 November 2009, eight Bears players and six Brother Elephants players pleaded guilty. In January

> 2010, the Brother Elephants' 'Golden Warrior', Chih-yan Chen, disclosed match-fixing earnings of nearly NT$ one million; additionally, Brother Elephants pitcher Yu-cheng Liao admitted to receiving NT$ 600,000 from the gambling dealer.

Gambling and match-fixing are linked, where gambling has remained a longstanding threat to the integrity of sport (Brooks and Lavorgna, 2018: 81):

> Playing up to the rules in sport or 'putting in the fix', and a desire to win at all costs, is not a problem of its time, or an historical artifact. Waging, regardless of the class of the person, was commonplace, as was trying to fix the result in advance for profit and/or a desire to enforce a sense of social superiority.

Gambling is the activity of predicting sports results and placing a wager on the outcome. Athletes and coaches can be bribed to influence sports results. Others might be bribed as well, for example, by allowing doped athletes at IBU events to participate with clean athletes (UNODC, 2023:14):

> Another example of sporting-related competition manipulation is provided by the sport of biathlon, where in 2021 accusations were made of a cover up of doping violations involving the governing body, with those responsible for ensuring a clean sport accused of taking bribes to allow some athletes to avoid being tested.

There exists diversity in sports, while there is often a lack of inclusion and recognition of minorities within that diversity. Diversity requires recognizing minority cultures and shaping institutions so that they mirror the global diversity of athletes. Inclusion refers to the extent to which individuals feel part of critical organizational processes (Næss, 2023). Discriminated deviants feeling disadvantaged may not only complain about a lack of equity and equality. They may also attempt to restore the perception of fairness and justice and to be treated equally (Leigh *et al.*, 2010). Then, for example, it might be tempting to restore perceived fairness and equality by bribing the president of the IBU with gifts, services, and money.

Leadership positions in sport organizations are primarily occupied by volunteers who are not compensated for their hard work. They are nominated and rarely receive compensation for the dedication and work carried out. Travel expenses are often covered, but other financial support and compensation are lacking. It is often expected that leaders in sports organizations are idealistic supporters without the incentive of decent pay. They may, however, find it strange that top athletes often earn significant sums of money in contrast to their own earnings. An example is Tarjei Bø, a 35-year-old Norwegian biathlete who has won three Olympic championships and eleven World Championship gold medals, as well as the World Cup. Recently, he bought a family home in a high-status area of Oslo for NOK 25 million (USD 2.5 million) after having done nothing else but biathlon in his adult life (Sellæg, 2024). It does not come as a surprise when volunteers in leading IBU positions simply feel entitled to some gifts and services offered to them in an attempt to alleviate the feeling of discomfort from perceived financial discrimination (Kamerdze *et al.*, 2014; Zvi and Elaad, 2018). It is interesting to note that Anders Besseberg, as IBU president, received only a symbolic salary, while his successor, Olle Dahlin, enjoyed a substantial increase in his financial compensation as IBU president. The compensation grew four times from EUR 30,000, which Besseberg received, to EUR 120,000, which Olle Dahlin received (Verstad and Rognerud, 2021).

A leadership style characterized by narcissism strengthens the feeling of entitlement to receive bribes. For example, if the IBU president has been in the position for too long, then narcissistic identification with the organization might occur. A narcissist is a person who exhibits an unusual trust in self, believing that they are uniquely special and entitled to more benefits than are legitimately available to them (Chatterjee and Pollock, 2017), typically rationalizing their misconduct (Schoen *et al.*, 2021). Narcissistic organizational identification implies seeing oneself as central to the organization's identity (Galvin *et al.*, 2015).

A lack of diversity and a lack of inclusion are two aspects of organizational culture. Other aspects of organizational culture might stimulate corruption as well, such as competition rather than cooperation among volunteers, secrecy rather than transparency within organizations like the IBU, improvisation rather than planning, and irrationality rather than rationality. Culture generally refers to the values, beliefs, preferences, and assumptions that provide the basis for interaction and shared understandings among group members and which differentiate one group of people from another (Malmi *et al.*, 2020).

Seven causes are presented here: (1) the rapidly increasing amounts of money involved in sports, (2) the rapidly increasing prestige and fame associated with hosting major sporting events, (3) the rapidly rising gambling and betting industry aligned with the modern sports industry, (4) the lack of recognition and organizational inclusion of diversity, (5) the lack of compensation for people in leadership positions, (6) the potential for narcissistic leadership styles, and (7) an organizational culture dominated by competition rather than cooperation and secrecy rather than transparency.

There are a few more reasons worth mentioning that address the individual level. Moral disengagement plays an important role in explaining generally why people are able to participate in corruption without feeling any sort of distress (Moore *et al.*, 2012). The theory of moral disengagement can be explained as humans' self-regulatory capabilities being undermined, resulting in the execution of wrongdoing without experiencing any kind of distress (Kihl, 2019). Self-regulatory processes can, for instance, include feelings of shame, guilt, and self-condemnation. These feelings usually lead people into avoiding actions that violate their own moral standards. This mechanism has been used in sports to facilitate doping cases. Athletes have used moral disengagement when trying to justify doping. In light of these cases, athletes try to frame their wrongdoing as less wrong by comparing it to more serious kinds of crime, such as murder and sexual assault (Kihl, 2019). Liu *et al.* (2024: 862) argued that individuals may have a tendency "to adopt moral disengagement strategies when facing decisions related to ethical conflicts".

The rational choice theory is central to criminology. The theory is based on how people will evaluate the utility versus the cost of criminal behavior (Beaudry-Cyr, 2015). Individuals will participate in corruption when the perceived benefits outweigh the perceived costs where it seems to be profitable to participate (Jancsics, 2014). The explanation of why individuals engage in corruption, in light of rational choice theory, connected to the phenomenon of doping, is the motivation for higher performance, better achievements, and winning competitions (Kihl, 2019).

Justification for one's behavior can be a prominent factor in explaining why people engage in corrupt behavior. They rationalize by justifying it as a mechanism to protect and safeguard their positive self-image. This means one finds good reasons for one's deviant behavior and actions, instead of looking inward for flaws. This type of justification is rooted in self-identity (Schoen *et al.*, 2021). The mechanism stimulates poor behavior and decision-making without hurting one's view of self. In a justification, the actor admits responsibility for the act in question while denying its pejorative and negative content (Schoen *et al.*, 2021: 730):

> People use justification mechanisms to protect their sense of self. People who sincerely believe that they are a specific kind of person but routinely demonstrate behaviors that indicate otherwise may avoid cognitive dissonance and maintain their sense of self by using justification mechanisms that allow them to "explain away" their behavior.

Silver and Garofalo (2024: 3) discussed the difference between an excuse and a justification:

> When confronting someone for acting wrongly, they may defend themselves by offering either a justification or an excuse. Scholars have disagreed about exactly how to capture this distinction both in the law and in morality, but a plausible and common way of understanding the distinction in the moral context is to say that an agent who is justified in performing some action has not acted wrongly, and an agent who is excused has acted wrongly but should not be blamed or punished.

The personal willingness is concerned with the impression that surprisingly few deviants believe they have done anything wrong. Most of them feel innocent and victims of injustice when sanctioned in some ways.

2.2 Consequences of Corruption in Sport

Corruption is defined as the giving, requesting, receiving, or accepting of an improper advantage related to a position, office, or assignment. Corruption is "an act of transgression" that refers to "a violation of the implicit and explicit rules that guide a relationship" (Kulczycki and Koenigstorfer, 2016: 546). Corruption serves the purpose of the briber to influence the bribed in a desired direction. For example, by bribing IBU officials, a nation attempts to host biathlon events in its country. Another example is bribing IBU officials in an attempt to become sponsors and obtain advertising space at biathlon events. Sometimes such attempts do not succeed, as IBU officials might make decisions that are not influenced by the bribe. However, when IBU officials are influenced, decisions may differ from what they would be without a bribe. To corrupt, in general terms, is to destroy or pervert the integrity or fidelity of a person in the discharge of their duty; it is to induce to act dishonestly or unfaithfully; it is to make venal; and it is to bribe (Gardiner *et al.*, 2017: 11):

> The root of corruption is generally thought to be the Latin *corruptus*, the state of being rotten, decayed, and transferrable to the morally unsound state of being degenerate, decadent and depraved.

Today, corruption is considered a mega sport event syndrome. There are negative effects on attitudes toward the event-governing body and attitudes toward the event (Kulczycki and Koenigstorfer, 2016). Corrupt regimes are assigned major sporting events (e.g., Russia and Qatar), while democratic nations do not get to have such events (Taylor, 2021; Garcia, 2014).

2.3 Actions against Corruption in Sport

Actions against corruption in sport should address the causes of corruption, as exemplified by the seven causes presented above. However, the research literature on remedies and reform seems to offer suggestions that do not necessarily derive from causal analyses of corruption (Kihl, 2017, 2019). Some of the suggestions found in the literature address organizational integrity, stakeholder concerns, and whistleblowing, as discussed in the following.

In the research literature, integrity is often emphasized as an important barrier against corruption in sport (e.g., Artello and Albanese, 2022; Gardiner *et al.*, 2017; Loyens *et al.*, 2022). Integrity is the quality of acting in accordance with moral values, norms, and rules considered valid, appropriate, and relevant within the context of the actor's operations (Loyens *et al.*, 2022). Organizational integrity reflects the organization's identity and values accurately and reliably (Gardiner *et al.*, 2017). Integrity is about conformity rather than compliance, as the former refers to acting in accordance with laws, rules, and regulations to maintain a legal license to operate, while the latter aspect refers to acting in accordance with norms, values, and beliefs to maintain a social license to operate (Durand *et al.*, 2019; Gottschalk, 2024). Compliance and conformity create legitimacy, defined as "a generalized perception or assumption that the actions of an entity are proper or appropriate within some socially constructed system of norms, values, beliefs, and definitions (…) that is widely accepted as necessary for a corporation's survival and success" (Oberhauser *et al.*, 2024: 1), where legitimacy revolves around the alignment of values, social norms, and expectations (Saenz, 2019).

Integrity is a matter of honesty and consistency between one's inner values and outward actions, ensuring that actions are viewed as honest and truthful reflections of those values. Gardiner *et al.* (2017: 8) suggested that the concept of corruption is an antithesis of integrity, wherein being corrupt is characterized by being "rotten, decayed, transferable to the morally unsound state of being degenerate, decadent and depraved". High moral standards should be reflected in actions as a sign of integrity. Integrity in fighting corruption needs to address: (1) the inherent integrity of sport, (2) personal integrity in sport, (3) organizational integrity of sport, and (4) procedural integrity in the sporting event, according to Gardiner *et al.* (2017: 18):

> First, and fundamentally, is the integrity of sport itself, focused on an identity maintained by a cooperative community that recognizes and respects the goods and excellences that are internal to the activity (…) Second, we can distinguish personal integrity in sport, in which the individual sportsperson, be they contestant, administrator, referee or so on, takes responsibility for representing this identity in their practice (...) Third, we can distinguish another form of integrity in sport focused in the organization or institution (...) Fourth, it is possible to distinguish the idea of procedural integrity.

Gardiner *et al.* (2017) argued that the term "integrity" has recently become common currency in the world of sports. Yet, the almost random use of the term, lacking definitions, is a problem since there is a gap between talking about integrity and acting it out. Therefore, all four efforts to combat corruption through integrity must be implemented before they can be considered trustworthy in the world of sports. It is a matter of restoring trust in sport (Ordway, 2023).

In addition to the requirements of integrity and accountability, there is also a requirement for credibility and reliability. Credibility refers to the consistent provision of accurate information and the fulfillment of commitments. Credibility implies demonstrating that the leader has the necessary expertise, experience, and resources to deliver on their promises. Reliability refers to being trustworthy, where trust is the willingness to be exposed to and the acceptance of vulnerability to another's actions (Baer *et al.*, 2021).

"In an attempt to restore trust following the scandal, the IBU has chosen, amongst other things, to put stricter anti-corruption regulations in place" (Riedl, 2021: 50). The IBU corruption scandal emerged in 2018, while new anticorruption regulations emerged at IBU in 2019. The rules include an obligation to report any alleged misconduct, while they do not specifically outline procedures and potential sanctions to be followed, clarifying the consequences of allegations and accusations based on evidence.

A second action against corruption in sports can be initiated by sponsors and other stakeholders who might worry. While some sponsors could be involved in bribery, as discussed above, other sponsors might be on the opposite side: expressing concern when rumors of corruption arise within the sponsored organization. The threat of withdrawing sponsorship could serve as an action against corruption in sports. Sponsors are important stakeholders, where the term "stakeholder" refers to someone with an interest or concern for something and who might influence or be influenced by corruption in sporting events (Kulczycki and Koenigstorfer, 2016; Philippou, 2022, 2023).

As presented later in this book, sponsors might be blamed for supporting corrupt events. The empirical study by Kulczycki and Koenigstorfer (2016: 566) regarding the football association FIFA concluded that "although the sponsors cannot be blamed directly for unethical behaviors, the mere support of, and cooperation with, the corrupt body likely causes negative spillover effects on individuals' attitudes". The secret world of FIFA – including bribery and vote rigging – was exposed a decade earlier by Jennings (2006).

A third action against corruption is the implementation of an efficient and effective whistleblowing system, potentially based on artificial intelligence technology. Such a system might enable the whistleblower initially to communicate with the system regarding allegations and accusations, clarifying matters before the message is eventually reported to someone. Traditionally, when people notice wrongdoing within an organization, they are reluctant to report it due to perceived reprisal and retaliation threats. The lack of whistleblowing in Europe has been explained by governments' refusal "to proactively recruit whistleblowers", as compared to the United States (Karpacheva and Hock, 2024: 9). Following discussion with the system, the whistleblower who claims to have observed wrongdoing can report the incident to someone who can take appropriate action, such as a compliance officer at the IBU. Such system features are useful, for example, when blowing the whistle on someone with a Machiavellian personality, which is associated with manipulation, cynicism, and deception aimed at achieving self-interested goals (Wijayanti *et al.*, 2024).

Other recommended actions in the literature include the development of an organizational culture in sport organizations characterized by diversity and inclusion (Næss, 2023), fair pay, general equity and equality (Leigh *et al.*, 2010), and a transparent governance structure (Philippou, 2022; 2023). A governance structure formalizes decision rights and workflow procedures. Whether formalization will lead to less corruption at organizations such as the International Biathlon Union is a relevant question addressing the relationship between formality and bribery (Vu *et al.*, 2024: 571):

> The relationship between firm formality and bribery has been extensively examined in the literature. Nevertheless, the findings are inconclusive. One strand of the literature indicates that bribery is a greater burden for formal firms in comparison to informal firms. These studies show that, since formal firms are more visible and have more direct contact with local governments, they are more susceptible to bribe demands. In addition, formal firms often resort to paying more bribes as a mindful strategy against the unfair competition from informal firms. Another strand of literature shows the opposite.

The most effective leadership style depends on the situation. In normal times, however, transformational and relational leadership seem more appropriate than authoritative and transactional leadership.

2.4 Issues in District Court Verdict

Causes, consequences, and remedies were touched upon in the 67-page verdict from the Buskerud district court (Buskerud tingrett, 2024). In terms of causes, it seemed for a while that Besseberg was "too big to fail" and "too powerful to jail" (Pontell *et al.*, 2014: 1). In terms of consequences, it seemed that Besseberg ignored doping involving Russian biathletes and also supported the holding of major biathlon events in Russia. In terms of remedies, the IBU claims it has introduced new ethical guidelines.

Yet, the most relevant issue is whether the alleged corruption, as described in ten criminal charges in the indictment from the Norwegian serious fraud office, Økokrim, could have been avoided (Buskerud tingrett, 2024: 2): "While Besseberg resided in Vestfossen in Norway and in connection with his position as president of the International Biathlon Union (IBU), he demanded, accepted, and received the following benefits in the period 2009–2018":

1. Sometime in 2011, likely in connection with board meeting number 100 of the IBU in March 2011 in Khanty-Mansiysk, Russia, he received an Omega watch (copper/black) from an official in Russian biathlon. The value of the watch was approximately NOK 195,000 (USD 19,500).
2. Sometime, probably in April 2013 and prior to the Winter Olympics in Sochi, Russia, in 2014, he accepted an offer of a prostitute who was procured for him from an official in Russian biathlon. This probably happened in connection with a biathlon show race in Moscow.
3. Sometime probably in 2013, during a biathlon event in Russia, he received a Hublot watch from a Russian official in the Ugra region. The watch was worth approximately NOK 70,000 (USD 7,000).
4. In April 2013, in connection with a trip to Tyumen, Russia, he was paid by Russian government officials to participate in a hunting and fishing trip at a hunting resort, where he was taken by helicopter. During the stay, moose, wild boar, and deer were hunted.
5. In 2014, at the end of the Biathlon World Cup in Holmenkollen, Norway, he received a Ulysses Nardin watch (black with a leather strap) from an official in Russian biathlon. The value of the watch was approximately NOK 78,000 (USD 7,800).
6. In October 2015, he was sponsored for a hunting trip to Tyumen, Russia, by an official from Tyumen. Besseberg also received a free trophy after killing a maral deer.
7. In the period 2015–2018, Besseberg, on several occasions, accepted offers of prostitutes organized and offered to him by government officials connected to the Russian biathlon. The stay with a woman

for several days and nights was arranged for him by such persons on at least two occasions, likely in March 2016 in Khanty-Mansiysk, Russia, in connection with an IBU World Cup event, and in March 2018 in Tyumen, Russia, in connection with the IBU World Cup finale.

8. In March 2018, on the occasion of a stay in Tyumen, Russia, Besseberg was entrusted by Russian government officials with a hunting and fishing trip, including accommodation and hospitality at a Russian hunting resort. During the trip, Besseberg hunted maral deer and wild boar.
9. In the period 2009–2018, Besseberg had a standing agreement to participate in hunting trips with the owner and general manager of the company APF Marketing Services GmbH (hereinafter "APF"), who subsequently served as a consultant for Infront Austria GmbH (hereinafter "Infront") and as a member of Infront's advisory board. Hunting stays and hunting trophies were free of charge for Besseberg and were paid for by the mentioned person, his company, or by Infront. The hunts occurred regularly, one to three times per year, in Austria and/or the Czech Republic at exclusive hunting sites. Usually, Besseberg also received trophies from the animals he killed. During this period, APF and later Infront had agreements with the IBU regarding marketing and sponsorship rights for IBU biathlon events or were in negotiations with the IBU on such agreements, which Besseberg approved or signed in his capacity as president of the IBU.
10. In the period 2011–2018, at his residence in Norway, Besseberg privately had a car of the type BMW X5 at his disposal, for which Infront covered the leasing costs. The value of this was approximately NOK 850,000 (USD 85,000).

As discussed above, one of the actions against corruption in sports is to address sponsors' concerns as stakeholders who dislike being associated with a corrupt organization. Sponsors may threaten to withdraw from their sponsorships unless the sponsored organization, such as the IBU, introduces compliance and conformity to ensure legitimacy. The primary sponsor of the IBU is the car manufacturer BMW, based in Germany. The compliance officer at BMW was asked about the company's reaction to allegations of corruption at the IBU. Answers to that question, in terms of an email exchange, are presented later in this book.

References

Artello, K. and Albanese, J.S. (2022). Culture of corruption: Prosecutions, persistence, and desistence, *Public Integrity*, 24, 142–161.

Baer, M.H., Frank, E.L., Matta, F.K., Luciano, M.M. and Wellman, N. (2021). Untrusted, overtrusted, or just right? The fairness of (in)congruence between trust wanted and trust received, *Academy of Management Journal*, 64(1), 180–206.

Beaudry-Cyr, M. (2015). Rational choice theory, in: Jennings, W.G. and Beaudry-Cyr, M. (editors), *The Encyclopedia of Theoretical Criminology*, John Wiley & Sons, UK: London.

Brooks, G. and Lavorgna, A. (2018). Lost Eden – The corruption of sport, in Kihl, L.A. (editor), *Corruption in Sport – Causes, Consequences, and Reform*, Routledge, UK: Abingdon, pp. 79–90.

Buskerud tingrett (2024). Court case number 23-03940MED-TBUS/THOK, *Buskerud tingrett* (Buskerud district court), professional judge Vidar Toftøy-Lohne, lay judges Kari Aasen Ingebo and Gunnar Sanden, Hokksund, Norway, verdict document, p. 67.

Chatterjee, A. and Pollock, T.G. (2017). Master of puppets: How narcissistic CEOs construct their professional worlds, *Academy of Management Review*, 42(4), 703–725.

Durand, R., Hawn, O. and Ioannou, I. (2019). Willing and able: A general model of organizational responses to normative pressures, *Academy of Management Review*, 44(2), 299–320.

Fifa (2023). *FIFA Sub-Committee on Human Rights & Social Responsibility. Report on remedy and legacy for workers in the context of the FIFA World Cup Qatar 2022*, The Fédération Internationale de Football Association, December 22, 58 p.

Galvin, B.M., Lange, D. and Ashforth, B.E. (2015). Narcissistic organizational identification: Seeing oneself as central to the organization's identity, *Academy of Management Review*, 40(2), 163–181.

Garcia (2014). *Report on the Inquiry into the 2018/2022 FIFA World Cup Bidding Process*, Report of Investigation, Investigatory Chamber, FIFA Ethics Committee, Switzerland: Zürich, 359 p.

Gardiner, S., Parry, J. and Robinson, S. (2017). Integrity and the corruption debate in sport: Where is the integrity? *European Sport Management Quarterly*, 17(1), 6–23.

Gillespie, N., Anesa, M., Lizzio-Wilson, M., Chapman, C., Healy, K. and Hornsey, M. (2024). How do sector level factors influence trust violations in not-for-profit organizations? A multilevel model, *Journal of Business Ethics*, 191, 373–398.

Gottschalk, P. (2024). *Crisis Management – Recovering the Social License by Corporate Conformity*, Oxford University Press, UK: Oxford.

Grafström, M. (2024a). *Fifa World Cup 2030 – Bid Evaluation Report*, The Fédération Internationale de Football Association, p. 178.

Grafström, M. (2024b). *Fifa World Cup 2034 – Bid Evaluation Report*, The Fédération Internationale de Football Association, p. 109.

Jennings, A. and Sambrook, C. (2000). *The Great Olympic Swindle – When the World Wanted its Games back*, Simon & Schuster publishing, UK: London.

Jancsics, D. (2014). Interdisciplinary perspectives on corruption, *Sociology Compass*, 8(4), 358–372.

Jennings, A. (2006). *Foul! The Secret World of FIFA: Bribes Vote Rigging and Ticket Scandals*, HarperSport, HarperCollins Publisher, UK: London.

Kamerdze, S., Loughran, T., Paternoster, R. and Sohoni, T. (2014). The role of affect in intended rule breaking: Extending the rational choice perspective, *Journal of Research in Crime and Delinquency*, 51(5), 620–654.

Karpacheva, E. and Hock, B. (2024). Foreign whistleblowing: The impact of US extraterritorial enforcement on anti-corruption laws in Europe, *Journal of Financial Crime*, 31(1), 1–13.

Kihl, L.A. (2017). *Corruption in Sport: Causes, Consequences, and Reform*, Routledge, UK: London.

Kihl, L.A. (2019). Individual-level explanations of corruption within an intercollegiate context, *Journal of Intercollegiate Sport*, 12(1), 43–72.

Kihl, L.A., Skinner, J. and Engelberg, T. (2017). Corruption in sport: Understanding the complexity of corruption, *European Sport Management Quarterly*, 17(1), 1–5.

Kulczycki, W. and Koenigstorfer, J. (2016). Why sponsors should worry about corruption as a mega sport event syndrome, *European Sport Management Quarterly*, 16(5), 545–574.

Lee, P.C. (2017). Understanding the match-fixing scandals of professional baseball in Taiwan: An exploratory study of a Confucianism-oriented society, *European Sport Management Quarterly*, 17(1), 45–66.

Leigh, A.C., Foote, D.A., Clark, W.R. and Lewis, J.L. (2010). Equity sensitivity: A triadic measure and outcome/input perspectives, *Journal of Managerial Issues*, 22(3), 286–305.

Liu, X., Wang, Y., Yang, F. and Huang, Q. (2024). When the punisher is both potential vicitm and (intended) beneficiary: Investigating observers' attitudianl and behavioral reactions toward organizational punishment severity for unethical pro-organizational behaviors, *Journal of Business Ethics*, 195, 859–877.

Locatelli, G., Mariani, G., Sainati, T. and Greco, M. (2017). Corruption in public projects and megaprojects: There is an elephant in the room! *International Journal of Project Management*, 35(3), 252–268.

Loyens, K., Claringbould, I., Heres-van Rossem, L. and Eekeren, Frank van. (2022). The social construction of integrity: A qualitative case study in Dutch football, *Sports in Society*, 25(9), 1714–1733.

MacInnes, P. (2024). Fifa ignores own report into Qatar World Cup over workers' compensation, *The Guardian*, www.theguardian.com, published November 30.

Malmi, T., Bedford, D.S., Brühl, R., Dergård, J., Hoozee, S., Janschek, O., Willert, J., Ax, C., Bednarek, P., Gosselin, M., Hanzlick, M., Israelsen, P., Johanson, D., Johanson, T., Madsen, D.Ø., Rohde, C., Sandelin, M., Stömsten, T. and Toldbod, T. (2020). Culture and management control interdependence: An analysis of control choices that complement the delegation of authority in Western cultural regions, *Accounting, Organizations and Society*, 86, 1–16.

Moore, C., Detert, J.R., Trevino, K. Baker, V.L. and Mayer, D.M. (2012) Why employees do bad things: Moral disengagement and unethical organizational behavior, *Personnel Psychology*, 65, 1–48.

Næss, H.E. (2023). Diversity and inclusion management in sport organizations: An integrative literature review, *Managing Sport and Leisure*, published first online https://doi.org/10.1080/23750472.2023.2213707.

Oberhauser, M., Conrad, M. and Holtbrügge, D. (2024). Apologize or deny? How companies defend legitimacy of Wall street, Main street, and Market street after corporate misconduct, *Corporate Social Responsibility and Environmental Management*, published first online https://doi.org/10.1002/csr.2951.

Ordway, C. (2023). *Restoring Trust in Sport: Corruption Cases and Solutions*, Routledge, UK: London.

Panja, T. (2021). Hunting trips, sex and cash: How grooming biathlon's leader paid off for Russia – An investigation accuses biathlon's longtime president of accepting gifts from Russians and then doing the country's bidding as a doping scandal swirled, *The New York Times*, www.nytimes.com, published January 28.

Philippou, C. (2022). Anti-bribery and corruption in sport mega-events: Stakeholder perspectives, *Sport in Society*, 25(4), 819–836.

Philippou, C. (2023). Expert perceptions on anti-bribery and corruption policies in sports governing bodies: Implications for ethical climate theory, *Journal of Business Ethics*, published first online https://doi.org/10.1007/s10551-023-05478-x.

Pontell, H.N., Black, W.K. and Geis, G. (2014). Too big to fail, too powerful to jail? On the absence of criminal prosecutions after the 2008 financial meltdown, *Crime, Law and Social Change*, 61(1), 1–13.

Riedl, E. (2021). How sport regulations are being used to restore trust following the International Biathlon Union scandal, in: Ordway, C. (editor), *Restoring*

Trust in Sport – Corruption Cases and Solutions, Routledge, UK: London, pp. 48–63.

Saenz, C. (2019). Building legitimacy and trust between a mining company and a community to earn social license to operate: A Peruvian case study, *Corporate Social Responsibility and Environmental Management*, 26(2), 296–306.

Schoen, J.L., DeSimone, J.A., Meyer, R.D., Schnure, K.A. and LeBreton, J.M. (2021). Identifying, defining, and measuring justification mechanisms: The implicit biases underlying individual differences, *Journal of Management*, 47(3), 716–744.

Sellæg, S.H. (2024). Tarjei Bø kjøper villa på Vinderen (Tajei Bø buys villa at Vinderen), daily Norwegian financial newspaper *Finansavisen*, www.finansavisen.no, published January 9.

Silver, K. and Garofalo, P. (2024). Excusing corporate wrongdoing and the state of nature, *Academy of Management Review*, published first online https://doi.org/10.5465/amr.2020.0236, pp. 1–23.

Stathopoulou, A., Quansah, T.K. and Balabanis, G. (2022). The blinding effects of team identification on sports corruption: Cross-cultural evidence from Sub-Saharan African countries, *Journal of Business Ethics*, 179, 511–529.

Taylor, J. (2021). *Final Report of the IBU External Review Commission*, ERC (External Review Commission), International Biathlon Union, Austria, 28 January, 220 p.

UNODC (2023). *A Practical Guide to the Prosecution of Cases of Competition Manipulation*, United Nations Office on Drugs and Crime, United Nations.

Verstad, A.B. and Rognerud, A. (2021). Bessebergs arvtaker fikk firedoblet lønnen (Besseberg's heir received four times his salary), Norwegian public broadcasting *NRK*, www.nrk.no, published February 3.

Vu, N.H., Nguyen, T.A., Hoang, T.B. and Cuong, N.V. (2024). Formal firms with bribery in a dynamic business environment, *Journal of Business Ethics*, 191, 571–589.

Wijayanti, D.M., Senjani, Y.P. and Farah, W. (2024). The role of Machiavellian personality, altruistic personality, religiosity, whistleblowing system, and accounting firm size in mitigating fraud intention, *Journal of Financial Crime*, 31(1), 119–134.

Zvi, L. and Elaad, E. (2018). Correlates of narcissism, self-reported lies, and self-assessed abilities to tell and detect lies, tell truths, and believe others, *Journal of Investigative Psychology and Offender Profiling*, 15, 271–286.

Chapter 3

The Prosecuted Sport President

Following the verdict at the district court (Buskerud tingrett, 2024), it was important for defendant Anders Besseberg to appeal the prison sentence (Christiansen, 2024b). Some had already considered him guilty without any sense of criminal justice through appeal, such as the World Anti-Doping Agency (WADA) stating that "WADA welcomes guilty verdict in Besseberg case" without affording Bassler the benefit of the doubt, which is a requirement in democratic countries with criminal justice systems (WADA, 2024):

> The World Anti-Doping Agency (WADA) welcomes the guilty verdict by a court in Norway in relation to the former President of the International Biathlon Union (IBU), Anders Besseberg, who was on trial in connection to criminal corruption charges related to accepting bribes and other inducements and favoring Russia while he was head of the IBU.

Witold Banka was the president at WADA, who ignored Besseberg's appeal and thus considered him guilty. Banka was a former Polish 400-meter sprinter who later became a politician. He served for several years as minister of sport and tourism in the cabinets of Beata Szydlo and Mateusz Morawiecki in Poland. In May 2019, he was elected president of WADA.

3.1 Replacing Defense Lawyers at Appeal

After the appeal written by defense lawyers Mikkel Toft Gimse and Christian B. Hjort was successfully accepted for a complete trial at the Borgarting Court of Appeal, defendant Anders Besseberg decided to change his defense lawyer by choosing attorney Fredrik Berg (Påsche, 2024). "He wants fresh eyes on the case, I think that might be wise, says Hjort" (Cederblad, 2024b). The law firms present their attorneys in this way by referring to them as partner (Hjort), managing associate (Gimse), and owner (Berg):

- Christian B. Hjort has extensive experience in a wide range of civil and financial criminal cases. Over the years, Christian has represented companies and private individuals in a number of high-profile financial criminal cases involving corruption, insider trading, market manipulation, financial misconduct, and tax fraud (www.hjort.no).
- Mikkel Toft Gimse specializes in criminal law and has provided legal assistance in a wide range of criminal and compensation cases. He possesses particular expertise in economic crimes, market abuse, and labor law-related offenses. Mikkel has represented both defendants and victims of financial crimes, working to safeguard their assets (www.hjort.no).
- Fredrik works as a litigation lawyer, serving as both a defense attorney in financial crime cases and in civil proceedings. He has assisted in several large, high-profile cases. Fredrik also has experience in the shipping and offshore industries. He has negotiated many contracts in shipbuilding (www.fend.no).

The attorneys seem to have similar profiles, as "financial crime cases", "economic crimes", and "financial crime cases" are emphasized in the presentations. Yet, the failure of Hjort and Gimse to successfully defend Besseberg (Gottschalk, 2024) might stimulate Berg to develop an alternative approach to the defense work in the courtroom as a theatrical scene (Gupta and Gottschalk, 2023).

The new defense lawyer, Fredrik Berg, was voted Norway's best lawyer in economic crime in 2024, as presented by journalist Oliver Orskaug in the business magazine Kapital's version regarding law (Cederblad, 2024c):

> Oliver Orskaug, responsible for the annual lawyer survey for Kapital Jus, tells Dagbladet that Berg climbed the list for several years, before he won this year's survey by the narrowest possible margin: one point.
>
> — He was very surprised when he received the award. He was humble and made it clear that it was not an individual effort. It was his entire office that was behind it, says Orskaug to Dagbladet.
> — How would you describe Berg as a lawyer?
> — He has always behaved very neatly. Great working capacity, and always speaks in the interests of his clients. He has worked for several large law firms before starting Fend, replies Orskaug.

In the interview, journalist Orskaug said that Berg ticks several boxes for what a lawyer who works with economic crime needs: criminal law, economics, business law, and international experience. The latter is important, as economic crime is not something that necessarily happens in Norway. Economic crime is international crime, such as the allegations against Besseberg related to deviant behaviors in Russia, Germany, and Austria, and it is not reserved for a single country, Orskaug said in the interview (Cederblad, 2024c).

On the other side, both Gimse and Hjort had been criticized for being too passive in the district court (Cederblad, 2024a):

> Anders Besseberg's (78) good friend Kjell Hovda (78) cannot believe that his friend was convicted of gross corruption for his role as president of the International Biathlon Union (IBU).
>
> — For me, it is completely meaningless that a person like Anders, whom I know so well, should be sentenced to three years in prison. When you know what work he has put in and how honest, proper and fair he is in many ways, they it is completely beyond, Hovda tells Dagbladet, just days after the verdict was handed down. He assured that "Anders is ready to fight on". As is well known, Besseberg appealed the merciless sentence on the spot in Buskerud district court on Friday last week. Since then, Hovda has spoken several times with Besseberg.
> — He was very, very disappointed. Especially with the fact that they were unable to come up with almost any arguments, says the close friend.

In fact, one of the reasons for the replacement of lawyers, Besseberg told me in a phone conversation I had with him on November 6, 2024, was the passive attitude of his defense lawyers. He said he had repeatedly conveyed written reminders to them on the defense bench, but those were ignored, and none of them had reacted. Especially when witnesses told stories in which Besseberg disagreed about the facts, he had handed over written reminders without any reaction from Gimse or Hjort. Both remained silent most of the time during the several weeks of trial. That made Besseberg really frustrated. Therefore, he was happy to work with attorney Berg in October 2024, instead of preparing for the appeal trial scheduled for the following year. In a press release from the Borgarting Court of Appeal in November 2024, the court announced that the trial would begin on April 23, 2025, and last 21 days (NRK, 2024; NTB, 2024a).

3.2 The International Biathlon Union

Anders Besseberg was president of the International Biathlon Union (IBU) from 1992 until he was laid off in 2018 following accusations of wrongdoing. During those years, the sport of biathlon evolved from being a sport for people who were particularly interested to becoming one of the most popular winter sports on television. Besseberg is considered the architect of the various successful forms of competition in biathlon, such as the hunting start, joint start, and mixed relays. He elevated the sport of biathlon to new heights during his tenure as president. Having served as president for such a long time, he became a powerful individual with great influence internationally. There were no restrictions on being the union president or how many terms he could serve in such a central position without being replaced. Besseberg has been a central figure in shaping the business, culture, ethics, structure, and compliance of right and wrong at IBU as an organization. The suspected fraud involved the president receiving favors and bribes from Russian biathlon union officials.

The IBU is headquartered in Salzburg, Austria (Ellingworth and Dunbar, 2018). Biathlon is a winter sport that combines cross-country skiing and rifle shooting. It is treated as a race, with contestants skiing through a cross-country trail whose distance is divided into shooting rounds. Major biathlon nations include France, Russia, Sweden, and Norway. Biathlon is a very popular sport among spectators, both present at shooting stadiums and in front of television screens all over the world. The business of biathlon events has grown significantly in recent decades, and rumors of both corruption and doping have flourished in the media for several years.

Russian doping whistleblower Grigory Rodchenkov told the media about organized doping of Russian athletes at the Sochi Winter Olympics (Ruiz and Schwirtz, 2016). He had been the head of Russia's national anti-doping laboratory (Pelley, 2018). Rodchenkov's allegations were confirmed by the independent McLaren (2016) report, leading to Russia's partial bans from the 2016 Summer Olympics and the 2018 Winter Olympics. Rodchenkov's allegations and the McLaren (2016) findings led to an investigation, particularly targeted at the management of the IBU. When the IBU report was released (Taylor, 2021), the *New York Times* reported on it under the heading "Hunting trips, sex, and cash: How grooming biathlon's leader paid off for Russia: An investigation accuses biathlon's longtime president of accepting gifts from Russians and then doing the country's bidding as a doping scandal swirled" (Panja, 2021):

> The president of the International Biathlon Union told the police that the young woman who had come to his hotel in Moscow was a prostitute, but he was hazy on the details. He did not remember the date or even who had paid for her services, he said, but it had assuredly not been him. The president, Anders Besseberg, had led biathlon's governing body for more than two decades by then, and he was accustomed to receiving gifts from his Russian hosts. Like a chocolate on his pillow or a gift bag placed on a chair in his hotel room, the company of a young woman during a trip to a World Cup biathlon event was not uncommon.

The potential offender in this case study is Anders Besseberg, who appears, in the view of the commission, to have had no regard for ethical values and no real interest in protecting the sport from cheating. Taylor (2021) claims that Besseberg was enabled by a complete lack of basic governance safeguards, leaving integrity decisions in the sole hands of himself and his allies on the IBU executive board, with no checks and balances, no transparency, and no accountability. Integrity is the quality of acting in accordance with moral values, norms, and rules considered valid and relevant within the context in which the actor operates (Loyens *et al.*, 2021). The external review commission found that Besseberg had been bribed by Russian officials for more than EUR 300,000.

3.3 Court Verdict of Sixty-Seven Pages

The document is dated April 12, 2024. It was written by District Court Judge Vidar Toftøy-Lohne, with participation from lay judges Kari Aasen Ingebo and Gunnar Andre Sanden. The prosecution was represented by state prosecutor Marianne Djupesland and police lawyer Marthe Stømner Smestad. The defense of Anders Besseberg was handled by attorneys Christian Fredrik Bonnevie Hjort and Mikkel Toft Gimse. That is information on the first page (Buskerud tingrett, 2024).

The second page details the indictment against Anders Besseberg, born February 25, 1946, residing at Besseberg Road 48 in the town of Vestfossen. The Norwegian penal code relevant to the case is § 388, which charges the defendant "for having for himself or others demanded, received or accepted an offer of an undue advantage on the occasion of the performance of a position, office or the performance of an assignment". "Position, office, or assignment" also includes position, office, or assignment abroad. Corruption is serious because particular emphasis is placed on the fact that the act was committed in breach of the special trust which comes with his position, office, or assignment and because it has resulted in significant financial benefit.

The verdict claims that Besseberg is responsible for connected criminal activities, which means that he has been exhibiting the tendency to commit crimes during all his years as the IBU president. This is very different from viewing the charges as independent incidents of corrupt behavior. The court claims in the verdict that there is a relationship between the charges in terms of the offender having a criminal mindset all those years as president at IBU. The verdict implies that he was open to bribes during those years. The Norwegian term for a connected punishable circumstance – "*et sammenhengende straffbart forhold*" – is repeated 16 times in the 67-page verdict.

Although the document is written in Norwegian, it contains several quotes in English regarding various matters outside of Norway. For example, the conflicts-of-interest regulation was introduced in ethical guidelines at the IBU in 2012 (Buskerud tingrett, 2024):

> All those acting on behalf of the IBU must make decisions in the interests of the IBU. All those whose personal interests might reasonably be perceived as being affected by a decision or policy concerning an IBU

> matter (including receiving material benefits) shall refrain from the decision-making process (page 12).
>
> Persons and organizations as listed in Art. 1.1 are expected to be aware of the importance of their task and shall be aware of their obligations and responsibilities. They shall pledge to behave in a dignified manner. They shall behave and act with complete credibility and integrity. They may not abuse their position as part of their function to take advantage of their function for private aims or gains, or in any other way (page 12).

Anders Besseberg had at his disposal a BMW car that was provided to him by the car manufacturer as the main sponsor of IBU events. However, auditors at the IBU found no documentation for the arrangement (Buskerud tingrett, 2024: 46):

> As you know, during our audit this past summer for the fiscal year 2011/2012 we discovered information which indicated that one of the IBU BMW cars is in Norway in your personal use. This was a surprise to the Auditors as we were totally unaware of such an arrangement.

Although corruption legislation in Norway does not require that the bribed change behavior to satisfy the briber, the court nevertheless discussed decisions regarding World Cup events in Russia (Buskerud tingrett, 2024: 53):

> Because of the detailed references to the manipulation of samples during the Olympic Winter Games Sochi 2014 the IOC asks all International Olympic Winter Sports Federations to freeze their preparations for major events in Russia, such as World Championships, World Cups or other major international competitions under their responsibility, and to actively look for alternative organizers.

Anders Besseberg appealed the verdict to the Borgarting Court of Appeal in Oslo, where the trial was scheduled to take place one year later in 2025. If later appealed to the Norwegian Supreme Court, then a final verdict was not expected until 2027.

While awaiting the response to the appeal from the Borgarting Court, the Norwegian Sports Federation announced the decision to rescind the award given to Besseberg when referring to the honorary distinction at a press conference on May 8, 2024. In the decision, it was stated that Besseberg, by having acknowledged objectionable circumstances in court, had damaged the reputation of the sport. Besseberg, now 78 years old, had been convicted on almost all charges and sentenced to three years and one month in prison for gross corruption while serving as president of the IBU. His lawyer, Toft Gimse, reacted strongly to the message that Besseberg was not allowed to retain his honorary distinction:

> — Anders Besseberg is not familiar with this. We react to the fact that he has not been contacted, but learn about this from the media, writes Gimse and elaborates: -Besseberg emphasizes that the verdict against him is not legally binding and sees this as part of the in-advance judgment against him.

The acting president of the Norwegian Sports Federation, Arne Bård Dalhaug, said at the press briefing that they had announced a review of the honorary distinctions following the corruption verdict at the district court. The review was now completed, and the conclusion of withdrawing the award of an honorary distinction was final.

3.4 The Rotten Apple Metaphor

Anders Besseberg lost his honorary membership in the Norwegian Sports Federation based on the verdict from a district court ruling that was not final. Similarly, WADA (2024) welcomed the guilty verdict in the Besseberg case without affording Besseberg the benefit of the doubt that is a requirement in democratic countries with criminal justice systems. The Norwegian Biathlon Union did not follow the example of the Norwegian Sports Federation. Besseberg kept his honorary membership in the union, as “the union is waiting with its assessments until the case is completed in the legal system” (NTB, 2024b).

Fourteen sponsors were at the time linked to the Norwegian Biathlon Union. None of them reacted to the accusations other than condemning Anders Besseberg’s behavior. The main Norwegian sponsor, Ice Communications, said that it distanced itself from what had emerged in the district court proceedings. The main global sponsor of the IBU in

Austria, the car manufacturer BMW, based in Germany, claimed that it had no compliance issues, as referenced and discussed in the following chapter. Kulczycki and Koenigstorfer (2016) argued that sponsors should worry about corruption as a mega-sport event syndrome. However, the sponsors did not seem to worry, as they attempted to consider Anders Besseberg a rotten apple rather than the IBU a rotten apple basket. White-collar offenders are often considered rotten apples; however, it may be more appropriate to describe the phenomenon of white-collar crime as a basket of rotten apples or a rotten apple orchard, as Punch (2003: 172) defined it:

> The metaphor of 'rotten orchards' indicates that it is sometimes not the apple, or even the barrel that is rotten but the system (or significant parts of the system).

A rotten-apple or a bad-apple perspective assumes that an individual member of an organization acts alone and that criminal activity might occur with or without the knowledge or participation of the organization as such (Bright *et al.*, 2024). The bad barrel refers to a situation "where the organization behaves unethically and is motivated to commit fraud for economic gain" (Manning *et al.*, 2024: 4).

In the beginning of the IBU scandal, Besseberg was accused of corruption while the general secretary at the IBU, Nicole Resch, was accused of covering up doping violations by Russian biathlete Evgeny Ustyugov at the 2014 Sochi Olympics (Taylor, 2021: 5):

> In April 2018, it was widely reported that the criminal authorities in Austria and Norway were investigating allegations that then-IBU President Anders Besseberg and IBU Secretary General Nicole Resch had buried evidence of Russian doping in return for improper benefits (including, in Mr. Besseberg's case, receipt of up to $300,000), and had conducted surprise raids of their respective residences and of the IBU offices to search for potential evidence.

Nicole Resch was never charged or prosecuted. Therefore, Anders Besseberg remained the single rotten apple in the eyes of biathlon stakeholders. The rotten-apple perspective is an individualistic approach to corruption and other forms of economic crime that views deviance as the work of isolated individuals who evade detection during their actions.

The rotten-apple view of white-collar crime is a comfortable perspective to adopt for organizations, as it allows them to look no further than suspected individuals. It is certainly an interesting issue whether to view white-collar misconduct as acts of individuals perceived as rotten apples or as an indication of systemic failures in sports organizations, the sporting industry, or the society as a whole. In this perspective, it is interesting to note that the media reported that "another president of the IBU is suspected of receiving bribes" (Perez, 2024):

> President of the International Biathlon Union, Olle Dahlin, is suspected of receiving bribes, as reported by NRK. According to sources, the Austrian police have already initiated a criminal investigation. The current president is suspected of potentially signing a sponsorship deal with Infront, a company that buys and sells television rights.

Infront was also subject to criminal investigation, where the investigation was focusing on Infront executives Stefan Kraus and Volker Schmid (Christiansen, 2024a):

> "We confirm that an investigation is ongoing in Austria into whether irregularities have occurred in connection with the business relationship between Infront Austria and the former IBU president. We are cooperating with the authorities in this matter", wrote a spokesperson for Infront to the newspaper.

While Besseberg might indeed be guilty, there seem to be more people involved in the systems failure at the IBU and at the union's business partners. As summarized by Gottschalk (2024: 88), following the district court trial in Norway:

> Several of the 24 witnesses had been or were still investigated by criminal police in Austria. One of them was the current IBU president, Olle Dahlin. He was suspected of corruption based on the assumption that the marketing firm InFront had simply continued its favorable deal with the IBU since the Besseberg period and still into the current Dahlin period.

The IBU and its business partners were participants in the rotten-apple basket evidences organizational problems regarding compliance and lack of conformity. Violations of legally binding statutes might have occurred at both the IBU and its partner, Infront, in the roles of potential bribed and briber in a corrupt relationship. Violations of norms and values might have occurred not only at the IBU and its partner, Infront, but also at various sponsors, including BMW as a global sponsor and Ice Communications, along with 13 more companies as local sponsors in Norway, which are presented in the following chapter.

Infront Sport & Media is a sports marketing company based in Zug, Switzerland. Infront presented itself as a global leader that shapes the future of sport at the time when Philippe Blatter was the president and chief executive officer at Infront (www.infront.sport):

> At Infront, we believe sport is one of the true unifying forces in the world. It transcends barriers and borders, inspiring billions of fans and participants from all walks of life every day. We see it as our role to act as a trusted partner for brands and rights holders to unite people in sport, so that they can live their passion and dreams. How do we achieve this? With a global team of professionals and as pioneer in sports marketing, we have been supporting sponsor brands, media companies, and the wider sports industry to connect with and build their audiences, and to grow their presence and impact for half a decade.

The rotten-apple metaphor finds support in social conflict theory, suggesting that the powerful and wealthy in the upper class of society define what is right and what is wrong. The ruling class makes laws for others, not for themselves. The justice system is biased and designed to protect powerful individuals (Daukere *et al.*, 2023). They are too big to fail and too powerful to jail (Pontell *et al.*, 2014). However, to maintain the legitimacy of laws in the eyes of others, they do sometimes need to punish their own. It is a matter of scapegoating (Faldetta and Gervasi, 2024) by attributing blame to target individuals (Sonnier *et al.*, 2015). However, whether or not Anders Besseberg was a victim of scapegoating by being attributed blame as a former member of the upper class of society is too early to tell.

The perception of a rotten apple is frequently linked to the perception of guilt by prejudgment. In democratic societies with criminal justice, however, a suspected individual is considered innocent until proven guilty beyond a reasonable and sensible doubt. Yet, the media and the public, and sometimes even the police and prosecution, may pass a verdict of guilt by blaming and shaming, independent of potential evidence and proof. Rumors, allegations, and accusations, among other forms of unsubstantiated claims, are allowed to surface and form a basis for the conclusion of guilt. It is therefore important to explore the complexities of criminal justice and challenge these harmful tendencies by applying the concepts of compliance and conformity to individual cases in respectful ways.

In the case of former IBU president Anders Besseberg, he became a victim of prejudgment several years before entering the courtroom for the first time in a trial against him as the defendant. At the time of writing this text, he has appealed the guilty verdict, which implies that he is still to be considered innocent. However, very few considered him innocent. A former biathlete was early on an exception. She criticized the prejudgment in the media ahead of the district court trial (Pedersen, 2024):

> Gunn Margit (50) about the corruption case: -Many men love to hunt and most men like women. Former biathlete Gunn Margit Andreassen does not like the prejudgment of Anders Besseberg. On Tuesday, the corruption case against Anders Besseberg (77) began in Buskerud district court. Former biathlete Gunn Margit Andreassen was very surprised when the case became known.

Another retired biathlete commented in the media three years ahead of the district court trial (Kolstad, 2021):

> — If this is true, then it is disgusting. I cannot – and will not – imagine such a world, says Liv Grete Skjelbreid (46) about the accusations against Anders Besseberg.

Skjelbreid has won eight gold medals in the world biathlon championships (six individual, one relay, and one in team competition), two Olympic silver medals (one relay), one Olympic bronze medal, and 22 individual victories in the Biathlon World Cup. Andreassen and Skjelbreid, in their fifties, had chosen different careers in 2024: Andreassen was now a real estate agent, while Skjelbreid offered lectures and training to business managers.

While prejudicing Anders Besseberg as a rotten apple was frequent in Norwegian media after the Taylor (2021) report, miscarriage of justice is a real concern. In fact, miscarriage of justice is typically a serious concern in Norway. Criminal justice refers to the delivery of justice to those who have been accused of committing crime. Doubt should always benefit the accused, and guilt has to be proven beyond any reasonable and sensible doubt to enable conviction by a court of justice. Miscarriage of justice by sentencing someone who is innocent is a risk that most criminal justice systems in democratic societies struggle to avoid. Rather than incarcerating an innocent person, a number of guilty criminals are never sent to prison. In countries with criminal justice systems, avoidance of miscarriage is so important that law enforcement officers may acquit defendants who obviously seem guilty to the public eye due to a lack of convincing evidence. This is the price to pay in democratic societies to avoid convicting innocent people. Until guilt is proven beyond any sensible and reasonable doubt, the defendant is to be considered innocent. Doubt, though, has never officially been quantified in any jurisdiction in terms of probability. Yet, a major likelihood, i.e., more than 50% probability, which is frequently applied in corporate investigations, is certainly not sufficient in criminal proceedings. If doubt accounts for less than 5% or 1% of the picture, then guilt must be evidenced and proven beyond 95% or 99% certainty.

Criminal justice is problematic in democratic societies with legal procedures as well since only wrongdoing and misconduct that happen to be described in legal statutes and codes can be considered by judges in criminal courts. Wrongdoing and misconduct that are not described cannot be considered in the criminal justice system in terms of police investigation, crime prosecution, or court trials. While most democratic societies attempt to criminalize what people think should be punished, there are obvious gaps and shortcomings. Therefore, conformity is not simply a matter of being consistent with norms and values but also a matter of refraining from crimes that are without legal basis but are considered bad and should be punished.

References

Bright, D., Sadewo, G., Cubitt, T.I.C., Dowling, C. and Morgan, A. (2024). Co-offending networks among members of outlaw motorcycle gangs across types of crime, *Trends in Organized Crime*, 27, 263–285.

Buskerud tingrett (2024). Court case number 23-03940MED-TBUS/THOK, *Buskerud tingrett* (Buskerud district court), professional judge Vidar Toftøy-Lohne, lay judges Kari Aasen Ingebo and Gunnar Sanden, Hokksund, Norway, verdict document p. 67.

Cederblad, C.A. (2024a). Advokatene får sterk kritikk (The lawyers receive strong criticism), daily Norwegian newspaper *Dagbladet*, www.dagbladet.no, published April 22.

Cederblad, C.A. (2024b). Kvitter seg med advokater (Gets rid of lawyers), daily Norwegian newspaper *Dagbladet*, www.dagbladet.no, published October 30.

Cederblad, C.A. (2024c). Henter "Norges beste" (Brings in Norway's best), daily Norwegian newspaper *Dagbladet*, www.dagbladet.no, published October 31.

Christiansen, A.K. (2024a). Tre vitner «mistenkt» i Besseberg-saken: Bekrefter etterforskning (Three witnesses «suspected» in the Besseberg case: Confirm investigation), daily Norwegian newspaper *VG*, www.vg.no, published January 30.

Christiansen, A.K. (2024b). Aktor: Besseberg trekker klokke-anke (Prosecutor: Besseberg withdraws watch appeal), Norwegian daily newspaper *VG*, www.vg.no, published October 15.

Daukere, B.E., Dankani, I.M., Yahaya, I.K., Sulaiman, T.M., Olaniyi, O.I. and Eniolorunda, N.B. (2023). A spatial patterning of the relationship between indigenous police force numerical strength, socioeconomic characteristics and crime rate in Nigeria, *Social Sciences & Humanities Open*, published online https://doi.org/10.1016/j.ssaho.2023.100644, p. 13.

Ellingworth, J. and Dunbar, G. (2018). Biathlon president steps down after police raid in Austria, *AP News*, www.apnews.com, published April 12.

Faldetta, G. and Gervasi, D. (2024). Escaping the scapegoat trap: Using René Girard's framework, *Journal of Business Ethics*, 191, 269–283.

Gottschalk, P. (2024). Economic crime in the courtroom: A case study of defense lawyers' arguments against prosecution evidence, *Journal of Economic Criminology*, 5, published first online https://doi.org/10.1016/j.jeconc.2024.100085.

Gottschalk, P. (2025). *Corruption, Criminal Justice, and Compliance in Sport – The Case of the International Biathlon Union*, Routledge, UK: Abbingdon.

Gupta, C.M. and Gottschalk, P. (2023). *Trusted White-Collar Defendants – The Courtroom as a Theater Scene*, Springer publishing, Switzerland: Cham.

Kolstad, J.G. (2021). Skjelbreid sjokkert over Besseberg: -Vi var naive da jeg var aktiv (Skjelbreid shocked by Besseberg: -We were naive when I was active), local daily newspaper *Bergensavisen*, www.ba.no, published January 28.

Loyens, K., Claringbould, I., Heres-van Rossem, L. and Eekeren, Frank van. (2021). The social construction of integrity: A qualitative case study in Dutch football, *Sports in Society*, published online https://doi.org/10.1080/17430437.2021.1877661.

Manning, L., MacLeod, A., James, C., Thompson, M., Oyeyinka, S., Cowen, N., Skoczylis, J. and Onarinde, B.A. (2024). Food fraud prevention strategies:

Building an effective verification ecosystem, *Comprehensive Reviews in Food Science and Food Safety*, 23, published first online https://doi.org/10.1111/1541-4337.70036.

McLaren, R.H. (2016). *Wada Investigation of Sochi Allegations*, independent person report to the world anti-doping agency, December 9, 151 p.

NRK (2024). Besseberg-anke for retten i april (Besseberg appeal in court in April), public Norwegian broadcasting *NRK*, www.nrk.no, published November 1.

NTB (2024a). Norges Skiskyterforbund gjør ikke som NIF – avventer vurdering av Bessebergs æresmedlemskap (The Norwegian Biathlon Union is not doing like NIF does – awaiting assessment of Besseberg's honorary membership), web-based Norwegian newspaper *Nettavisen*, www.nettavisen.no, published May 8.

NTB (2024b). Ankebehandlingen i korrupsjonssaken mot Anders Besseberg starter 23. april (The appeal hearing in the corruption case against Anders Besseberg starts on April 23rd), web-based Norwegian newspaper *Nettavisen*, www.nettavisen.no, published November 1.

Panja, T. (2021). Hunting trips, sex and cash: How grooming biathlon's leader paid off for Russia – An investigation accused biathlon's longtime president of accepting gifts from Russians and then doing the country's bidding as a doping scandal swirled, *The New York Times*, www.nytimes.com, published January 28.

Pedersen, R. (2024). Gunn Margit (50) om korrupsjonssaken: -Mange menn elsker å jakte og de fleste menn liker damer (Gunn Margit (50) about the corruption case: -Many men love to hunt and most men like women), local daily newspaper *Ringerike Blad*, www.ringblad.no, published January 9.

Pelley, S. (2018). The Russian doping mastermind on the run, *CBS News*, www.cbsnews.com, published February 11.

Perez, S. (2024). Another president of the IBU is suspected of receiving bribes, *Daily Sports*, www.dailysports.net, published February 27.

Pontell, H.N., Black, W.K. and Geis, G. (2014). Too big to fail, too powerful to jail? On the absence of criminal prosecutions after the 2008 financial meltdown, *Crime, Law and Social Change*, 61(1), 1–13.

Punch, M. (2003). Rotten Orchards: "Pestilence", police misconduct and system failure, *Policing and Society*, 13(2), 171–196.

Påsche, E.S. (2024). Dagbladet: Besseberg bytter advokat (Newspaper: Besseberg switches lawyer), daily Norwegian newspaper *VG*, www.vg.no, published October 30.

Ruiz, R.R. and Schwirtz, M. (2016). Russian insider says state-run doping fueled Olympic gold, *The New York Times*, www.nytimes.com, published May 12.

Sonnier, B.M., Lassar, W.M. and Lassar, S.S. (2015). The influence of source credibility and attribution of blame on juror evaluation of liability of industry specialist auditors, *Journal of Forensic & Investigative Accounting*, 7(1), 1–37.

Taylor, J. (2021). *Final Report of the IBU External Review Commission*, ERC (External Review Commission), International Biathlon Union, Austria, 28 January, 220 p.

Wada (2024). WADA welcomes guilty verdict in Besseberg case, *The World Anti-Doping Agency (WADA)*, www.wada-ama.org, published April 12.

Chapter 4

Case: BMW as Biathlon Sponsor

It has been argued that sponsors will reconsider their support and possibly withdraw their financial support when the supported entity and events become subject to allegations of economic crime. The International Biathlon Union (IBU) and its world cups and championships have been accused of corruption for a decade, and the former president of the union is being prosecuted in court. Yet, the German car manufacturer BMW did not change its position as the main sponsor. In the email exchange presented in this chapter, the compliance officer at BMW responded, "We confirm that BMW AG is the official title sponsor of the BMW IBU World Cup Biathlon". The case study presented in this chapter is interesting, as it illustrates limited stakeholder concerns as long as the sponsor perceives sufficient benefits from the sponsorship. However, the case study also illustrates that the company has some interest in addressing compliance while demonstrating no apparent interest in addressing conformity.

In many jurisdictions globally, both the bribed and the briber are considered criminals in a corruption relationship. While the bribed has committed the offense of accepting an improper and undue advantage, the briber has committed the offense of providing such an advantage. There is necessarily no legal requirement that the briber was able to or even successful in influencing the bribed, as legislation varies among jurisdictions. In the current case study of the former president of the IBU prosecuted in Norway, there was no such requirement. He had at home a BMW X5 car free of charge for his private and exclusive use from 2011 to 2018

(Ingle, 2023, 2024; Panja, 2021; Riedl, 2021). In the Norwegian district court, he was convicted of corruption due to the car and other illegitimate benefits he had received (Buskerud tingrett, 2024).

The German car manufacturer BMW was the main sponsor of IBU World Cup events. This article addresses the following research question: *How did the sponsor, as a stakeholder, react to the allegation of being the briber in the IBU corruption scandal?* This research question is relevant because sponsors, as stakeholders, may or may not react to corruption allegations against the sponsored organization. In this case study, the company BMW in Germany was the official title sponsor of the IBU Biathlon World Cup, while the marketing firm Infront in Austria was the contractual partner for the German car manufacturer, responsible for allocating vehicles to IBU top officials (Associated Press, 2024; Buskerud tingrett, 2024; Gottschalk, 2024; Ingle, 2023, 2024). The research method employed in this study involved email exchanges between the researcher and the compliance officer at BMW in Germany. This article adds to the research stream on stakeholder concerns regarding economic crime, generally, and on sponsors as stakeholders, particularly.

4.1 Concern by Sponsors as Stakeholders

Cheong *et al.* (2019: 288) argued that "the global market sees the rapid rise of sports promotion as a major component of the marketing mix" through advertising and sponsorship:

> While advertising refers to a two-way communication process between advertiser and consumer, sponsorship includes a three-way communication process among sponsor, property, and consumer. Accordingly, sponsorship is defined as a business relationship between a provider (sponsor) of funds, resources or services and an individual, event or organization (property) which offers in return some rights and association that may be used for commercial advantage. Sport sponsorship may represent the form of attaining the right of entitlement to events (e.g. Virgin Money London Marathon), athletes (e.g. Adidas's endorsement deal with football celebrity David Beckham), or a facility (e.g. Etihad Stadium).

Similar to this definition of sport sponsorship as a business relationship (Cheong *et al.*, 2019), Parganas *et al.* (2017: 460) referred to sport sponsorship as "an investment, in cash or in kind, in an activity, in return for access to the exploitable commercial potential associated with that activity" that "involves sponsoring sport associations, leagues, teams, athletes, facilities, events, and competitions".

The term "stakeholder" refers to individuals or groups with an interest or concern in something. A stakeholder is someone who can affect or be affected by something or who associates with something and does or does not derive utility from that association. A stakeholder can be someone who derives their own identity to some extent from the attributes of something. Lange *et al.* (2022) argued that a stakeholder should not necessarily be viewed as someone having a single-minded focus on their own utility, but rather as someone having an outcome in mind that often will be of utility for groups of people based on a kind of solidarity.

At sporting events, Philippou (2022) identified two groups of stakeholders who relate to athletes and sponsors. Among stakeholders related to athletes, she listed fans, media, sport governance officials, sport governing bodies, residents of host cities, politicians, and law enforcement personnel in those cities. Among stakeholders related to sponsors, she listed advertising companies, construction companies, concession and service providers, and betting companies. In her empirical study of stakeholder perspectives on anti-bribery and corruption, she interviewed individuals from three internationally dispersed groups: anti-bribery specialist practitioners, sport governance officials, and stakeholders working in sport.

Participants in the interviews were asked whether they would expect specific anti-bribery measures around sport events. Two strands emerged from the responses: governance and competition. Kourula *et al.* (2019: 1104) defined governance as consisting of organizational leaders who direct behaviors of business conduct through rulemaking, enforcement, and sanctions:

> By "governance", we refer not to corporate governance, but to the wider concept of societal governance, that of the collective means to give "direction to society" which we take to include direction to society's politics and markets.

While there are stakeholder concerns regarding corruption, a number of factors influence sponsors' dealings with corruption, as listed by Chadwick *et al.* (2018: 115):

> What is clear is that sponsors seem to operate with a 'wait-and-see' or 'it depends' mentality when it comes to dealing with corruption in sport. The variables of the severity and frequency of any transgressive or corrupt act (i.e. repeat offenders), the media interest in and the sport affected by the case, the level at which the corrupt act occurred (i.e., a major global competition as opposed to a less popular or commercialized sport or a lower league competition), the cost of withdrawing from a sponsorship agreement both in terms of the financial cost and the costs to the image of the brand, the level of investment, and the length of the relationship with the rights-holder all impact upon the decision that would be made by a sponsor in light of the scandal.

Concerns by sponsors, as stakeholders, are based on social judgments and evaluations that "encompass a broad spectrum of concepts that reflect individual and collective perceptions of an organization or other entities" (Bitektine *et al.*, 2025: 1). Relevant concepts include legitimacy (an assessment of an entity and its actions as desirable and appropriate), trustworthiness (an assessment of the ability to function reliably with integrity), reputation (an assessment of the entity's past actions), status (an assessment of the order or rank of the entity), and authenticity (an assessment of the consistency between the entity's internal values and its external expressions). Sponsors, as evaluators, might base their assessments on first-hand inputs, borrowed inputs, and taken-for-granted views of the entity.

According to Philippou (2022), anti-bribery in sport through governance begins by assessing risk factors. Lack of hierarchy and lack of transparency were two risk factors; lack of hierarchy implies that sanctions against deviance are difficult to implement, and lack of transparency implies that the wrong things might be done or that things are done for the wrong reasons or based on the wrong considerations. Transparency can lead to ensuring that the right things are done for the right reasons, based on the right considerations.

The competition perspective is concerned with the actual events in host nations. Stakeholder concerns here might be addressed through due diligence of all contracts and projects, a whistleblower hotline, and a professional group to investigate allegations and accusations. Furthermore, when investigations conclude with misconduct, enforcement of sanctions and penalties is important. Enforcement might include cooperation with law enforcement by reporting incidents to the police, as happened in the IBU case to be presented later in this chapter.

Whistleblowing is the disclosure by an individual within an organization or society of deviant practices to someone who can do something about it. Whistleblowing is an action by employees who believe their business or colleague(s) are involved in activities of misconduct or crime, causing unnecessary harm, violating human rights, or contributing to otherwise immoral offenses (Mpho, 2017). Whistleblowers stand out as a group of reporters who have made observations and are willing to disclose them. However, stakeholders may try to withhold bad news (Bao *et al.*, 2019) and punish whistleblowers through reprisals and retaliation. Ondrackova and Verschuuren (2021: 134) emphasized whistleblowing platforms as a solution to fight corruption in sport, stating that "internal reporting mechanisms are now considered as a leading fraud detection mechanism".

Stakeholders tend to have multiple concerns, as they are typically a heterogeneous rather than a homogeneous group. Stakeholders may have both rational and emotional concerns that need attention. Rational concerns address how the organization can align with laws and norms to eliminate deviance. Emotional concerns address the negative affect toward the organization and how badly stakeholders feel about the organization (Iqbal *et al.*, 2024: 302):

> As opposed to rational concerns that are focused on what happened and who was responsible, emotional concerns are fundamentally about how the stakeholder feels about the crisis and organization. While emotional concerns may not be outwardly communicated, they are critical components of stakeholders' perceptions of organizations and thus need to be mitigated by organizations during a crisis. Finally, stakeholders' moral concerns arise when a crisis signals value incongruence between an organization and its stakeholders.

Rational, emotional, and moral concerns should be addressed through accountability and attention, according to Iqbal *et al.* (2024). Accountability refers to the organizational acceptance of responsibility for its role, while attention refers to organizational efforts to focus on stakeholder concerns. Governance mechanisms are needed to "induce or force management to internalize the welfare of stakeholders" (Stoelhorst and Vishwanathan, 2024: 109).

Sponsors associate with individual biathletes, biathlon organizations, and biathlon events to gain positive responses in their own markets.

Sponsorship of sports events is a popular marketing tool to connect companies and brands with potential customers in favorable contexts, allowing for positive associations to be formed. If the sponsored individual, unit, or event turns out to be corrupt, associating with them may cause negative reactions among target group members and sponsors. That is why, according to Kulczycki and Koenigstofer (2016), sponsors should worry about corruption in sports.

While this negative link between corruption and perceptions of sponsors at events might be true, there was no evidence of the link at the World Cup events in biathlon, which is the main case study in this chapter. Journalist Bergh (2024: 34) reported from a biathlon world cup event in Nove Mesto, in the Czech Republic, that while "the Anders Besseberg case is receiving massive attention in Norway", "in the circus that he built up, he is a non-theme for many athletes". Similarly, advertisements from the German car manufacturer BMW were visible everywhere. BMW had even located real cars at the ski track where television viewers would see the cars every time biathletes were skiing on the track past the cars. BMW, as a sponsor of the IBU for many years, did not at all seem concerned about the corruption allegations that had been visible in the media for some years and the main suspected offender was now on trial in criminal court in Norway. In addition to watches, hunting trips, and prostitutes, the former IBU president was also charged with access to a BMW car at his home in Norway. The car had been provided to him free of charge by the local BMW vendor in Norway, following instructions from BMW headquarters in Germany through the marketing firm Infront. The trial did not seem to affect BMW's sponsorship of international biathlon events and international biathlon associations.

Maybe the described IBU situation regarding BMW as a sponsor is an exception. Kulczycki and Koenigstofer (2016: 548) discussed the negative effects of perceived corruption on attitudes toward sponsorship, as they argued generally:

> Moral wrongdoing triggers negative emotions in individuals (e.g., anger, contempt, and disgust) and links violations of moral standards to moral behavior. These emotions are directed at the entity that is blamed as responsible for the transgression (...) The perception of corrupt behaviors of event-governing bodies might thus cause negative emotions in individuals. The perception of corrupt corporate behaviors may also translate into the evaluation of products and services.

Kulczycki and Koenigstorfer (2016: 549) formulated the following research hypothesis: "Perceived corruption of the event-governing bodies has a negative effect on attitude toward mega sport event sponsorship via attitude toward the event-governing body and attitude toward the event". The researchers found support for their hypothesis because the indirect effects via attitude toward the event and the indirect effect via attitude toward the event-governing body were negative and significant on attitudes toward event sponsorship. However, no direct negative effect was found linking perceptions of corruption within the event-governing body to attitudes toward event sponsorship.

The empirical study by Kulczycki and Koenigstorfer (2016) was based on a sample of respondents. Two hundred and two Brazilian residents were the respondents. The sample was recruited in a pedestrian area in Rio de Janeiro. They were stopped on the street and offered a small incentive for their participation. Participants filled in a written survey. The survey referred to the FIFA World Cup 2014, held in Brazil, as the sporting event, with FIFA as the event-governing body. Kulczycki and Koenigstorfer (2016: 566) concluded that "although the sponsors cannot be blamed directly for unethical behaviors, the mere support of, and cooperation with, the corrupt body likely causes negative spillover effects on individuals' attitudes". The secret world of FIFA – including bribery and vote rigging – was exposed a decade earlier by Jennings (2006).

Chadwick *et al.* (2018: 119) mentioned an example of immediate withdrawal by a sponsor:

> Although not especially prevalent as a response, there have been some examples of immediate withdrawal in sport. This is appropriately demonstrated by the case of Dutch bank ING, which withdrew from its sponsorship of the Renault Formula 1 Grand Prix team following a proven case of race-fixing that the team perpetrated. Immediate withdrawal is generally perceived by many sponsors as being a response of last resort. There are several reasons for this. Having often made significant investments in a property (both in terms of contract value and activation spend), many sponsors believe that immediate withdrawal undermines the return on investment in a sponsorship.

Chadwick *et al.* (2018) mentioned many more reasons for avoiding withdrawal while rather operating with a "wait-and-see" or "it depends" approach. One of the few reasons in favor of withdrawal is the severe media attention and interest. When people express their negative reactions on social media, in the press, and during street demonstrations, corporate management becomes afraid of losing its social license to operate due to a lack of conformity. The boycott of a company quickly mobilizes on social media (Horn, 2024), potentially causing a rapid withdrawal of sponsorship.

A case of rapid withdrawal from sponsorship occurred in 2025 following the Nordic Ski World Championship in Norway. The event outside the city of Trondheim concluded on Sunday, March 9, 2025. On the following Monday, March 10, both Help, an insurance company, and Nammo, a manufacturing company, terminated their sponsorship arrangements with the Norwegian ski jumping team. Norway's ski association had admitted to cheating but claimed the scandal at this stage involved the suits of just two ski jumpers in a single competition. A secret video taken through a keyhole or door slit showed the illegal re-stitching of extra seams into Norwegian ski jumping suits to enhance their stability, representing a serious scandal and subsequent crisis. Help and Nammo requested the immediate removal of their logos from any materials related to the Norwegian ski-jumping team. A new sponsor, Adidas, was expected to reconsider its engagement (Berglund, 2025; Endal *et al.*, 2025; Wiersen and Larsen, 2025).

The main sponsor of the IBU at its world cup events and world championships was the German car manufacturer BMW. The corruption allegations against IBU officials and others often mention BMW since the former IBU president, Anders Besseberg, had a BMW car at his disposal for free at his home in Norway (Ingle, 2023). The German car manufacturer was visible at every event with its advertising posters and displayed cars (Associated Press, 2024; Dahlkamp and Latsch, 2024a, 2024b; Taylor, 2021; Ingle, 2023; Panja, 2021).

4.2 Notification to Compliance Officer

Between 2011 and 2018, at his residence in Norway, Besseberg had privately and exclusively the right of disposal of a BMW X5 car, for which Infront covered the leasing costs. The value of this benefit was approximately NOK 850,000 (USD 85,000). Auditors at IBU questioned the practice in a letter to Besseberg in 2012 (Buskerud tingrett, 2024: 45):

> The answers and the information which have been provided to the Auditors make it necessary for us to investigate the situation further.

> We need to make sure that the contract is clear and that there is absolutely no conflict of interest which might have a negative effect on the IBU. As it is a serious concern, we ask you to provide a clear explanation about the details of arrangements of this car. Specifically including, how long have you had an IBU car, what is the contractual status, who are the involved parties and who is aware of the situation?

Besseberg responded that "I have never asked the IBU or a car sponsor of IBU to have a car", while the auditors expressed in return that "the circumstances of the case make it a conflict-of-interest situation and a violation of the IBU Code of Ethics" (Buskerud tingrett, 2024: 24).

There was no media report visible that covered how the company BMW reacted to being mentioned in a corruption scandal. Therefore, this author wrote an email to the company's compliance function at compliance@bmwgroup.com on Thursday, March 21, 2024:

> Please allow me to ask a question to the compliance department at BMW:
>
> Anyone prosecuted in Norwegian court is considered innocent until guilt is proven beyond reasonable and sensible doubt. Any doubt that exists should benefit the defendant. I followed the six weeks trial where the verdict is expected in the middle of April. Whether he will be convicted of corruption is an open question, and the losing party will for sure appeal the verdict. Maybe it is a case of principle interest. Then the Norwegian Supreme Court will review it, and a final verdict cannot be expected until 2026 or 2027.
>
> BMW is a main sponsor of the IBU but not in any way involved in the charges. However, in addition to hunting trips, watches, and prostitutes, the prosecution argued in court that a BMW at the defendant's home represents a bribe potentially via the marketing firm Infront.
>
> My question is whether you have reviewed your company's sponsorship in light of the corruption allegations? Thank you for your reply.

A few hours later, the author received the following response from the BMW Group Compliance contact:

> Thank you for your email to the BMW Group Compliance Contact. We would like to inform you that we have forwarded your inquiry to the responsible compliance department. We ask for your understanding that we are unable to provide any information on the processing status by telephone. Where necessary, the person responsible there will get back

> to you. If you have any further questions, please do not hesitate to contact us from Monday to Friday, 7:00 a.m. to 8:00 p.m. (CET).
> Best regards,
> BMW Group Compliance Contact
> 80788 München
> Phone: +49-89-382-60000

The following day, the author received another email, this time from notifications@bmwgroup.com:

> Thank you very much for contacting the BMW Group Compliance. We received your message. We take your concerns seriously and will look into the matter. In order to process the matter more efficiently, we would appreciate your support by answering following questions:
>
> - What exactly did the prosecutor argue?
> - Whom did BMW bribe?
> - How and at which occasion did BMW bribe?
> - Who at BMW was involved from prosecutor's perspective?
> - What is the connection between BMW and Infront with regard to the alleged bribery?
> - Are there any publicly available sources (news articles, press statements etc.)?
>
> Thank you and best regards,
> Anastasia Berger, BMW Group
> Dr. Anastasia Berger
> Recht, Patente, Group Compliance, Compliance Investigations,
> E-Discovery (AC-4)
> Compliance Managerin, Syndikusrechtsanwältin, Dostierstr. 3,
> 80809 München
> Postanschrift: 80788 München
> Telefon: +49-151-601-94798
> Mail: anastasia.berger@bmw.de
> Web: http://www.bmwgroup.com

The author replied the same afternoon:

- What exactly did the prosecutor argue? The prosecutor argued that the BMW car at Besseberg's free disposal in Norway at his home represented a bribe.
- Whom did BMW bribe? The court did not review the briber, only the bribed.
- How and at which occasion did BMW bribe? The court did not review the briber, only the bribed.

- Who at BMW was involved from prosecutor's perspective? The name mentioned was Volker Schmid at Infront who managed the sponsorship arrangement with your company BMW.
- What is the connection between BMW and Infront with regard to the alleged bribery? The sponsorship arrangement with the International Biathlon Union via Infront.
- Are there any publicly available sources (news articles, press statements etc.)?: Yes: Dahlkamp, J. and Latsch, G. (2024a). Prozess gegen ehemaligen Biathlon-Weltverbandchef: Uhren, Prostituierte, Trophäenjagden (Process against former biathlon union chief: Watches, prostitutes, trophy hunts), German magazine *Der Spiegel*, www.spiegel.de, published January 12. Dahlkamp, J. and Latsch, G. (2024b). Blattschuss beim Pinkeln (Leaf shot while peeing), German magazine *Der Spiegel*, number 8, February 17, pages 84–85. Associated Press (2024). Prosecutors seek prison term for former biathlon boss on last day of corruption trial in Norway, *The Washington Post* (www.washingtonpost.com), published February 15. Panja, T. (2021). Hunting trips, sex and cash: How grooming biathlon's leader paid off for Russia – An investigation accuses biathlon's longtime president of accepting gifts from Russians and then doing the country's bidding as a doping scandal swirled, *The New York Times*, www.nytimes.com, published January 28. Ingle, S. (2023). Hunting trips, sex and a BMW: Former biathlon chief charged with corruption – Anders Besseberg accused of taking gifts from Russia – If convicted he could face 10 years in prison in Norway, *The Guardian*, www.theguardian.com, published April 17.

Anastasia Berger as compliance manager at BMW replied the same evening:

> Thank you very much for the prompt reply. We will look at the matter and come back to you at a later point.

The author then confirmed receipt in an email the same evening, adding that Volker Schmid was being prosecuted in Austria. The author also wrote in the email:

> Some may argue that allegations of corruption at the IBU belong to the past. However, the case is still relevant as the current IBU president became subject to police investigation starting in February this year in Austria. The current president Olle Dahlin at the IBU is charged with renewing a contract very favorable to Infront where BMW has an

> agreement with Infront. Again, the name Volker Schmid is mentioned.
> I hope this helps in your inquiry.

While awaiting a response from Berger at BMW Compliance, the author emailed the correspondence with BMW to journalists Dahlkamp and Latsch (2024a, 2024b) at the German magazine *Der Spiegel* on Tuesday, March 26, 2024, and Dahlkamp responded immediately:

> Thank you for your information about your inquiry to BMW. I can imagine what the answer will be (contract allowed Infront at their disposal to give cars to IBU officials, the interest of BMW was to prevent that IBU officials are connected with other car brands while driving to IBU events), but please hold us in the loop.

On April 22, 2024 – one month after the first contact – Dr. Anastasia Berger at Compliance Investigations within the BMW Group stated in an email:

> Dear Professor,
> We are still looking into this matter. I will come back to you as soon, as we have completed the review.
> Best regards,
> Anastasia Berger

Anastasia Berger at BMW Compliance Investigations came back to me on May 5, 2024:

> We have reviewed the contractual relationship and spoken to involved persons. We confirm that BMW AG is the official title sponsor of the BMW IBU World Cup Biathlon. Our contract partner however is the marketing company Infront Austria GmbH. Please understand that we do not comment on contract details. We can furthermore confirm that the use of BMW vehicles by IBU officials – even outside of events – is contractually permitted. The allocation of vehicles is the responsibility of our contractual partner. Please, let us know if there are any concrete allegations against Infront Austria GmbH or BMW AG employees.

I replied to her the same day: “Do you only consider compliance, or do you also consider conformity?” “See this book by Gottschalk and Hamerton (2023)”, I also wrote in my reply. While compliance refers to the legal license to operate, conformity refers to the social license to operate. Compliance is concerned with laws and regulations, while conformity is concerned with norms and values.

Former IBU president Anders Besseberg was convicted of corruption on several accounts in the district court, one of them being the free use of a BMW car at his home in Norway (Buskerud tingrett, 2024). Corruption implies that someone is bribing and someone is being bribed. The bribed individual was Besseberg. Who was the briber? Contractually, the car was assigned to him by Infront. So, Infront was the briber. However, it was a BMW car, where Anastasia Berger at BMW stated above in her email that "We confirm that BMW AG is the official title sponsor of the BMW IBU World Cup Biathlon". But then she disclaimed being the briber by stating that "Our contract partner however is the marketing company Infront Austria GmbH". As confirmed in the district court, "It is clear that the invoice was sent from BMW directly to Infront" (Buskerud tingrett, 2024: 51).

When this text was ready to be published, I emailed Anastasia Berger on October 23, 2024:

> Dear Anastasia Berger,
> I have written a book manuscript entitled "Corruption, Criminal Justice, and Compliance in Sport – The Case of the International Biathlon Union". The role of BMW is discussed in Chapter 11 of the book. I have included our email exchange in the chapter. I assume that you are in favor of openness and transparency, and that you therefore do not mind having your emails included in my new book. If you have any comments to the attached text, I will need your response before the end of this month. The book manuscript has been blind reviewed by other scholars and accepted for publication by a famous publishing house. The book manuscript will follow my sequence of books published by DeGruyter that I have mentioned to you earlier, as well as the forthcoming book published by Oxford University Press. I look forward to your response regarding potential changes you would like to see in Chapter 11 by the end of October. Best wishes.

Anastasia Berger replied one week later, on October 30, 2024:

> Thank you for sending over the manuscript. I do not consent to the publication of my personal data and expressly object to this as a precautionary

> measure. I therefore ask you in particular to remove from your manuscript any information that could allow conclusions to be drawn about myself and identify myself. Please confirm, that my personal data and any information that could allow conclusions to be drawn about myself and identify myself will be removed. Please also note that this e-mail does not represent an approval or endorsement of your manuscript by the BMW Group. Finally, please direct your emails to the email address notifications@bmwgroup.com instead of my address starting from tomorrow.
> Kind regards,
> Anastasia Berger, BMW Group
> Dr. Anastasia Berger
> Recht, Patente, Group Compliance, Compliance Investigations, E-Discovery (AC-4)
> Compliance Managerin, Syndikusrechtsanwältin. Dostlerstr. 3, 80809 München
> Postanschrift: 80788 München
> Telefon +4915160194798
> Mail: anastasia.berger@bmw.de
> Web: http://www.bmwgroup.com
> Bayerische Motoren Werke Aktiengesellschaft
> Vorstand/Board of Management: Oliver Zipse (Vorsitzender/Chairman), Jochen Goller, Ilka Horstmeier, Walter Mertl, Milan Nedeljkovic, Joachim Post, Frank Weber
> Vorsitsender des Aufsichtsrat/Chairman of the Supervisory Board: Norbert Reithöfer

The same evening, I sent her the following email:

> Dear Anastasia Berger,
> You are the compliance officer at BMW. In my book, I discuss compliance and conformity related to the BMW sponsorship of the IBU. Included in the discussion are your comments, and you are the source of information. Why do you object to it? In my previous email I asked you to suggest changes in the text. Best wishes.

Anastasia Berger replied to me six minutes later:

> I am not a public person. There is no reason to use my personal data. I do not consent to the publication of my personal data and expressly object to this as a precautionary measure. I therefore ask you in particular to remove from your manuscript any information that could allow conclusions to be drawn about myself and identify myself. Please confirm, that

my personal data and any information that could allow conclusions to be drawn about myself and identify myself will be removed. Please also note that this e-mail does not represent an approval or endorsement of your manuscript by the BMW Group.
Thank you and best regards,
Anastasia Berger

In the verdict, the district court discussed whether the car represented corruption (Buskerud tingrett, 2024: 51):

> It is all in all clear that Infront covered the leasing costs for the defendant's car, related to the BMW X5. The court cannot see any reasonable cause or background for Infront covering the costs. The defendant claims that it is a sponsored car from BMW, which, however, there is no trace of in the writings. The court also questions why Infront had an interest in giving him a free car. The court has not been presented with a reasonable answer to that.

Corruption in Norwegian legislation is a matter of providing or receiving an undue and improper advantage. The district court found that the BMW X5 represented such an undue advantage. The verdict argued that the advantage had substantial value, that it was a special treatment for the president, and that there was a lack of transparency surrounding the scheme. The defense had argued that it was of obvious interest to BMW that the president drove that particular car. According to the defense, it was only reprehensible that Besseberg did not pay taxes on the fringe benefit to Norwegian tax authorities. The court found it suspicious, however, that the wording regarding the car had been removed from all documents. There was no advertising or other profiling on the car, which would indicate that BMW received no advantage from it at any time. As regards the possibility of influence, although not explicitly required for corruption in Norwegian legislation, the court referred to the relationship between Infront and IBU, where the president had the possibility of influencing the future role of BMW as a sponsor of IBU world cups and thus the business opportunities for Infront with the IBU (Buskerud tingrett, 2024).

4.3 Compliance – Conformity – Transparency

Former IBU president Anders Besseberg successfully appealed the corruption sentence in the Norwegian criminal justice system. The trial was scheduled for April 2025 (Christiansen, 2024; NRK, 2024). He also replaced his defense lawyers with new ones (Cederblad, 2024b, 2024c) after criticism of their performance (Cederblad, 2024a) since they failed in their arguments in favor of the defendant in the district court (Gottschalk, 2024). Until a final verdict of guilt is eventually passed to him, he is supposed to be considered innocent, and his innocence of corruption should be respected. However, scholars have already considered him innocent (e.g., Riedl, 2021). This chapter as well might have created such an impression. The reason is that the assumption of corruption was required in this research to confront the sponsor as a stakeholder with the potential role of being the briber.

As is evident in the presented email exchanges, BMW disclaimed responsibility for the alleged corruption and continued in the role of main sponsor of IBU world cups. They pointed at their business partner Infront, and the compliance officer was unwilling to make the contract between BMW and Infront transparent regarding cars for free to top IBU officials. BMW officials seemed to be hiding behind the marketing outsourcing through the IBU, facilitated by the marketing firm Infront, to engage with sponsor BMW. This kind of marketing outsourcing was discussed by Manoli and Hodgkinson (2017: 437), who referred to outsourcing as the hiring of another entity to perform a service:

> Since motivations for outsourcing include cost reduction, focus on core activities, access to resources/skills, performance improvement, innovation, and development of employees, it is viewed by sport organisations as having a fundamental role in their economic value.

The issue of conformity did not seem relevant to the compliance officer at BMW in Germany.

However, sportswashing can make sponsors, fans, and athletes complicit in injustices, such as human rights abuses in Qatar and corruption in biathlon. Some actors in the sports industry attempt sportswashing, which refers to the use of athletic events to divert attention from wrongdoing. The term was introduced when Azerbaijan diverted attention away from concerns over human rights violations in the country in 2015 by emphasizing sporting events. Sportswashing is often seen as a rebranding effort by a nation or organization to disassociate from undesirable circumstances. The moral violation, from the perspective of the sportswasher, is problematic primarily because it is publicly known and condemned, creating a moral strain that requires cleansing. Sportswashing goes beyond image-building, as it addresses reputational damage caused by visible moral issues. It works to distract from, minimize, or normalize an injustice for which the sportswasher is responsible. Sportswashing diverts attention away from compliance and conformance violations, thereby reducing pressure on those responsible and allowing injustices to continue. Those involved in sports – such as the company BMW as a sponsor of the IBU – may unintentionally support the deviant process, allowing injustices to persist (Fruh *et al.*, 2022).

Trautendorfer *et al.* (2025) distinguished between *de jure* transparency and *de facto* transparency, where "transparency" is referred to as complying with information disclosure requirements. While *de jure* transparency comprises laws and regulations that are formally in place to be followed, *de facto* transparency comprises being responsive to requests and proactively providing information. Greater active transparency goes beyond regulatory compliance into conformance with expectations. The extent of transparency can be measured by responsiveness to information requests and proactive disclosure of information. Crepaz and Arikan (2024: 897) argued that transparency reduces information asymmetries in principal-agent relationships, and it "signals honesty and openness, thereby positively affecting evaluations and trust".

Sponsors face increasing pressure to respond appropriately to issues of corruption. Bribery raises serious concerns about ethics, morality, integrity, and trust, which are key topics in marketing and sponsorship discussions. These concerns are especially important to sponsors because ethics, integrity, and trust may influence sponsorship effects. Sponsors face important decision-making when linked to athletes, teams, or events involved in corruption. Some sponsors continue their support, such as BMW as discussed above, and Ice, as discussed in the following section. Other sponsors might terminate agreements, depending on the specific situation and its potential impact on their brand image. Roberts *et al.* (2017) argued that sponsors can no longer ignore or distance themselves from corruption. Rather, they must respond. Sponsors then seem to apply market-driven morality, where stakeholder concerns about corruption push them to act. The challenge for sponsors is to find the right way to respond and then to take appropriate action.

4.4 Ice Communications as Biathlon Sponsor

While BMW is the main sponsor of IBU events, there are many more sponsors involved in biathlon. One of the sponsors is Ice Communications, which supports financially the Norwegian national biathlon team. Ice is a Norwegian telecommunications company that provides mobile and broadband services. It has become the third-largest operator in the telecommunications market in Norway, competing with Telenor and Telia. On its website www.ice.no, the company answers in a message posted August 18, 2022, their own question "Why does Ice sponsor the Norwegian Biathlon team?" in the following statement:

> Although Norway is a small country, we are not a small biathlon nation – quite the opposite! We can boast a number of gold medals and achievements that others can only dream of. From Ole Einar Bjørndalen's eight Olympic medals, to Johannes Tingnes Bø's five combined victories in the World Cup. With a unique driving force, biathletes challenge the boundaries of the sport and constantly take it to new heights. …just like Ice! Ice's network is involved in continuously developing technology, because we are the challenger who dares to think new things. With good team morale and an innovative mind, Ice is constantly developing new and modern services and products that challenge the market in new digital guidelines.

When asked about Ice's response to corruption allegations against former IBU President Besseberg, communication manager at Ice, Andreas Veggeland (andreas.veggeland@lyse.no), responded in an email on December 19, 2024:

> The trial against Anders Besseberg concerns matters from before 2019, which is when Ice entered into a sponsorship partnership with the Norwegian Biathlon Union. We have a close and good dialogue with the Norwegian Biathlon Union, which, like Ice, strongly distances itself from what has emerged in the district court proceedings in the case.

The motive for sponsorship is to be associated with positive attitudes in sports. Important values are "a unique driving force", "an innovative mind", "generosity", and "determination", as stated in their long message. Values are important to achieve conformity, where conformity is a matter of being consistent with norms and values (Durand *et al.*, 2019).

I emailed Andreas Veggeland at Ice again on the same day regarding another motive for sponsorship. The motive is the possibility of special events for customers and employees linked to biathlon. As a sponsor, Ice has access to facilities and spectator seating locations at venues where biathlon competitions take place. The sponsor invites people to venues where they are served, entertained, and educated. The latter is important, as events can be labeled seminars so that attendees do not have to pay tax on benefits received in terms of travel, accommodation, meals, sightseeing, and entertainment. When bringing along someone who can give a presentation, then the entire event is labeled a seminar.

I have myself, as a Norwegian business school professor, been brought along overseas to major events in Germany, where a sponsor paid me to give a lecture to their guests. While the lecture was a minimal part of the whole package for the participants, they nevertheless avoided income tax on the benefit of traveling with the sponsor, valued at typically USD 2,000–4,000. Some might argue that this is a form of arranged tax evasion by the sponsor for their guests. Others might argue that participation in such events is a form of corruption, where the sponsor is bribing their guests, especially when those guests represent important customers. However, such arrangements were never the case at Ice Communications, as described in the following response from Veggeland.

The chief executive officer (CEO) of Ice Communications, Eivind Helgaker, initiated the sponsorship of the Norwegian biathlon team in 2019. He was the CEO of Ice for 14 years, from 2009 to 2023. Helgaker is a graduate of the Norwegian Business School. On LinkedIn, he said about himself that "Eivind is a visionary leader who also focuses on the fact that strategy must be operationalized and that the organization is crucial to success". In 2022, Helgaker renewed the sponsorship of the Norwegian biathlon team through 2026. The union stated in a press release posted at www.media.skiskyting.no that:

> Ice renews agreement with the Norwegian Biathlon Union. The most popular sport in Norway thus retains its main sponsor in an agreement that is valid until spring 2026. The sponsorship agreement applies to elite teams for women and men, as well as junior, recruit and Para. The launch of the renewed collaboration will take place during the Blink festival. The press meeting is scheduled for 12:00–12:30 on Friday, August 5th at SR Bank's premises. Address: Elvegata 23, 4306 Sandnes. CEO of Ice, Eivind Helgaker, secretary general of NSSF [Norwegian Biathlon Union], Morten Djupvik, and Johannes Thingnes Bø will be

> present as well as biathletes Ida Lien, Filip Fjeld Andersen and Åsne Skrede for reasons that will be announced at the launch. Maybe there will be a laser shooting duel between Johannes Thingnes Bø and Eivind Helgaker?

While the mentioned Morten Djupvik (morten.djupvik@skiskyting.no) was the secretary-general of the Norwegian Biathlon Union, Therese Engebråten was the sponsorship manager for the union. I asked her in an email (therese.engebraten@skiskyting.no) about her thoughts regarding compliance and conformity.

Ice Communications was owned by the American company Access Industries. The Norwegian energy company Lyse acquired Ice in 2023, paying NOK 5.6 billion (USD 560 million) for it. Helgaker resigned shortly after the takeover (Finstad, 2023).

I had emailed Andreas Veggeland at Ice again on the same day regarding another motive for sponsorship. The added motive is the possibility of special events for customers and employees linked to biathlon. I sent him an earlier draft of the text above. He responded on Friday, December 20, in an email:

> I think the first part of the draft here looks fine. However, I think it is quite peculiar that in your text you then go on and refer to the as yet unanswered follow-up question about customer events that you sent yesterday, before you make a subjective assessment of general sponsorship practices related to seminars/events. The text could quickly be perceived as you describing Ice's practice here. Overall, I find that the entire highlighted (in yellow) part of your text appears incoherent. And the fact that you write that "others might argue that participation at such events is a form of corruption where the sponsor is bribing their guests, especially when the guests are representatives of important [telecom] customers" can hardly be interpreted as anything other than a serious accusation against Ice without any basis in reality.
>
> Ice's main purpose in sponsoring the Norwegian biathlon team is increased visibility for the Ice brand. Sponsorships also provide an opportunity to cultivate relationships with customers and partners in addition. This is of course done in line with laws and regulations. Ice has a very limited number of customer events related to sponsorships. In general, we tend to be present at the following arenas: Sjusjøen during

the start of the season – then we have activities aimed at private customers, with a stand, raffle, etc. This is open to everyone present at the arena. During the races in Holmenkollen, we have a sober event aimed at our corporate customers with invited customers who cover their own travel and possible accommodation.

In addition, I can also point out that it is a bit strange that you highlight so much about Eivind Helgaker, who no longer works for us. Even though Eivind was a spokesperson and representative of the Ice brand when he was with us, it was not he who personally sponsored the biathlon union.

While I corrected the text above to remove any suggestion of accusation against Ice and will emphasize that my personal experience is not at all related to Ice, I left the description of the former CEO since he was such an important actor at the time of the sponsorship.

In a follow-up email, I asked whether Ice also has biathlon events abroad. Veggeland said no. Then, I asked whether such events took place for employees. Veggeland said no. Then, I asked if he had ever been to a biathlon event abroad. Veggeland said no. Then, I asked how much they pay for the sponsorship. Veggeland replied that they do not disclose the costs of their commercial collaborations.

Ice Communications seemed to be the main sponsor of the Norwegian Biathlon Union. Other sponsors listed on the union's webpage for the biathlon season 2024–2025 included Eidsiva Energi (energy), AF Gruppen (construction), YX Energi (gas stations), VB Gruppen (plumbing), Craft Sportswear, Nammo AS (ammunition), Byggmakker/Onninen (building materials), ASKO (furniture stores), BMW, Bama Gruppen AS (fruits), Hurtigruta Carglass, MENY (grocery chain), and ALI Kaffe (coffee). It is interesting to note here that BMW is also a sponsor locally in Norway and not only globally a sponsor of the IBU. The question emerges whether the car provided privately to Anders Besseberg in Norway, for which he was convicted in district court, originated from a global or local sponsorship.

The various minor sponsors have posted statements on their websites about their sponsorships:

- Eidsiva says that "our collaboration with the Norwegian Biathlon Union has built pride, created joy and helped us raise awareness about mental health over the past four years".

- AF says that "the Camp AF is an annual event where AF employees are invited to bring family and friends to World Cup biathlon in Holmenkollen".
- YX says that "we have been inspired by a common set of values".
- VB says that "the collaboration between us and the national biathlon team will make us more visible, create relationships and build internal pride".
- Craft says that "together with the ski sports elite, we have developed a new groundbreaking collection that raises the bar for quality, flexibility and functionality".
- Nammo says that "for athletes, having the right ammunition can mean the difference between an Olympic gold medal – or twentieth or thirtieth place".
- Byggmakker/Onninen says that "just like the ski greasers and support staff are up early and always present for the athletes, Byggmakker and Onninen are always there for the craftsmen".
- Asko says that "Asko is committed to health and well-being by being active".
- BMW says that "our focus on innovation and development coincides".
- Bama says that they "reach out widely with the message about Eat Move Sleep to both children, young people and their parents".
- Hurtigruta says that "we have always been concerned with how we work and providing something back".
- MENY says that "we look up to the biathletes".
- ALI says that they are "proud to be able to continue working with the great athletes who represent Norway in biathlon".

Thirteen sponsors are listed here, in addition to Ice. Being associated with successful national biathletes is obviously important when the brands are showcased at world cup events in biathlon. Kulczycki and Koenigstorfer (2016) argued that sponsors should worry about corruption as a mega-sport event syndrome. However, the sponsors did not seem to worry, as they attempted to consider Anders Besseberg a rotten apple rather than the IBU a rotten apple basket. As discussed in the previous chapter, white-collar offenders are often considered rotten apples; however, it may be more appropriate to describe the phenomenon of white-collar crime as a basket of rotten apples or a rotten apple orchard, as Punch (2003) defined it. A rotten-apple or a bad-apple perspective assumes that an individual member of an organization acts alone, and that criminal activity might occur with or without the knowledge or participation of the organization as such (Bright *et al.*, 2024). The bad barrel refers to a situation "where the organization behaves unethically and is motivated to commit fraud for economic gain" (Manning *et al.*, 2024: 4).

A spokesperson at a former major sponsor of the Norwegian biathlon team, Jacob Lund of the Norwegian bank DNB, expressed skepticism regarding the allegations against Anders Besseberg. His views were in many ways opposite of those expressed by all other biathlon sponsors, the biathlon union, and anti-doping units, who seemed convinced that Besseberg was guilty of corruption. Lund claimed that Besseberg was tricked into a Russian trap that included bear hunting and prostitutes (Christiansen and Thorkildsen, 2023):

> Corruption defendant Anders Besseberg (77) was subjected to revenge and a package of crap as part of a power struggle, believes former DNB sponsorship manager Jacob Lund (...) He cites a concrete example to illustrate what he believes was a power struggle between Besseberg and the Russian who constantly challenged him in the fight for power: Aleksander Tikhonov. In the early 2000s, Tikhonov drooled over his job as president of the IBU, Lund believes. And during the end of the season in Russia, he and Besseberg were invited on a helicopter hunt in Siberia.

Lund said in the interview that they drank and enjoyed themselves. But the clock was ticking. This was the closing day of the World Cup, and Besseberg was supposed to give a speech. Both Besseberg and Lund requested a quick return by helicopter, but nothing happened. When they finally returned to the biathlon event, it was all over. Lund is convinced that the late arrival of Besseberg was arranged so that stakeholders should think that Besseberg prioritized hunting and drinking over biathlon events. Unfortunately, two months after this newspaper interview, on February 16, 2024, at the age of 71, Jacob Lund died (Strøm and Friberg, 2024). His thoughts regarding sponsors' potential influence on compliance and conformity at sponsored sports organizations and their biathletes could have been valuable input to the research presented in this book.

References

Associated Press (2024). Prosecutors seek prison term for former biathlon boss on last day of corruption trial in Norway, *The Washington Post*, www.washingtonpost.com, published February 15.

Bao, D., Kim, Y., Mian, G.M. and Su, L. (2019). Do managers disclose or withhold bad news? Evidence from short interest, *The Accounting Review*, 94(3), 1–26.

Bergh, N. (2024). Anders Besseberg-saken får massiv oppmerksomhet i Norge. I sirkuset han bygget opp, er han et ikke-tema for mange utøvere (The Anders Besseberg case is receiving massive attention in Norway. In the circus that he built up, he is a non-theme for many athletes), daily Norwegian newspaper *Aftenposten*, Wednesday, February 21, pp. 34–35.

Berglund, N. (2025). Norwegians admit to cheating, FIS probes ski-jumping scandal, head coach suspended, *News in English*, www.NewsinEnglish.no, published March 10.

Bitektine, A., Gillespie, N. and Lange, D. (2025). From the evaluator's perspective: A functional approach to social judgments, *Academy of Management Review*, published first online https://doi.org/10.54657amr.2020.0405.

Bright, D., Sadewo, G., Cubitt, T.I.C., Dowling, C. and Morgan, A. (2024). Co-offending networks among members of outlaw motorcycle gangs across types of crime, *Trends in Organized Crime*, 27, 263–285.

Buskerud tingrett (2024). Court case number 23-03940MED-TBUS/THOK, *Buskerud tingrett* (Buskerud district court), professional judge Vidar Toftøy-Lohne, lay judges Kari Aasen Ingebo and Gunnar Sanden, Hokksund, Norway, verdict document 67 p.

Cederblad, C.A. (2024a). Advokatene får sterk kritikk (The lawyers receive strong criticism), daily Norwegian newspaper *Dagbladet*, www.dagbladet.no, published April 22.

Cederblad, C.A. (2024b). Kvitter seg med advokater (Gets rid of lawyers), daily Norwegian newspaper *Dagbladet*, www.dagbladet.no, published October 30.

Cederblad, C.A. (2024c). Henter "Norges beste" (Brings in Norway's best), daily Norwegian newspaper *Dagbladet*, www.dagbladet.no, published October 31.

Chadwick, S., Roberts, S. and Cowley, R. (2018). The impact of sports corruption on organizational stakeholders, in Kihl, L.A. (editor), *Corruption in Sport – Causes, Consequences, and Reform*, Routledge, UK: Abingdon, pp. 110–125.

Cheong, C., Pyun, D.Y. and Leng, H.K. (2019). Sponsorship and advertising in sport: A study of consumers' attitude, *European Sport Management Quarterly*, 19(3), 287–311.

Christiansen, A.K. (2024). Aktor: Besseberg trekker klokke-anke (Prosecutor: Besseberg withdraws watch appeal), Norwegian daily newspaper *VG*, www.vg.no, published October 15.

Christiansen, A.K. and Thorkildsen, C. (2023). Bjørnejakt og prostituert: Hevder Besseberg ble lurt i russisk felle (Bear hunting and prostitute: Claims Besseberg was tricked into a Russian trap), Norwegian daily newspaper *VG*, www.vg.no, published December 22.

Crepaz, M. and Arikan, G. (2024). The effects of transparency regulation on political trust and perceived corruption: Evidence from a survey experiment, *Regulation & Governance*, 18, 896–913.

Dahlkamp, J. and Latsch, G. (2024a). Prozess gegen ehemaligen Biathlon-Weltverbandchef: Uhren, Prostituierte, Trophäenjagden (Process against former biathlon union chief: Watches, prostitutes, trophy hunts), German magazine *Der Spiegel*, www.spiegel.de, published January 12.

Dahlkamp, J. and Latsch, G. (2024b). Blattschuss beim Pinkeln (Leaf shot while peeing), German magazine *Der Spiegel*, number 8, February 17, pp. 84–85.

Durand, R., Hawn, O. and Ioannou, I. (2019). Willing and able: A general model of organizational responses to normative pressures, *Academy of Management Review*, 44(2), 299–320.

Endal, E.G., Nesset, J.B. and Persen, K. (2025). Nammo fjerner logoen sin fra hopplandslaget (Nammo removes its logo from the national ski jumping team), Norwegian broadcasting channel *TV2*, www.tv2.no, published March 10.

Finstad, Ø. (2023). Lyse etablerer teleselskap – utfordrer Telenor og Telia (Lyse establishes telecommunications company – challenging Telenor and Telia), Norwegian financial newspaper *Finansavisen*, www.finansavisen.no, published November 14.

Fruh, K., Archer, A. and Wojtowicz, J. (2022). Sportswashing: Complicity and corruption, *Sport, Ethics and Philosophy*, 17(1), 101–118.

Gottschalk, P. (2024). Economic crime in the courtroom: A case study of defense lawyers' arguments against prosecution evidence, *Journal of Economic Criminology*, 5, published first online https://doi.org/10.1016/j.jeconc.2024.100085.

Gottschalk, P. and Hamerton, C. (2023). *Corporate Social License – A Study in Legitimacy, Conformity, and Corruption*, Palgrave Macmillan publishing, UK: London.

Horn, J.M. (2024). Accident, scandal, disaster: The media framing of corporate crime, *Crime, Law and Social Change*, 81, 203–229.

Ingle, S. (2023). Hunting trips, sex and a BMW: Former biathlon chief charged with corruption – Anders Besseberg accused of taking gifts from Russia – If convicted he could face 10 years in prison in Norway, *The Guardian*, www.theguardian.com, published April 17.

Ingle, S. (2024). Coe defends World Athletics' move to award $50,000 to Olympic gold winners, *The Guardian*, www.theguardian.com, published April 10.

Iqbal, F., Pfarrer, M.D. and Bundy, J. (2024). How crisis management strategies address stakeholders' sociocognitive concerns and organizations' social evaluations, *Academy of Management Review*, 49(2), 299–321.

Jennings, A. (2006). *Foul! The Secret World of FIFA: Bribes Vote Rigging and Ticket Scandals*, HarperSport, HarperCollins Publisher, UK: London.

Kourula, A., Moon, J., Salles-Djelic, M.L. and Wicker, C. (2019). New roles of government in the governance of business conduct: Implications for management and organizational research, *Organization Studies*, 40(8), 1101–1123.

Kulczycki, W. and Koenigstorfer, J. (2016). Why sponsors should worry about corruption as a mega sport event syndrome, *European Sport Management Quarterly*, 16(5), 545–574.

Lange, D., Bundy, J. and Park, E. (2022). The social nature of stakeholder utility, *Academy of Management Review*, 47(19), 9–30.

Manning, L., MacLeod, A., James, C., Thompson, M., Oyeyinka, S., Cowen, N., Skoczylis, J. and Onarinde, B.A. (2024). Food fraud prevention strategies: Building an effective verification ecosystem, *Comprehensive Reviews in Food Science and Food Safety*, 23, published first online https://doi.org/10.1111/1541-4337.70036.

Manoli, A.E. and Hodgkinson, I.R. (2017). Marketing outsourcing in the English premier league: The rights holder/agency interface, *European Sport Management Quarterly*, 17(4), 436–456.

Mpho, B. (2017). Whistleblowing: What do contemporary ethical theories say? *Studies in Business and Economics*, 12(1), 19–28.

NRK (2024). Besseberg-anke for retten i april (Besseberg appeal in court in April), public Norwegian broadcasting NRK, www.nrk.no, published November 1.

Ondrackova, A. and Verschuuren, P. (2021). Whistleblowing platforms as a solution to fight corruption, in Ordway, C. (editor), *Restoring Trust in Sport – Corruption Cases and Solutions*, Routledge, UK: London, pp. 132–144.

Panja, T. (2021). Hunting trips, sex and cash: How grooming biathlon's leader paid off for Russia – An investigation accuses biathlon's longtime president of accepting gifts from Russians and then doing the country's bidding as a doping scandal swirled, *The New York Times*, www.nytimes.com, published January 28.

Parganas, P., Papadimitriou, D., Anagnostopoulos, C. and Theodoropoulos, A. (2017). Linking sport team sponsorship to perceived switching cost and switching intentions, *European Sport Management Quarterly*, 17(4), 457–484.

Philippou, C. (2022). Anti-bribery and corruption in sport mega-events: Stakeholder perspectives, *Sport in Society*, 25(4), 819–836.

Philippou, C. (2023). Expert perceptions on anti-bribery and corruption policies in sports governing bodies: Implications for ethical climate theory, *Journal of Business Ethics*, published first online https://doi.org/10.1007/s10551-023-05478-x.

Punch, M. (2003). Rotten Orchards: "Pestilence", police misconduct and system failure, *Policing and Society*, 13(2), 171–196.

Riedl, E. (2021). How sport regulations are being used to restore trust following the International Biathlon Union scandal, in Ordway, C. (editor), *Restoring Trust in Sport – Corruption Cases and Solutions*, Routledge, UK: London, pp. 48–63.

Roberts, S., Chadwick, S. and Anagnostopoulos, C. (2017). Sponsorship programmes and corruption in sport: Management responses to a growing threat, *Journal of Strategic Marketing*, 26(1), 19–36.

Stoelhorst, J.W. and Vishwanathan, P. (2024). Beyond primacy: A stakeholder theory of corporate governance, *Academy of Management Review*, 49(1), 107–134.

Strøm, O.K. and Friberg, J. (2024). Jacob Lund er død: – Han var en bauta (Jacob Lund is dead: – He was a bauta), Norwegian daily newspaper *VG*, www.vg.no, published February 17.

Taylor, J. (2021). *Final Report of the IBU External Review Commission*, ERC (External Review Commission), International Biathlon Union, Austria, 220 p., January 28.

Trautendorfer, J., Hohensinn, L. and Hilgers, D. (2025). From de jure to de facto transparency: Analyzing the compliance gap in light of freedom of information laws, *Regulation & Governance*, 19, 253–283.

Wiersen, S.Å. and Larsen, M.G. (2025). Sponsor trekker seg fra avtale (Sponsor withdraws from contract), daily Norwegian newspaper *Dagbladet*, www.dagbladet.no, published March 10.

Chapter 5

Facing Harassment Accusations

This chapter presents a case study from Norway that supplements previous research in other jurisdictions, such as Australia, Canada, the Netherlands, and the United Kingdom, regarding a lack of justice when corporate investigators conduct internal examinations in client organizations. A university violated its social license to operate due to a lack of conformity when handling personnel issues involving a faculty member. The case concerns a university researcher who was investigated after allegations of violating the National Labor Relations Act. Investigators applied a likelihood of fifty percent rather than the criteria of incident beyond any reasonable doubt. There was no real contradiction offered, and many more deviations from a fair process occurred when compared to the public criminal justice system. The presented maturity model, with four stages, is applied to illustrate the low level of investigative performance in the case. This research does not, in any way, claim that the presented case is representative of work by corporate investigators conducting internal examinations in client organizations. Nevertheless, this research is important, as it illustrates the lack of justice caused by the absence of regulation of the private investigation industry, as performed by law firms, audit firms, consulting firms, and others.

The business of internal investigations by audit firms and law firms is a growing industry within many jurisdictions. Private investigators take on the task of reconstructing past events and sequences of events for client organizations when there is suspicion of misconduct or wrongdoing.

Scholars have studied the problematic roles and varying performances of private investigators in countries such as Australia (King, 2020a, 2020b, 2020c, 2020d, 2021a, 2021b), Canada (Schneider, 2006), the Netherlands (Meerts, 2014, 2018, 2019, 2020, 2021, 2023), Norway (Gottschalk, 2016, 2017, 2021, 2023), and the United Kingdom (Brooks *et al.*, 2009; Button, 2020; Button and Gee, 2013; Button and Stiernstedt, 2017, 2018; Button *et al.*, 2007a, 2007b, 2015, 2023; Johnston *et al.*, 2008; Williams, 2005a, 2005b; and Wood, 2020).

Internal investigation reports tend to be kept secret for a variety of reasons (Gottschalk and Tcherni-Buzzeo, 2016). Some reports have become publicly available and were reviewed in the past. Examples include investigations into suspicions of economic wrongdoing in organizational settings (e.g., Gottschalk, 2018, 2019, 2020). The internal investigation report by Lilli and Sunde (2023) regarding suspected workplace wrongdoing, reviewed in this article, was disclosed and made publicly available by a colleague of the accused who found the treatment of the accused unacceptable.

This chapter applies the maturity model to assess the performance of private investigators. Stages of growth models for assessing maturity levels can help evaluate various phenomena (e.g., Iannacci *et al.*, 2019; Röglinger *et al.*, 2012; Solli-Sæther and Gottschalk, 2015). Stage models can predict the development or evolution of investigative maturity from basic performance to superior results (Iannacci *et al.*, 2019: 310):

> They also suggest that this development is progressive (i.e., each successive stage is better than the previous one), stepwise (i.e., each step is a necessary prerequisite for the following step in the sequence), and prescriptive (i.e., each step must occur in a prescribed order in accordance with a pre-existing plan or vision), thus emphasizing the chain of successful events rather than the mechanisms by which subsequent stages come about.

This chapter seeks to examine an important area of private policing and investigations. It contributes to the body of knowledge on workplace deviance and employment investigations. This research is important as it explicitly, rather than implicitly, applies criteria to study potential lack of justice in private investigations. At lower levels of the presented maturity model, there is more lack of justice than at higher levels of maturity.

5.1 Top Academic Coming to Norway

Internal investigation reports tend to be kept secret for a variety of reasons (Gottschalk and Tcherni-Buzzeo, 2016). Access to the current report was granted by an email from a professor of medical ethics at the Institute of Medical Ethics, Faculty of Medicine, University of Oslo (UiO) on February 16, 2023:

> I am writing to you on behalf of a brilliant female researcher from Turkey who has been exposed to accusations of harassment, but where the university management denies her full access to insights. This has led to her being stripped of her right to manage work as the project manager as of today over two large projects funded by the Norwegian research council that she was awarded last year. I have followed her situation closely since July 2019, when she approached me about harassment from her superior. At that time, I immediately contacted the science ombudsman at the university, Knut W. Ruyter, who reviewed the matter and wrote a sharp report to the then dean at the faculty of medicine, but to no avail. The harassment accusations against the researcher started last autumn, and in the investigation of the accusations, the university management has, as far as I can understand, failed to follow the most basic rules of the game how such accusations should be investigated, among others, she has been denied full access to the charges that have been brought against her, a denial she has appealed to the joint complaint board at the university. In its letter of February 1, the board says: "The joint complaint board has come to the conclusion that the university has not met the requirements for due process in the Public service act and the Public administration act when processing the request for access".

The researcher, in the role of main supervisor, was accused of unacceptable behavior toward doctoral students in supervision. Accusers claimed that her behavior included outbursts of rage when presenting negative results and condescending comments about the doctoral students' draft texts for publications and dissertations. The doctoral students frequently felt harmed by personal remarks as about their incompetence, that they worked too little to progress in their scientific work and that they did not deliver the expected research outcomes. The university hired corporate investigators at CMS Kluge, a law firm, to examine the allegations.

The researcher came to Norway to join the Norwegian Center for Molecular Medicine at UiO. The center consists of several research groups led by internationally recruited team leaders. The researcher successfully secured research funding to establish her own group. The research group used soft biomaterials, such as lipid membranes, in their laboratory to mimic the behavior of living cells. By modeling a complex cell with minimal features in the experiments, the group aimed to gain a deeper understanding of certain biological processes, including migration, mechanical damage and repair, endoplasmic reticulum dynamics, and related processes.

In September 2017, the researcher moved from Harvard University to UiO to start as a group leader and establish her research laboratory. She works in life sciences, a very demanding research field with a high pace. All group leaders, including the researcher born in Turkey, had temporary five-year positions, renewable for four additional years upon vigorous evaluation by international referees and a panel. She passed this evaluation in 2021, and her contract was renewed until the end of 2025. In Norwegian employment practice, such a long period of temporary employment can lead to a justified claim for permanent employment.

In one of her publications, written together with colleagues, she employed model protocell networks for evaluating molecular transport through lipid nanotubes as a potential means of communication among primitive cells on early Earth. Network formation was initiated by the deposition of lipid reservoirs onto a surface in a special environment. These reservoirs autonomously developed into surface-adhered protocells interconnected via lipid nanotubes, encapsulating solutes from the ambient buffer. The researchers could observe the uptake of DNA and RNA and their diffusive transport between lipid compartments via interconnected nanotubes.

In another of her publications, the researcher explored the origin of life as one of humankind's great mysteries. At the transition between non-living and living matter, protocells – initially featureless aggregates of abiotic matter – gain the structure and functions necessary to fulfill the criteria of life. Research addressing protocells as a central element in this transition is diverse and increasingly interdisciplinary. The authors reviewed current protocell concepts and research directions, addressing milestones, challenges, and existing hypotheses in the context of conditions on the early Earth.

UiO is a public research university located in Oslo, Norway. It is the highest-ranked and oldest university in Norway. The university was ranked 126th in the world in 2023.

5.2 CMS Kluge Report Accusation Findings

The CMS Kluge report by attorneys Marco Lilli and Liss Sunde at CMS Kluge begins with a summary of the main findings and conclusions. The university director had asked the law firm to investigate two whistle-blower complaints against the researcher, who served as the group leader at the Norwegian Center for Molecular Medicine, based on notifications from four research fellows in her research group. The summary was as follows:

- We have identified 13 different incidents in which the researcher behaves so censurable that it is in breach of Working Environment Act, Section 4–3 (3), which prohibits exposing employees to "improper behavior".
- In addition to these 13 incidents, there are several cases of censurable behavior from the researcher which are not so serious that they can be characterized as "improper behavior", but which is in breach of the duty to ensure that the working environment is fully satisfactory, cf. the Working Environment Act, Section 4-1 (1).
- The sum of these incidents implies that the researcher's behavior must be characterized as "harassment" of several PhD students in her group, cf. the Working Environment Act, Section 4-3 (3). These conditions have persisted for a long time, and many of the incidents must be considered as very serious.
- On one occasion, the researcher exposed one of her PhD students to illegal retaliation, after the person concerned had notified according to the Working Environment Act, Chapter 2A. This is in breach of the prohibition of retaliation under the Working Environment Act, Section 2 A-4. The retaliation has had major consequences for the person concerned. There are also other aggravating circumstances, which makes it a very serious case of retaliation.
- The researcher has broken her work obligations on two occasions; one time by refusing to carry out a guidance interview after one of the PhD students had made justified criticism against the researcher and the other time by terminating the supervision of a PhD student because the

PhD-student did not live up to her expectations in the final phase of the work on the PhD thesis.

- The researcher has broken UiO's internal regulations by not conducting appraisal interviews.
- The seriousness of the situation is reinforced by the fact that the researcher seems completely unable to see anything censurable in her own behavior. Even when she is confronted with how the whistleblowers have experienced her behavior, she takes no form of self-criticism, but does instead meet the whistleblowers with mockery. On some issues, her explanation of her own behavior also appears to be unreliable.

One of the incidents is presented in the report as follows (Lilli and Sunde, 2023: 26):

> According to NN1, the researcher said the following (which NN1 states that she wrote down word for word right after the group meeting). *"NN5's submission was horrible. I had to stay up day and night and live on pizza to help her. I told her that if she can skip the 45 min coffee breaks, she would make it. But she didn't listen to me and see what happened. I told you not to do things last minute, but everyone thinks that stupid one will fix it in the end. It was the same with NN6's submission.*

Lilli and Sunde (2023) selectively presented certain elements in the researcher's contradiction to their report. She argued that nothing the accusers said was trustworthy and that she could prove they were lying on multiple counts.

5.3 CMS Kluge Report Maturity Assessment

Attorneys Marco Lilli and Liss Sunde at law firm CMS Kluge wrote a 49-page report dated February 1, which was handed over to the client, UiO, represented by its internal auditor and personnel manager. The accused researcher received the report from the personnel manager on February 16, along with a message that the researcher was to attend a meeting with the personnel manager on February 21 regarding the report. Quite surprisingly, the personnel manager canceled the meeting on short notice.

To assess the maturity of the CMS Kluge report, it is important to identify characteristics that match one of the four levels in the maturity model. The assessment procedure starts by assuming that a report is of top quality and thus at the top level of stage 4. Then, potential shortcomings are identified that might reduce the maturity level from stage 4 to stage 3 and potentially further down to stage 2 or stage 1. The following shortcomings were identified in the investigation work conducted by Lilli and Sunde:

1. The Norwegian Labor Inspection Authority does not recommend "*faktaundersøkelse*" as an investigation method. The CMS Kluge report, written in Norwegian, claims that it follows guidelines from the inspection authority regarding a specific method for fact-finding missions. There are no such guidelines. They do not exist. The praxis of the specific method has received massive criticism, resulting in the withdrawal of support for the method from the inspection authority several years ago. Claiming to follow guidelines that no longer exist can be based on ignorance or manipulation, with the hope that readers are unaware of the non-existence of such guidelines from the Norwegian labor inspection authority. The initial parties involved in developing the method, including unions, have also withdrawn their recommendation of the method due to conflict escalation while it was in use across various organizations.
2. There has been massive criticism of method praxis in recent years (Antonsen and Løkling, 2020; Hallgren and Trædal, 2022; Jebens and Dorans, 2019; Lerø, 2021; Nordrik and Kuldova, 2021; Slettemark and Kvamme, 2022; Topdahl and Akhtar, 2018; Trædal, 2021). Choosing to apply such a method thus represents misconduct on the part of the investigators. The investigation praxis has been criticized from various perspectives, including legal, criminological, sociological, psychological, and management perspectives. Investigated individuals have become victims of their investigations. The investigations did not resolve anything. Conflicts escalated rather than disappeared due to the chosen procedure. The criticism appeared in victim statements in the media and in books and articles in Norway. Labor unions expressed concern for their members when they became subject to this method, and scholars expressed concern regarding the lack of training for those conducting such inquiries. In fact, there was no knowledge or educational requirement for taking on the role of a

fact examiner. Some facts examiners had only attended a weekend course with a textbook completely lacking substance. For example, there was no training requirement regarding interviewing techniques, while everyone knows – including police detectives – that the most important source of information is people who are to be encouraged to describe what happened, how it happened, when it happened, and why it happened. Confrontation as applied by some attorneys as fact examiners does not work in an interview situation when collecting information.

3. Taking on all three roles of investigator, prosecutor, and judge constitutes a violation of justice. In democratic nations such as Norway, which has a well-functioning criminal justice system, there is a distinct separation between police detectives who conduct criminal investigations, state attorneys who conduct prosecutions, and judges in the courtroom who administer trial hearings and draw conclusions in a verdict document regarding the sentence. In the private business of corporate investigations, such role separation should be maintained. as well. However, Lilli and Sunde (2023) took on all three roles by collecting information, confronting the accused, and drawing a conclusion that the researcher had violated the Norwegian Working Environment Act. The behavior of the corporate investigators represents a serious violation of justice for the accused.
4. Concluding on law violations represents a consultancy failure. While attorneys acting as corporate investigators might argue that their conclusions about violations of the law represent only advice to the client and not a verdict, clients typically trust those conclusions and believe in the existence of legal violations. In this case, the personnel manager will trust that Lilli and Sunde are right in their conclusion and confront the researcher with the conclusion that she has violated the Norwegian Working Environment Act. The conclusion that the accused is a criminal becomes trusted and applied by the client accordingly. No due process had occurred before the verdict emerged in the investigation report. Due process would require something similar to arguments and counterarguments presented before a judge in a public courtroom.
5. There is no real mandate enabling the evaluation of investigative work. There are certain requirements for a text to qualify as a mandate. The mandate has to describe initiatives and activities to reach a certain goal or goals. The mandate text by Lilli and Sunde does not

satisfy this requirement. Rather, the text claiming to be a mandate is a description of the situation at the relevant part of the university. Furthermore, the mandate must be formulated with objectives that the client in the aftermath can review to determine whether or not the investigators have been successful or failed. There is no way the client can evaluate the work of the investigators based on whether they have completed it in accordance with the mandate.

6. There is a presentation of incidents, one by one, without substance. A storytelling as presented by the investigators is not a reconstruction of past events or sequences of events. A reconstruction requires a focus on issues that are defined in the mandate. Since the mandate lacks focus and does not satisfy basic requirements as discussed above, the consequence is a lack of focus in the reconstruction. For example, if harassment is the focus, then only incidents that might reflect harassment should be assessed in the report. Harassment refers to behavior that demeans, humiliates, or embarrasses a person. The phenomenon is not concerned with isolated incidents as reported by Lilli and Sunde, but rather with the repeated behavior of disturbing, upsetting, or threatening the victim.
7. Contradiction by the accused returned to the whistleblowers is subject to criticism. An investigation should begin by identifying information sources and deriving relevant information from them. Then, the accused is to be invited to comment on the accusations. This refers to a contradiction in the accused's statements in response to accusations. Then, the investigation report should be written. The examiners made the mistake, however, of returning to the accusers to obtain their comments on the statements from the accused. The accused was never invited to a final round of comments. This constitutes a violation of fair and due process in private internal investigations.
8. Contradiction was prevented by denied access to relevant documentation. The accused complained that she had no access to relevant documents pertaining to her case. She filed her complaint with the personnel manager, and her appeal was, according to the personnel manager's instructions, "You may appeal the decision within 3 weeks after receiving this reply. The appeals body is the central complaint committee, but the appeal shall be directed to UiO". The accused thus filed her complaint with the joint board of appeals at the university. The board concluded that her right to access had wrongfully been denied. Nevertheless, she never gained access before the final CMS

Kluge report was sent to the university and subsequently presented to the accused. The accused felt that the university had mishandled her request for case-related documentation according to Norwegian public law. She referred to the decision by the Directorate for Higher Education and Competence regarding the university's response to her freedom of information request. It appeared that the university was in violation of the law because it had refused to transfer the requested documents to her, preventing her from properly contradicting. It was clear to her that the university applied several measures to restrict her opportunity to contradict properly. Furthermore, her option to contradict was not real since she was initially given 48 hours to respond to 55 pages of available documents. This was the initial request, which, due to the accused's objection and complaint, was extended to first two weeks and then to one month by swapping her appointment for a meeting with a university lawyer regarding the allegations against her, which – in Lilli's own words – needed more preparation from the accused's side. The fact that the accused had a full-time job and commitments was obviously ignored by the investigators and bureaucrats.

9. An investigation report should separate a part on all facts from the part on assessments. A statement of facts can be agreed upon by both accusers and the accused, while interpretations and conclusions typically cause disagreement. Therefore, a separation is important in the report. Unfortunately, the CMS Kluge report is a continuous storytelling mixing facts and opinions.
10. Selective inclusion of statements makes the report biased. It is open to guesswork as to which episodes are included and which are excluded. The impression is created that matters included are random accounts provided by whistleblowers and deemed serious enough to warrant inclusion by examiners. Examiners have been on the passive receiving end of stories rather than actively searching for incidents relevant to the mandate. Again, the lack of clear guidance from a mandate has contributed to failures regarding relevant incidents. The collection of incidents seems both random and biased, as whistleblowers have been in control of what episodes were presented to the examiners, and the examiners have been in control of what information to mention and not mention in their report.
11. Examiners demonstrate a lack of insight into supervision dynamics. The core content of the CMS Kluge report is concerned with

communication between the accused and the accusers. While the accused held a senior position, most accusers were in junior positions. For example, while the accused was an associate professor in charge of a major research project, most accusers were working on the research project as doctoral students supervised by the accused. The core matter is the extent to which the accused has communicated directly, explicitly, and truthfully to accusers when those accusers have underperformed in their work and the extent to which the accused's communication has involved harassment, threats, ridicule, and other hostile behaviors. While the examiners acknowledge that there might be some tension in academic relationships, they do not demonstrate any insights into the dynamics of such relationships. Things can be said and done that may indeed seem strange to outsiders. For example, a blind review process combined with rejection of work is common. Similar procedures are sometimes applied in non-blind review processes where a panel or a single expert simply expresses rejection of presented work. Examiners seem to believe that this is unacceptable behavior, as they argue that there should be not only constructive comments but also helpful ones. In many situations, academics among themselves simply provide critique. This is important so that the recipient understands they may be on the wrong path. Attorneys Lilli and Sunde seem simply to lack an understanding of critique as useful among academics in their communication. Furthermore, rivalry and competition among scholars is a constructive force in academia, where individuals at the same level and those at different formal levels within the organization strive to be better researchers than others. The competitive environment encourages researchers to work more thoroughly and quickly and be more goal-oriented to get their research output published in more prestigious journals. For example, the researcher's feedback to someone that "You cannot just show pictures, because we cannot understand it" represents a completely acceptable form of academic critique, while the CMS Kluge report concludes that the feedback represents a violation of the law regarding the working environment.

12. Examiners should have consulted with supervision experts to review whistleblower statements. Based on the previous point, examiners lacking insights into supervision dynamics should obviously have sought advice among academics with supervision experience. Anyone who has supervised PhD and master's students knows that they

sometimes communicate not only directly and explicitly but also extremely negatively to ensure that the supervised understands the feedback. Feedback can be a matter of suggesting a change in direction, and it is important to clearly convey the expert's opinion to the recipient. Receiving criticism can be hard to swallow as one may have worked for days, weeks, or even months on something that now seems completely a waste of time. Rather than reflecting on the feedback and considering how to change the direction of one's research, it is, of course, tempting for the recipient to externalize the problem by blaming the expert for negative and destructive comments. In fact, one of the accusers acknowledged in an email the usefulness of explicit critique: "Yes, you are totally right, there is no communication problem among us. Actually, you express yourself very clearly. I recognized that my self-awareness was totally interrupted. And yes, I recognized that (for a reason) I postpone the things until a moment that is actually late to start. I haven't figured out what is the reason but I am working on every aspect". Everyone who has supervised students at this level knows that students will have to go through some kind of depressive phase before returning to self-reflection and revising their research approach and working procedures, as indicated by this quote from an email. It would indeed not be helpful to have an enthusiastic supervisor who was always supportive, regardless of the candidate's presentation. Fake enthusiasm could in fact be detrimental to reaching a student's goal, which is to achieve a degree as a master or doctor. That goal is only possible to reach when external reviewers ultimately find the work acceptable. Enthusiasm on the way can lead to a devastating depression when a candidate is confronted by rejection from external reviewers after one or more years of work. An important task for senior academics is therefore to be explicit in their critique so that negative feedback from others at a later point in time comes as no surprise to them. Attorneys Lilli and Sunde demonstrate a complete lack of understanding here. They seem to favor enthusiasm rather than realism and to favor protection against being hurt rather than correction.

13. It is subject to criticism to apply a simple probability of 51 percent when drawing conclusions. To draw conclusions regarding law violations that could lead to criminal charges, the requirement in Norway is probability beyond any reasonable doubt. Beyond any reasonable doubt is a legal standard of proof required to validate a criminal

assessment in most adversarial legal systems. It is a far higher standard than the balance of probabilities used in civil cases because the stakes are much higher in a criminal case. Accusing someone of violating a penal law is not a civil case, even if it is presented by lawyers in the role of corporate investigators. Rather than a likelihood of 51 percent for wrongdoing, the likelihood should be above 90 percent or even 95 percent. If the accusation is not obviously evidenced and proven to 90 or 95 percent certainty, then examiners shall conclude that wrongdoing has not been confirmed. Unfortunately, this was not the praxis of Lilli and Sunde. Rather, they applied a rule that someone is guilty if it is more likely than not that the suspect has committed wrongdoing. Therefore, the CMS Kluge report violates a basic criminal justice principle.

14. The working language at this level is English, and the report should therefore be in English. Lilli and Sunde, however, wrote their report in Norwegian. This seems arrogant and ignorant toward the investigated person. At UiO, the working language among researchers is English, not Norwegian. In the research group headed by the researcher, there are almost no Norwegians. The researchers come from different parts of the world, often with basic degrees from prestigious universities. Confronting an international research capacity, such as the researcher facing accusations in Norwegian, is simply not acceptable. It demonstrates a lack of respect and a lack of competence among the two investigators.
15. It is a violation of the accused's right to justice to present a report in Norwegian. Justice is a matter of equal treatment for everyone. It is an act of discrimination when the CMS Kluge report is written in a local language not used in the research environment at UiO. Discriminating someone not knowing the local language while working in English as an international language used by everyone else in an academic setting seems to be an expression of ill will. The accused became a victim of a language she did not understand and was not expected to understand. UiO has no mandatory courses in Norwegian for researchers coming temporarily or permanently to this country. It is the choice of each researcher whether or not to spend time learning the local language. Since all work is conducted in English – such as communications with colleagues, publications in research journals, committee work for degrees, and committee work for promotions – it may in fact be a waste of time to attend Norwegian courses to learn

the language. Foreign researchers do not come to Norway to speak Norwegian to the local population. They do not come primarily to enjoy skiing or other activities typical of Norwegians. They come primarily because UiO has the ambition to make its research internationally competitive by recruiting scientists with excellent track records who can perform groundbreaking research, stimulate their teaching, and conduct professional supervision.

16. There is no knowledge strategy (people) or information strategy (sources). Selection of relevant corporate investigators depends on the knowledge needs for each specific examination challenge. The challenge in the current case was to establish the facts about the working environment in terms of climate, culture, and output. The last aspect was completely ignored by Lilli and Sunde, as they did not identify the extent of success of the researcher's group relative to the climate and culture in the group. Furthermore, to reconstruct past events and sequences of events, the most important source of information was what involved persons would tell investigators. Therefore, the most important knowledge requirement in a knowledge strategy would be interviewing skills that are typically well developed among psychologists and management consultants but typically underdeveloped among attorneys trained in the application of law. Nevertheless, the university director, together with the person responsible for internal audits at the university, hired attorneys at a law firm to conduct the investigation. It seems obvious from the investigation documents that Lilli and Sunde applied confrontation rather than cooperation and conducted interrogations rather than interviews that can lead to hostile behavior and non-cooperation among the victims of their approach. After a confrontational conversation, investigators obtained the results of the defense rather than the truth, which further diminished the reliability of investigative findings. Information strategy is concerned with the selection of information sources during an investigation. Examiners Lilli and Sunde should have started their work by interviewing some university professors about their experiences with academic communication in research dialogues and supervisory situations. Probably, they would have learned that the tone can vary to a large extent depending on the situation. Therefore, examiners should have a benchmark for acceptable behavior that might be very different from other kinds of workplaces. Unfortunately, the

investigators did not conduct such initial interviews. Instead, they applied some unknown and implicit criteria for unacceptable behavior, which seemed strange to people accustomed to life in academic institutions.

17. There is no configuration strategy (procedure) or system strategy (digital). There are two basic configurations, i.e., sequential and iterative. The sequential configuration is often labeled a value chain, where activities are predefined in a sequence for examiners to follow. The iterative configuration is often labeled a value shop, where activities tend to repeat themselves in a spiral. The term "value" is used to indicate value creation for clients. Traditionally, the value chain has been the dominant configuration. However, in knowledge work such as internal investigations, the value shop is more appropriate, where tasks follow each other iteratively, returning to earlier tasks for clarification. A value shop is an iterative approach in which examiners identify relevant issues in an iterative sequence consisting of problems, alternatives, choices, interpretations, and evaluations. Unfortunately, CMS Kluge investigators applied the value chain rather than the value shop in their sequential, incident-by-incident investigation. System strategy represents a choice of digital tools in the internal investigation to create improved insights into the issues. For example, words used by individuals can be linked to words used by other individuals, and individuals can be linked to each other in terms of topics. Unfortunately, CMS Kluge investigators applied no systematic strategy at all.
18. The report contributes to conflict escalation rather than problem-solving. A report drawing conclusions based on failing foundations tends to escalate conflicts and make involved people defend themselves rather than contribute to clarification and solutions. Innocent individuals can wrongfully be attributed blame for misconduct. A feasible and better solution is often to enter into dialogue internally at an early stage to resolve problems. Maybe an external management consultant could have been brought in to create a climate of communication and mutual understanding, where the consultant does not take on the task of reconstructing events or drawing conclusions, particularly regarding potential legal violations. Unfortunately, the internal auditor and the personnel manager at the university did not pursue such a constructive path. The internal auditor seemed to be the

bureaucrat shuffling the documents around, while the university director wrote to CMS Kluge, stating that it was his decision to forward the case.

19. Information analysis is completely absent from the report. The information collected in various interviews should have been subject to thematic analysis, which involves identifying, reflecting, and reporting patterns of themes within the complete sample of interviews with interviewees. Thematic analysis is one of the most common qualitative analysis techniques and an appropriate method for demonstrating understanding of presented memories, experiences, thoughts, views, and behaviors across a set of interviews. As is known to most internal investigators, they have a choice between inductive and deductive analysis. The inductive approach involves deriving meaning and creating themes from information without preconceptions, thus allowing themes to emerge from the information. A deductive approach can be applied to the legal discussion using pre-existing codes informed by terms derived from legal statutes. None of this was done by Lilli and Sunde. Only presenting incidents, one by one, as done by Lilli and Sunde in their report, is simply below any professional standard. An initial code could allow distinguishing between issues where the researcher is accused of criticizing a person and issues where the researcher is accused of rejecting work. There are in the report a total of 27 issues assessed in the report under the heading "Our assessment". Six are not considered serious. Twenty-one are considered serious, of which 12 are concerned with criticizing a person, while 9 are concerned with rejecting work. The CMS Kluge report claims that there are 13 issues considered serious, while this review identifies 21 issues that investigators found serious. However, the number difference is not important here. Rather, it is the complete lack of thematic classification that is so problematic. For example, it would be useful to have an initial discussion of the seriousness of unfavorable comments about the person compared to the seriousness of unfavorable comments about their work. To conduct a professional assessment of themes, several assessors are needed. For example, while the review here suggests that 12 issues are concerned with the person and 9 issues are concerned with their work, the medical ethics professor found far fewer issues concerned with the person and far more issues concerned with the work.

20. The content of the report lacks reliability as well as validity. Reliability refers to the extent of exact replication of incidents. There is no analysis of potential discrepancies between allegations and events, or of statements potentially contradicting each other. There is no triangulation of claims. Simply stated, it is not obvious that the interviewees said what they meant, that investigators understood what the interviewees said or meant, that investigators have replicated incidents by relevant context, or that investigation interpretations are relevant. Validity refers to the extent of accuracy in the presented results. There is no content analysis of terms used, and there are no explicit interpretations of those terms by the investigators. Validity can only be claimed if a new set of internal investigators are likely to arrive at the same conclusions as the first set of internal investigators. Given the criticism in this review, it seems obvious that a qualified team of investigators will arrive at significantly different conclusions.
21. It is an activity-oriented investigation lacking problem solutions, detection outcomes, and investment value. The investigation, with all its shortcomings as listed above, ends up at the bottom stage, representing the lowest level of maturity for internal investigations. Overall, the report seems to be the result of commissioned work, where conclusions are in line with expectations of the client. The university management, as the client, seemed interested in confronting the accused with conclusions from a law firm stating that the accused had violated Norwegian law. If the accused were to accept such a statement from lawyers acting as private investigators, then the accused might have no other choice but to leave her position at the university in complete absence of fair justice to bring her case in front of Oslo District Court. The escalating conflict level caused by Lilli and Sunde is yet another indication of the substandard, outsourced work that they conducted for the university.

5.4 Maturity Assessment Outcome

While it is not a direct shortcoming of the CMS Kluge report, it is yet another deficiency that Lilli and Sunde did not involve impartial managers at the university during the investigation process. Managers can guide investigators toward knowledge regarding what is typically not considered harassment in academic settings and how to approach top academics regarding their behaviors and reactions. The main criticism in this respect, however, has to be directed at the internal auditor and the personnel manager, along with the university director and the dean of the medical faculty, for their abdication of leadership by leaving the matter entirely to an external consultancy. External investigation represents an abdication of leadership by UiO management. Abdication refers to a failure to fulfill a responsibility and a duty.

It is important, however, to acknowledge the special characteristics of leadership roles held by individuals such as university directors, internal auditors, faculty deans, and personnel managers within their respective university settings. Basically, while they have various leadership responsibilities, their roles have little to no importance to faculty members. They do not decide whether a master's thesis is of sufficient quality, as that is decided by an external examiner. They do not decide whether a doctoral dissertation is of sufficient quality, as that is decided by an external committee. They do not decide whether an applicant is qualified for positions such as associate professor or professor, as this is determined by an external committee. They do not provide access to research funding, as that is provided by external national and international agencies. They do not decide whether your research output should be accepted or rejected by a research journal since that is decided by external referees in blind reviews. "Decision-making skills and strategic abilities are not as important in academia as in business" (Strand and Lie, 2023). In light of all these role limitations, it is indeed surprising that the UiO leadership outsourced an important task for which they are responsible and thus abdicated leadership.

In conclusion, given all the shortcomings and thus the substandard quality of the CMS Kluge report, UiO management should consider whether or not they are obliged to pay for the work. Since there is no clear mandate that can be used to conclude that Lilli and Sunde did not perform a proper job, it might be difficult to refuse to pay. Nevertheless, the internal auditor and the personnel manager at the university might consider not paying for the CMS Kluge work or ask to get UiO money back from the law firm.

The suggested consideration might be strengthened by the biased CMS Kluge investigation against the researcher, while there was a lack of investigation against a university lawyer. In an email from Lilli to the researcher, Lilli stated that "for the sake of good order, I repeat that we will start our handling of your complaint against the university lawyer after our interview with you". While this email was dated November 2022, the researcher had been informed of nothing regarding Lilli's handling of her complaint against a university lawyer by the end of February 2023.

Figure 5.1 illustrates the assessment procedure for allocating the 21 shortcoming items that reduce maturity level from stage 4 via stages 3 and 2 to stage 1. The characteristics are listed in Table 5.1, where they are assigned relevant stages of growth for internal investigations. In summary, the above assessment of the CMS Kluge report maturity should lead to the lowest possible level of an activity-oriented investigation, as illustrated in Figure 5.2.

While this review is mainly concerned with the CMS Kluge report, it is relevant to emphasize the role of university leadership that made it even worse for the accused to respond in a relevant and constructive manner. As mentioned above, university executives should have guided investigators toward knowledge sources to understand communication in academic settings. They should have avoided abdication of leadership. They should, in fact, not have outsourced the investigation task but rather established

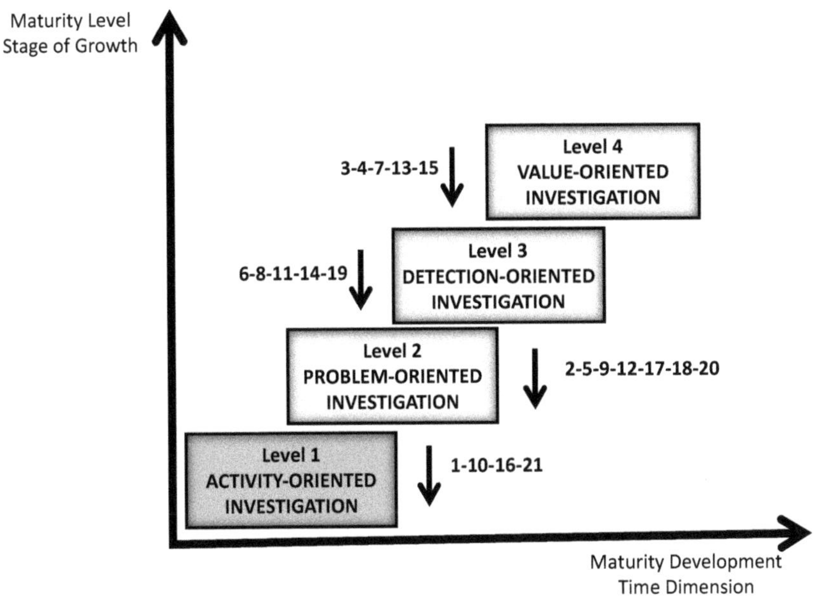

Figure 5.1. Maturity reductions by investigation shortcoming items.

Table 5.1. Characteristics reducing the CMS Kluge report maturity.

#	Characteristic of Conducted CMS Kluge Investigation	Violation of Activity-Oriented Investigation	Violation of Problem-Oriented Investigation	Violation of Detection-Oriented Investigation	Violation of Value-Oriented Investigation
1	Fact finding	Claim support from authority			
2	Fact finding		The praxis of investigations		
3	Three roles				Criminal justice
4	Sentencing				Criminal justice
5	No mandate		Unknown what to solve		
6	Sequential			No overview to detect	
7	Recycling				Unfair treatment
8	Denial			No option to suggest	
9	Separation		No focus on issues		
10	Bias	Not transparent			
11	Non-familiar			Wrong benchmark	
12	Experts		Misleading focus		
13	Probability				Criminal justice
14	Language			Barrier to participation	
15	Language				Criminal justice
16	Knowledge	Shortcoming interviews			

Table 5.1. (*Continued*)

#	Characteristic of Conducted CMS Kluge Investigation	Violation of Activity-Oriented Investigation	Violation of Problem-Oriented Investigation	Violation of Detection-Oriented Investigation	Violation of Value-Oriented Investigation
17	Configuration		Shortcoming understanding		
18	Escalation		No consensus achieved		
19	Analysis			No themes identified	
20	Reliability		No relevant representation		
21	Problem	Escalation of allegations			

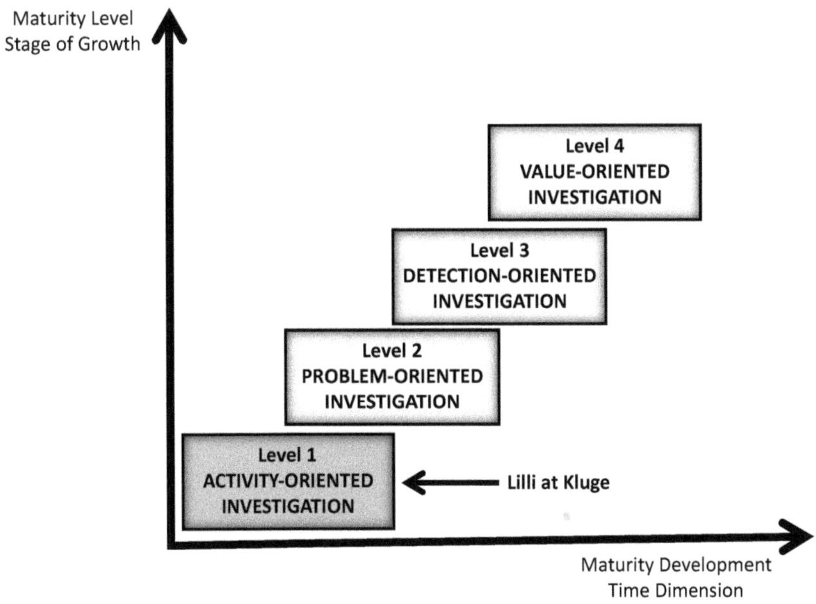

Figure 5.2. Maturity assessment of the Lilli and Sunde report at law firm CMS Kluge.

an internal investigation with people trusted by both the accusers and the accused.

Furthermore, the university should not have left the researcher alone to handle the accusations. She was entitled to support from her employer. For example, if she faced legal allegations, she was entitled to a defense lawyer paid for by the university. If she were facing other kinds of allegations, she was to have access to experts free of charge. This is a matter of security and justice for an employee, for which the university, as employer, is responsible.

Also, the denial of access to documents made it more difficult for the accused to defend themselves during the contradiction phase. In fact, as stated in issue number 8 above, the contradiction was prevented by denying access to relevant documentation. The accused complained to the university leadership that she had no access to relevant documents pertaining to her case. She filed her complaint, and the joint complaint commission rejected the university's arguments against not giving the researcher full access to all the documents related to the different allegations.

5.5 Problematic Internal Investigation

The secrecy of most internal reports by corporate investigators at law firms and audit firms (Gottschalk and Tcherni-Buzzeo, 2016) is a problem since there tends to be a lack of justice when compared to the criminal justice system (Button, 2020; Gottschalk, 2020; King, 2020c; Meerts, 2020). As emphasized in the case study, a number of problematic issues arise when corporate investigators are hired by client organizations. One issue is the threefold role of many investigators, who assume the responsibilities of investigation, prosecution, and sentencing. Another issue is the requirement of evidence that an incident is more likely than not. A requirement of 51 percent probability of being an offender in law violation is far from the justice requirement of being an offender beyond any reasonable doubt. A third issue is the use of investigation reports by clients who do not treat them as consulting work but rather as court verdicts.

In many jurisdictions, the business of corporate investigators is not at all regulated. While lawyers in the role of attorneys have certain guidelines to follow, there are no guidelines when they are acting as corporate investigators. Becoming a voluntary member of the Association of Certified Fraud Examiners (ACFE) in the United States, for example, or any other similar association does not imply a role obligation where deviance can be sanctioned. Meerts (2018: 6) found that the legal framework is almost non-existent or non-functioning for corporate investigators in the Netherlands:

> Respondents indicate that the state has very little insight into what happens in the corporate security sector (...) The legal framework that applies is dependent on the label an investigator wears (…) Although forensic accountants and legal investigators are regulated by a general legal framework, these laws are not constructed to deal with investigative activities – rather, they are focused on traditional accounting activities and the traditional role of the lawyer. (…) The diversification in the corporate investigations arena and in legal frameworks and control create a fragmented field in which the state has very little knowledge about actual activities. Democratic control over the corporate security sector is very limited. Control over corporate investigations is, for an important part, reliant on the ethics of individual investigators and on the client. This places much responsibility on organizations using the services of corporate investigators.

This description of the non-existence of a legal framework for corporate investigators in the Netherlands resonates completely with the situation in Norway. When forensic accountants and auditors conduct fraud examinations, they only relate to general rules applicable to accountants and auditors. When investigating lawyers conduct fraud examinations, they only relate to general rules that apply to the legal profession. Although lawyers can claim the client-attorney privilege of secrecy even toward public authorities, this is not possible for certified accountants and auditors, even when they all carry out exactly the same kind of work in fraud examinations (Gottschalk, 2017, 2018, 2019, 2020, 2021).

This research does not, in any way, claim that the presented case is representative of work by corporate investigators conducting internal examinations in client organizations. Nevertheless, this research is important, as it illustrates the lack of justice caused by the absence of regulation of the private investigation industry as performed by law firms, audit firms, consulting firms, and others. While judges issue verdicts to defendants in court, corporate investigators may arrange settlements in private investigations. Clients often want to settle a matter quietly, for example, by a contract in which parties agree on an amount payable by the involved person. It may also include conditions, such as the termination of the labor contract. Non-disclosure clauses are fairly standard in settlement agreements where parties commit themselves to the confidentiality of the agreement and the circumstances surrounding termination. There is no public scrutiny of the potential justice violations involved.

The final destiny of the accused scholar was not known at the time of writing this case study. Unfortunately, she started another altercation at UiO in June 2023 regarding authorship of a research publication. Although she may be correct, her attack can also be interpreted as a desperate reaction to the treatment she has suffered from the university for a long time. We know that if you are unfairly treated, you may want to hit back wherever you can. That is very human indeed.

5.6 Preparing for Oslo Court Trial

At the time of writing about the case study above in 2023, the fate of the accused scholar was not known (Gottschalk, 2024). However, upon revisiting the case one year later in 2024, the situation was characterized by an upcoming court trial in which the accused Irep Gözen sued UiO for having terminated her by giving her a dismissal notice in the previous year. According to Norwegian law, an employee is entitled to remain in their job until a court verdict is issued when the employee takes the initiative of bringing the case in front of a judge. The trial was scheduled at the Oslo district court at the end of September 2024.

Ahead of the trial, the parties were preparing themselves in various ways and presenting their competing narratives in the media. A "narrative" refers to a way of organizing and speaking to the world; it is the way in which meanings unfold in and through time (Fox *et al.*, 2022; Torbor *et al.*, 2024). While the university attorney suggested that Gözen in every way had behaved terribly, unacceptably, and beyond anything excusable, the defense attorney for Gözen argued that she had simply done nothing wrong when supervising PhD students and deciding on authorship regarding publication of research from the Gözen group in the university.

The first news report, with the heading "A UiO researcher was dismissed after a factual investigation – Now there will be a trial", focused on the criticism of the CMS Kluge investigation report discussed above (Lindqvist, 2024a):

> I was asked if I was willing to look at the report that Kluge had made. I was, and when I went through it I discovered that, unfortunately, like very many such reports, it appeared to be commissioned work. All accusations against the woman have been taken at face value, and the lawyers leave no room for doubt, Gottschalk says. He does not base his assessment solely on a reading of the report. In the article "Workplace deviance investigations: A case study of the application of maturity model to a university investigation", the professor has systematically gone through the Kluge report.

The second news report, headlined "UiO's Kluge lawyer was reported to the police after facts review", focused on CMS Kluge's response to the criticism (Lindqvist, 2024b):

> I have no comments to the article, apart from the fact that Gottschalk has a number of views both on the actual circumstances of the case and on how such investigations should be carried out, with which I fundamentally disagree, writes Lilli in an e-mail to Uniforum. Law firm Kluge has had a framework agreement with UiO for a number of years, and Lilli has advised the university in many cases. The factual investigation in this case has been carried out under the direction of Lilli with the assistance of another Kluge lawyer.

The third news report focused on the criticism of the CMS Kluge report (Olsen, 2024):

> Professor at BI gives the CMS Kluge review the smooth finish: - Mixes facts and opinions. Partner at CMS Kluge, Marco Lilli, says he 'fundamentally disagrees' with a number of the views of the professor.

The fourth news report focused on the research manager accused of abuse of power and harassment of fellows (Svarstad, 2024a):

> The circumstances had persisted for a long time, and many of the incidents are very serious, says the investigation report. The university has dismissed the research leader, who responds with a lawsuit.

The fifth news report addressed arguments the university might use in the trial (Lindqvist, 2024c):

> Dismissed UiO researcher referred to as "incorrectable". The researcher who is suing UiO for invalid dismissal completely lacks the ability and will to realize her own problematic behavior, claims the government attorney.

Since UiO is a public university, it was to be defended by a government attorney. The selected government attorney, Magnus Johan Færø, had been at the Norwegian government attorney's office for four years. The lawyer prosecuting Irep Gözen in the civil lawsuit was Ingvild Opøien. Attorney Opøien wrote in her final statement to the court ahead of the trial that her client Gözen refused to accept the dismissal and therefore took legal action against UiO to have the dismissal decision declared invalid and to receive compensation (Svarstad, 2024b):

> The researcher stated, among other things: "Peer assessment is extremely critical and almost pedantic. I am employed at UiO to bring my standards into my group, not the other way around. I certainly have no intention of adapting to the 'feelings' of a bachelor student who thinks that difficult questions are rude".

The head of the Research Ethics Committee at UiO claimed that the previous year had been very intense. A major reason was that Irep Gözen, who had been twice rejected by the committee, was subsequently acquitted by the National Investigation Committee in one of the cases. "This caused headaches for the UiO committee", while "In addition to the report drawn up by the law firm CMS Kluge following two reports against the woman, UiO will be able to show in court that she was later found guilty of scientific misconduct in the National Committee for the Investigation of Research Misconduct" (Lindqvist, 2024d).

5.7 Reporting from Oslo Court Trial

The court proceedings were scheduled for five days, starting on Monday, September 23. The government attorney was Magnus Johan Færø, and the defense lawyer was Ingvild Opøien. Ingebjørg Tønnessen was the district court judge. The media attention was limited to digital newspapers focusing on university activities such as *Uniforum* and *Khrono*. Lindqvist (2024e) at Uniforum reported from the first day of trial at Oslo District Court:

> Kluge has submitted a comprehensive report in the case, which ended in dismissal. But the court really only needs to decide on one thing, the government attorney pointed out. Last year, a female researcher and research group leader was dismissed from UiO for repeatedly "violating her duties". On Monday, the trial started in the Oslo district court, where the woman is demanding that the dismissal be declared invalid and compensation. Around 15 listeners – more than there were seats for – turned up to hear the parties' introductory speeches.

While some doctoral students had blown the whistle on Irep Gözen, she had herself blown the whistle on her superior, Janna Saarela. Therefore, Gözen denied that she had violated her duties. Rather, she claimed that the university leadership had denied their duties as she was entitled to a different supervisor after having blown the whistle on her current whistleblower. However, the university leadership never replaced her supervisor (Lindqvist, 2024e).

Svarstad (2024c) at Khrono reported from the first day in court the statement by defense attorney Ingvild Opøien regarding Irep Gözen, "it seems that they have been looking for things that can be used against her":

> In her introductory talk, her lawyer Ingvild Opøien reminded of the peculiarities of academia as a workplace, that it can be tough to be a research fellow, and of academic freedom of speech.
>
> — She has spent a lot more time on guidance and contact with the fellows than has been usual. Her goal has been to get the students through a race, she said. Opøien mentioned that the researcher has a background from, among others, Harvard and has an international way of thinking.

Irep Gøzen had been working at the university since 2016. Opøien said in court that Gözen is certainly familiar with the high workload and stress associated with doctoral work. Doctoral students must learn how to receive and deal with criticism, she said in court. Opøien said that the CMS Kluge report appears as a commissioned work, where Marco Lilli at CMS Kluge drew conclusions as requested by Irene Sandlie and Arne Benjaminsen at the university (Lindqvist, 2024e; Svarstad, 2024c). This first day in court was dominated by competing narratives presented against Gözen by government attorney Færø and in favor of Gözen by defense lawyer Opøien. As mentioned above, a "narrative" refers to a way of organizing and speaking to the world; it is the way to make sense of meanings that unfold in and through time (Fox *et al.*, 2022; Torbor *et al.*, 2024). "The law, focused on putting facts in the world into coherent form and presenting them persuasively – to make a case – always results in particular narratives that differ between the defense and the prosecution" (Brooks, 1996: 14).

The second day in court was for the plaintiff to argue her case that the termination of her employment could not be justified and that she was therefore entitled to remain in her position at the university. She also claimed financial compensation for the harm inflicted upon her by the university, as her employer. When asked about the CMS Kluge report, she said in court (Lindqvist, 2024f):

> As Uniforum has written previously, Kluge's fact-finding was slaughtered by professor emeritus at BI, Petter Gottschalk.
>
> — How did you feel when you got the Gottschalk review of the Kluge report? Opøien asked.
>
> — It was the first time I felt some support. Gottschalk revealed that there was no real contradiction, that the whistleblowers got the last word, and that Kluge lawyer Marco Lilli changed his role from external expert to representing the university in the case. I was happy when, for the first time, I experienced that more people than me saw what was happening, answered the woman. Like Gottschalk, the woman also claims that the Kluge law firm twisted events described to fit the image of her as a problem. Several things in the report are exaggerated and misleadingly presented in order to make the events as dramatic as possible, she claimed.

In court, plaintiff Irep Gözen played several audio recordings of meetings with the students who had blown the whistle on her. The recordings should indicate that events did not occur as presented in the CMS Kluge report. For example, she played a recording that showed a positive atmosphere with laughter during the same meeting. Gözen also brought recordings and read aloud text, where it was obvious that she had high expectations of the PhD students in her group, apparently higher expectations than the students themselves (Lindqvist, 2024f).

At the end of the second day in court, a witness called by the plaintiff made his testimony in court. It was Esteban Pedrueza-Villalmanzo, a senior research engineer in nanofabrication at Chalmers University of Technology in Sweden. He said in court that he had cooperated quite a bit with Gözen. He explained a collaborative effort that was friendly and productive, and that Gözen was a person it was easy to get along with and work with. He said he was surprised when he learned about the termination case at UiO (Svarstad, 2024d).

Wednesday, September 25, 2024, was the third and final day in court. The day started with a witness statement by Jo Døhl, a dean at the university who had participated in the hiring process of Irep Gözen in 2016. Døhl said that there had been 71 applicants for two positions as group leaders. He told that Gözen had made a strong, positive impression as energetic and visionary with interesting research ideas. "Leader vision can be broadly defined as the expression of an idealized image of the future based on the organization's core values" (Kislov *et al.*, 2024: 4). The next witness was Kjetil Taskén, who also confirmed that Gözen was both clever and problematic. The final witnesses were Jan Helge Solbakk and Janna Saarela, who said that the Gözen group was special in many ways (Toft, 2024). Following the witness statements, both defense lawyer Ingvild Opøien and government attorney Magnus Johan Færø made their final remarks. The CMS Kluge report was again mentioned on the final third day in court (Svarstad, 2024e):

> To a student who never manages to deliver on time, never manages to prepare for a presentation, she must be able to take it in and say that "now you have to sharpen up".
>
> There has been disagreement about the interpretation of events in the investigation report, and about details, for example in a situation with shouting and slamming a door. Government attorney Magnus Johan Færø believed that the report is, in its core, correct, although there may be disagreements about details.

In her closing remarks, lawyer Opøien argued that the CMS Kluge report was part of a procedure that could not have been objective and neutral (Lindqvist, 2024g):

> It represents a criminal justice problem that one attempts to produce an objective report when there are so many leads involved, said Opøien. The fact that the Kluge lawyer behind the report has followed the case further after the report had been submitted means that the process overall constitutes an administrative law case management error which renders the decision invalid, claimed Opøien.

The final day of court was September 25, 2024. The verdict from Oslo District Court was dated two weeks later, on October 7, 2024. The verdict, signed by judges Ingebjørg Tønnessen, Jan Murvold, and Anne-Marte Brevig Vaagan said (Oslo tingrett, 2024: 30):

> The state by the University of Oslo is acquitted. The university's dismissal decision will take effect from October 15, 2024. Irep Gözen is sentenced to pay NOK 355,255 in legal costs to the state by the University of Oslo. The amount is due for payment within two weeks after the verdict has been released.

The report by Marco Lilli at CMS Kluge was mentioned 42 times in the verdict of the district court, for example (Oslo tingrett, 2024: 4):

> In a telephone conference between the court and the legal representatives, it was agreed that the members of the court should read the Kluge report in advance. It was also agreed that the whistleblowers' explanations to Kluge could be used as a basis by the court, so that it would not be necessary to bring the whistleblowers as witnesses during the main hearing. The agreement on this procedure did not imply that Gözen agreed with what the whistleblowers had explained to Kluge.

By agreeing to the court's procedure of reading the CMS Kluge report in advance of the trial, and by agreeing that the whistleblowers' explanations in the report could be used as a basis by the court, attorney Opøien simply reduced and possibly ruined her chances for winning the case on behalf of Gözen. Opøien made the implicit mistake of approving the report as a legitimate legal document. A more effective alternative strategy that could have been much more successful would be to deny the CMS Kluge report's relevance to the trial and demand that whistleblowers testify in court. As Gottschalk and Hamerton (2023: 69) have explained regarding lawyer roles, the relevant role would be as an enabler rather than a defender or attacker:

> The lawyer in the role of enabler is concerned with protecting and defending the rights of the client as well as helping the client achieve their personal and business objectives in a potential conflict with individuals, organizations, and public authorities. The lawyer in this role tends to apply substance communication, symbolic influencing, and information selection and control.

Information control is a matter of what and how crucial information is presented to make it difficult, and sometimes impossible, for counterparts to get the complete picture. Information in favor of the client should be presented, while information that might harm the client should be avoided. Given the premise that judges Tønnessen, Murvold, and Vaagan read the CMS Kluge report in advance of the trial, it became a core source of information for the court. The court reflected on the document in various ways (Oslo tingrett, 2024):

> Nor can the court see that Kluge has violated the guidelines that the Norwegian Bar Association has given for private investigations. However, the court agrees with some of the general criticism that has been leveled against investigations and that Gözen has pointed to in her argumentation. (page 13).
>
> The court shall not review whether Kluge's assessment of these circumstances is correct. (page 14).
>
> As previously mentioned, the Kluge report identifies a number of episodes where Gözen allegedly violated the students' right to a safe working environment. Many of the episodes are about Gözen allegedly expressing frustration that the fellows were too poorly prepared and/or had unnecessarily many breaks. It appears from the report that Gözen must also have expressed frustration that the fellows blamed stress or illness. (page 18).

Lindqvist (2024h) reported in the university newspaper that the "dismissed research group leader lost in Oslo district court". One month later, Svarstad (2024f) reported that Irep Gözen appealed the verdict from the Oslo District Court to the Borgarting Court of Appeal.

References

Antonsen, T. and Løkling, T. (2020). Fremgangsmåten forsterker konflikter (The procedure strengthens conflicts), daily Norwegian business newspaper *Dagens Næringsliv*, www.dn.no, published July 28.

Brooks, P. (1996). The law as narrative and rhetoric, in Brooks, P. and Gewirtz, P. (editors), *Law's Stories*, Yale University Press, CT: New Haven.

Brooks, G., Button, M. and Frimpong, K. (2009). Policing fraud in the private sector: A survey of the FTSE 100 companies in the UK, *International Journal of Police Science & Management*, 11(4), 493–504.

Button, M. (2020). The "new" private security industry, the private policing of cyberspace and the regulatory questions, *Journal of Contemporary Criminal Justice*, 36(1), 39–55.

Button, M. and Gee, J. (2013). *Countering Fraud for Competitive Advantage – The Professional Approach to Reducing the Last Great Hidden Cost*, John Wiley & Sons, Chichester, UK.

Button, M. and Stiernstedt, P. (2017). The evolution of security industry regulation in the European Union, *International Journal of Comparative and Applied Criminal Justice*, 41(4), 245–257.

Button, M. and Stiernstedt, P. (2018). Comparing private security regulation in the European Union, *Policing and Society*, 28(4), 398–414.

Button, M., Frimpong, K., Smith, G. and Johnston, L. (2007a). Professionalizing counter fraud specialists in the UK: assessing progress and recommendations for reform, *Crime Prevention and Community Safety*, 9, 92–101.

Button, M., Johnston, L., Frimpong, K. and Smith, G. (2007b). New directions in policing fraud: The emergence of the counter fraud specialists in the United Kingdom, *International Journal of the Sociology of Law*, 35, 192–208.

Button, M., Nicholls, C.M., Kerr, J. and Owen, R. (2015). Online fraud victims in England and Wales: Victims views on sentencing and the opportunity for restorative justice, *The Howard Journal of Criminal Justice*, 54(2), 193–211.

Button, M., Kapend, R. and Stiernsted, P. (2023). Investigative private policing beyond the police: An exploratory study, *Policing and Society*, 33(2), 150–169.

Fox, N., Wise, J.D. and Brehm, H.N. (2022). Following heavenly orders: Heroic deviance and the denial of responsibility in narratives of rescue, *Deviant Behavior*, 43(11), 1385–1405.

Gottschalk, P. (2016). Private policing of financial crime: Key issues in the investigation business in Norway, *European Journal of Policing Studies*, 3(3), 292–314.

Gottschalk, P. (2017). Private police legitimacy: The case of internal investigations by fraud examiners, *Policing: An International Journal of Police Strategies and Management*, 40(3), 628–640.

Gottschalk, P. (2018). Blame game in private investigation reports: The case of Deloitte examination at Telenor VimpelCom, *Journal of Investigative Psychology and Offender Profiling*, 15(2), 99–108.

Gottschalk, P. (2019). Evaluation of fraud examinations: The case of inappropriate accounting practices at Fuji Xerox, *Deviant Behavior*, 40(11), 1421–1427.

Gottschalk, P. (2020). Private policing of white-collar crime: Case studies of internal investigations by fraud examiners, *Police Practice and Research*, 21(6), 717–738.

Gottschalk, P. (2021). *Private Policing of Economic Crime – Case Studies of Internal Investigations by Fraud Examiners*, Routledge, London, UK.

Gottschalk, P. (2023). *Fraud Examinations in White-Collar Crime Investigations*, Routledge, London, UK.

Gottschalk, P. (2024). Workplace deviance investigations: A case study of the application of maturity model to a university investigation, *Deviant Behavior*, 45(8), 1081–1094.

Gottschalk, P. and Hamerton, C. (2023). *Lawyer Roles in Knowledge Work – Defender, Enabler, Investigator*, Intersentia publishing, UK: Cambridge.

Gottschalk, P. and Asting, C. (2020). Entitled to embezzlement? The case of successful executives working for rich heirs, *Deviant Behavior*, 41(3), 269–277.

Gottschalk, P. and Tcherni-Buzzeo, M. (2016). Reasons for gaps in crime reporting: The case of white-collar criminals investigated by private fraud examiners in Norway, *Deviant Behavior*, 38(3), 267–281.

Hallgren, A. and Trædal, T.J. (2022). Ledende forsker ved rettsmedisin sa opp etter å ha varslet (Leading forensic scientist resigned after giving notice), daily Norwegian newspaper *Aftenposten*, www.aftenposten.no, published December 9.

Iannacci, F., Seepma, A.P., Blok, C., and Resca, A. (2019). Reappraising maturity models in e-government research: The trajectory-turning point theory, *Journal of Strategic Information Systems*, 28, 310–329.

Jebens, A. and Dorans, H. (2019). Utfordringer ved faktaundersøkelser (Challenges at facts investigations), lawyer association *Juristforbundet*, www.juristforbundet.no, published March 18.

Johnston, L., Button, M. and Williamson, T. (2008). Police, governance and the private finance initiative, *Policing & Society*, 18(3), 225–244.

King, M. (2020a). What makes a successful corporate investigator: An exploration of private investigators attributes, *Journal of Financial Crime*, 27(3), 701–714.

King, M. (2020b). Out of obscurity: The contemporary private investigator in Australia, *International Journal of Police Science & Management*, 22(3), 285–296.

King, M. (2020c). Private investigation into economic crime: Regulation of a multidisciplinary field, *Journal of Applied Security Research*, published first online https://doi.org/10.1080/19361610.2020.1832018.

King, M. (2020d). Financial fraud investigative interviewing – Corporate investigators' beliefs and practices: A qualitative inquiry, *Journal of Financial Crime*, published first online https://doi.org/10.1108/JFC-08-2020-0158.

King, M. (2021a). Profiting from a tainted trade: Private investigators' views on the popular culture glamorization of their trade, *Journal of Criminological Research Policy and Practice*, published first online https://doi.org/10.1108/JCRPP-07-2020-0050.

King, M. (2021b). *Pathways and Partnerships: A Study of Private Policing Economic Crime in Australia*, dissertation submitted in fulfilment of the requirements for the degree of Doctor of Philosophy, School of Justice, Faculty of Law, Queensland University of Technology, Australia.

Kislov, R., Bresnen, M. and Harvey, G. (2024). Getting your message across? The evolution of leader vision and managed pluralization of leadership, *Human Relations*, published first online https://doi.org/10.1177/00187267241301720, 1–29.

Lerø, M. (2021). Dropp faktaundersøkelser (Skip facts investigations), web-based media *Dagens Perspektiv*, www.dagensperspektiv.no, published May 31.

Lilli, M. and Sunde, L. (2023). Rapport vedrørende påstander om kritikkverdige forhold (Report regarding allegations of objectionable conditions), *CMS Kluge Advokatfirma*, Bryggegata 6, 0250 Oslo, Norway, 49 p.

Lindqvist, H. (2024a). UiO-forsker ble sagt opp etter faktaundersøkelse – nå blir det rettssak (A UiO researcher was dismissed after a factual investigation – Now there will be a trial), university newspaper *Uniforum*, www.uniforum.uio.no, published September 6.

Lindqvist, H. (2024b). UiO's Kluge-advokat ble politianmeldt etter faktaundersøkelse (UiO's Kluge lawyer was reported to the police after facts review), university newspaper *Uniforum*, www.uniforum.uio.no, published September 6.

Lindqvist, H. (2024c). Oppsagt UiO-forsker omtales som «ukorrigerbar» (Dismissed UiO researcher referred to as "incorrectable"), university newspaper *Uniforum*, www.uniforum.uio.no, published September 11.

Lindqvist, H. (2024d). Fjoråret ble «intenst» for Forskningsetisk utvalg på UiO (Last year was «intense» for the Research Ethics Committee at UiO), university newspaper *Uniforum*, www.uniforum.uio.no, published September 20.

Lindqvist, H. (2024e). Oppsigelsessaken: -Hun hørte ikke på Benjaminsen, hørte ikke på Sandlie (The dismissal case: -She did not listen to Benjaminsen, did not listen to Sandlie), university newspaper *Uniforum*, www.uniforum.uio.no, published September 24.

Lindqvist, H. (2024f). Leste høyt fra «avslørende» e-poster fra UiOs administrasjon (Read aloud from «revealing» e-mails from UiO's administration), university newspaper *Uniforum*, www.uniforum.uio.no, published September 25.

Lindqvist, H. (2024g). Advarte retten mot å høre på oppsagt kvinne og støttespillerne hennes (Warned court not to listen to fired woman and her supporters), university newspaper *Uniforum*, www.uniforum.uio.no, published September 26.

Lindqvist, H. (2024h). Oppsagt forskningsgruppeleder tapte i Oslo tingrett (Dismissed research group leader lost in Oslo district court), university newspaper *Uniforum*, www.uniforum.uio.no, published October 8.

Meerts, C. (2014). Empirical case studies of corporate security in international perspective, in Walby, K. and Lippert, R.K. (editors), *Corporate Security in the 21st Century – Theory and Practice in International Perspective*, Palgrave Macmillan, UK: Hampshire, Houndmills, pp. 97–115.

Meerts, C.A. (2018). The organization as the cure for its own ailments: Corporate investigators in the Netherlands, *Administrative Sciences*, 8(25), 1–15.

Meerts, C.A. (2019). *Corporate Investigations, Corporate Justice and Public-Private Relations: Towards a New Conceptualisation*, Springer Nature, Palgrave Macmillan, Switzerland.

Meerts, C.A. (2020). Corporate investigations: Beyond notions of public-private relations, *Journal of Contemporary Criminal Justice*, 36(1), 86–100.

Meerts, C.A. (2021). Struggles in cooperation: Public-private relations in the investigation of internal financial crime in the Netherlands, in Lord, N., Inzelt, E., Huisman, W. and Faria, R. (editors), *European White-Collar Crime: Exploring the Nature of European Realities*, Bristol University Press, UK: Bristol.

Meerts, C.A. (2023). The private policing of economic crime – Corporate investigations and settlement, *Journal of Economic Criminology*, published first online https://doi.org/10.1016/j.jeconc.2023.100016.

Nordrik, B. and Kuldova, T.Ø. (2021). Faktaundersøkelser – Et «hybrid konfliktvåpen» på norske arbeidsplasser (Facts investigations – A «hybrid conflict weapon» at Norwegian workplaces), Gyldendal publishing, Oslo, Norway.

Olsen, S. (2024). Professor på BI gir CMS Kluge-undrsøkelse det glatte lag: -Blander fakta og meninger (Professor at BI gives the CMS Kluge review the smooth finish: - Mixes facts and opinions), lawyer news *AdvokatWatch*, www.advokatwatch.no, published September 6.

Oslo tingrett (2024). Dom avsagt 7.10.2024 (Verdict released October 7, 2024), *Oslo tingrett (Oslo district court)*, Oslo, Norway, 30 p.

Röglinger, M., Pöppelbuss, J. and Becker, J. (2012). Maturity model in business process management, *Business Process Management Journal*, 18(2), 328–346.

Schneider, S. (2006). Privatizing economic crime enforcement: Exploring the role of private sector investigative agencies in combating money laundering, *Policing & Society*, 16(3), 285–312.

Slettemark, G. and Kvamme, H. (2022). Arbeidsmiljøsaker bør tas ut av varslingsordningen (Working environment matters should be removed from the notification system), daily Norwegian business newspaper *Dagens Næringsliv*, www.dn.no, published June 7.

Solli-Sæther, H. and Gottschalk, P. (2015). Stages-of-growth in outsourcing, offshoring and backsourcing: Back to the future? *Journal of Computer Information Systems*, 55(2), 88–94.

Strand, H.K. and Lie, T. (2023). "Man må se på det å få ledere utenfra som et større mangfold og økt kompetanse" ("You have to see getting managers from outside as greater diversity and increased competence"), web-based university newspaper *Khrono*, www.khrono.no, published May 13.

Svarstad, J. (2024a). Forskningsleder anklages for maktmisbruk og trakassering av stipendiater (Research manager accused of abuse of power and harassment of fellows), university newspaper *Khrono*, www.khrono.no, published September 10.

Svarstad, J. (2024b). UiO-ansatt til sak etter "en usedvanlig og unødvendig brutal oppsigelsesprosess" (UiO employee initiates trial after «an exceptionally and unnecessarily brutal dismissal process»), university newspaper *Khrono*, www.khrono.no, published September 15.

Svarstad, J. (2024c). – Det virker som man har lett etter ting som kan brukes mot henne (It seems that they have been looking for things that can be used against her), university newspaper *Khrono*, www.khrono.no, published September 23.

Svarstad, J. (2024d). – UiO presser meg til å innrømme ting jeg aldri har gjort (-UiO is pressuring me to admit things I have never done), university newspaper *Khrono*, www.khrono.no, published September 24.

Svarstad, J. (2024e). Regjeringsadvokaten: -Hun mangler evne til å håndtere menneskelig samhandling (The government attorney: -She lacks ability to handle human interaction), university newspaper *Khrono*, www.khrono.no, published September 25.

Svarstad, J. (2024f). Oppsagt UiO-forsker anker til lagmannsretten (Dismissed UiO researcher appeals to the court of appeals), university newspaper *Khrono*, www.khrono.no, published November 11.

Toft, M. (2024). – Eg rådde henne til å lata vera å senda lange epostar (-I advised her not to send long e-mails), university newspaper *Uniforum*, www.uniforum.uio.no, published September 26.

Topdahl, R.C. and Akhtar, S.A.S. (2018). Rapporten som endret alt (The report that changed everything), Norwegian public broadcasting *NRK*, www.nrk.no, published December 1.

Torbor, M., Sarpong, D., Ofosu, G. and Boakye, D. (2024). In defense of the indefensible: Exploring justification narratives of corporate elites accused of corruption, *Journal of Business Ethics*, published first online https://doi.org/10.1007/s10551-024-05703-1.

Trædal, T. (2021). Forskere mener faktaundersøkelser er farlige (Researchers claim facts investigations are dangerous), web-based news media Khrono, www.khrono,no, published April 28.

Williams, J.W. (2005a). Reflections on the private versus public policing of economic crime, *British Journal of Criminology*, 45, 316–339.

Williams, J.W. (2005b). Governability matters: The private policing of economic crime and the challenge of democratic governance, *Policing & Society*, 15(2), 187–211.

Wood, J.D. (2020). Private policing and public health: A neglected relationship, *Journal of Contemporary Criminal Justice*, 36(1), 19–38.

Chapter 6

The Fraud Investigation Business

Corporate investigators conducting fraud examinations within client organizations review the extent of compliance and conformity within those organizations. When Taylor (2021) reviewed corruption allegations at the International Biathlon Union (IBU) in Austria, the review considered both compliance and conformity. Corruption is criminalized for both the briber and the bribed, and it is thus a relevant issue for compliance. However, the circumstances might prevent a valid conviction in court, which makes acquittal a possible final outcome in the case of former IBU president Anders Besseberg, as presented and discussed in Chapter 3.

Therefore, regardless of whether the legal license was violated, people considered the social license to be violated by Besseberg and others at the IBU (Dahlkamp and Latsch, 2024a, 2024b). Therefore, to achieve conformity at the IBU, integrity units with ethical guidelines were established to prevent deviance that represents violations of norms and values and to secure IBU legitimacy (Gottschalk, 2025b). Taylor (2021: 1) argued that integrity was a critical issue: "Enabled by a complete lack of basic governance safeguards that left integrity decisions in the sole hands of the President and his allies on the IBU Executive Board, with no checks and balances, no transparency, and no accountability whatsoever to keep them honest, Mr. Besseberg's proclaimed commitment to clean sport was, in the Commission's view, a charade". "Charade" refers to an absurd pretense intended to create a pleasant or respectable appearance, while "integrity" refers to the quality of acting in accordance with moral values, norms, and rules considered valid and relevant within the context in which the actor operates (Loyens *et al.*, 2022). So far in 2025, without any legally binding conviction, the termination of Anders Besseberg as president of the IBU in 2018 resulted from a conformity violation rather than a compliance violation.

Similarly, after corporate investigations at Danske Bank by Bruun Hjejle (2018) and Swedbank by DiBari (2020) regarding lack of antimoney laundering measures, chief executives Birgitte Bonnesen and Thomas Borgen were terminated from their positions and from the banks, despite never being convicted in court. Both banks were fined several years later for violating their legal licenses due to lack of compliance. Previously then, both executives were terminated for violation of the social license due to lack of conformity (Gottschalk, 2025a).

In addition to the Taylor (2021) investigation, this book has also presented the Pilgaard (2020) investigation and the Lilli and Sunde (2023) investigation. As discussed in this book, all three corporate investigations were highly problematic. Therefore, this chapter shifts its focus from those being investigated to those investigating.

6.1 Deviance by Corporate Investigators

This chapter turns from focusing on investigated individuals and organizations over to focusing on the investigating individuals and organizations that conduct corporate investigations. The question is to what extent the fraud investigation business also violates both the legal license and the social license to operate by a lack of compliance and a lack of conformity, respectively. Research into corporate investigations is growing, particularly in Australia (King, 2021), Canada (Schneider, 2006), the Netherlands (Meerts, 2023), Norway (Gottschalk, 2020), and the United Kingdom (UK; Button, 2020; Button *et al.*, 2023). The research emphasizes a number of challenges in managing corporate investigations. For example, King (2021) discussed the need to professionalize investigators, including their skills in investigative interviewing, in Australia. Meerts (2021) discussed the struggles in cooperation in public–private relations in the investigation of internal financial crime in the Netherlands. Gottschalk (2024) emphasized the challenges of identifying and applying relevant knowledge in investigative work and answering questions without escalating problematic situations in client organizations in Norway.

Button (2020) discussed the need for regulation of the private sector of corporate investigations in the UK.

Researchers in Australia (King, 2020), the Netherlands (Meerts, 2020), and the UK (Button, 2020; Button and Stiernstedt, 2017, 2018) have emphasized the failings of self-regulation in the corporate investigation industry. Research in Norway indicated a lack of independence, as investigators tended to deliver commissioned work whose outcomes aligned with client expectations and desires (Gottschalk, 2024). At the same time, research from these countries, as well as Canada and the United States (Lau and Flasher, 2025), indicated that law enforcement in public criminal justice systems struggles with their own legitimacy problems.

From the management perspective of examinations, corporate investigation managers need to professionalize their businesses to address both compliance and conformity issues within their industry. Compliance refers to acting in accordance with laws, rules, and regulations for the legal license to operate (Gottschalk, 2025a; Lehman *et al.*, 2020; Teichmann and Wittmann, 2024; Thottoli, 2021). "Conformity" or "conformance" refers to meeting and potentially exceeding societal and other informal norms and obligations for the social license to operate (Durand *et al.*, 2019; Gottschalk, 2025a; Hollebeek *et al.*, 2022; Lewis and Carlos, 2022). The legal license then refers to compliance with laws, regulations, and rules that apply within a jurisdiction, while the social license refers to conformity with norms, values, and guidelines that apply within a society. Conformity by corporate investigators includes being accountable with integrity. Accountability refers to liability, answerability, and blameworthiness (Lewis and Carlos, 2022). As stated above, integrity is the quality of acting in accordance with rules that are considered valid and relevant (Loyens *et al.*, 2022). Conformity can lead to legitimacy, which refers to the acceptance of behavior by corporate investigators. Business activities in the corporate investigation industry are then considered legitimate in the eyes of society (Saenz, 2019).

In the UK, a number of research studies on corporate investigations were conducted by Brooks *et al.* (2009), Button (2020), Button and Stiernstedt (2017, 2018), Button *et al.* (2007a, 2007b, 2023), and Kapend *et al.* (2024). The main focus was on investigators' self-perceptions regarding their own deviance in the course of conducting corporate reviews and examinations. When Kapend *et al.* (2024: 1) asked corporate investigators about the extent of illegal information gathering, miscarriages of justice, and other illegal and unethical activities, they claimed that there is "a very small minority of largely private investigators who engage in such activities".

However, many corporate investigators are suspected of illegal information gathering (Kapend *et al.*, 2024). In 2023, corporate investigators in the UK were accused of illegally bugging phones, intercepting communications, and "blagging" – impersonating someone else to gain access to restricted areas or systems and obtain information. Private investigators make "widespread use of illegal information-gathering tactics including phone hacking, landline interception and the blagging of personal information", exemplified by private investigator Gavin Borrows, who said that "he and his team obtained information, hacked voicemails, tapped landline phones and bugged cars" (Waterson, 2023).

Many corporate investigators are suspected of causing miscarriages of justice (Kapend *et al.*, 2024: 2): "The largest miscarriage of justice to date in the UK, involving the wrongful prosecution of over 500 postmasters, was the result of both a private investigation and prosecution". One of the corporate investigators in the Horizon scandal, Stephen Bradshaw, was accused of acting like a mafia gangster when securing false convictions against post office masters (Boffey, 2024): "In several instances, the accused were told they could avoid a jail sentence if they kept quiet about the accounting system's fault". For example, "Jacqueline McDonald, who was sentenced in 2011 to 18 months' imprisonment and handed a confiscation order for the sum of £99,759.60, accused Post Office investigators, including Bradshaw, of behaving like mafia gangsters in a witness statement" (Boffey, 2024).

Nevertheless, when Kapend *et al.* (2024: 1) asked corporate investigators – as quoted above – about the extent of illegal information gathering, miscarriages of justice, and other illegal and unethical activities, they claimed that there is "a very small minority of largely private investigators who engage in such activities". The study was based on an online survey of private investigators, where the researchers received 331 responses. When questioned about unlawful surveillance, 3 investigators admitted to doing it frequently, 22 occasionally, 33 rarely, and 266 never. When asked about the use of forged credentials, 3 admitted to doing it frequently, 8 occasionally, 15 rarely, and 298 never. When asked about planting evidence, none admitted to doing it frequently, 2 occasionally, 6 rarely, and 316 never. While it might seem surprising that someone admits to criminal behavior as a corporate investigator, the numbers are probably higher than these self-reported figures for frequently, occasionally, and rarely.

The survey instrument used by Kapend *et al.* (2024) to study deviant behavior among corporate investigators was also used by Button *et al.* (2023) to study the outcomes of investigative work. In their responses, 331 corporate investigators reported on their backgrounds, roles, tools, and outcomes. There was a dominance of older, well-educated men in their second careers. The research distinguished between four groups of corporate investigators: private investigators hired on a fee basis (38%), in-house public investigators (30%), private in-house investigators (20%), forensic accountants (9%), and others (3%). Among the investigations conducted in the past three years, 324 out of 331 respondents said they had conducted fraud investigations within that same period, and 297 respondents said they had carried out corruption/bribery investigations, followed by cybercrime investigations, staff theft investigations, money laundering investigations, intellectual property investigations, corporate espionage investigations, and criminal defense investigations.

It comes as no surprise that self-perceptions within an industry differ from external perceptions of actors within the same industry. When King (2023: 112) interviewed 33 corporate investigators in Australia, the interviewees claimed knowledge of investigative interviewing but had difficulty explaining what cognitive interviewing implied:

> All participants acknowledged that interviewing was a critical component of their role and were broadly aware of cognitive interviewing as a technique, however, 20 (60%) had difficulty explaining what it involved. Only 12 (36%) had attended additional investigative interviewing courses after obtaining a license. These courses ran for 3–5 days in a classroom environment and were based on the PEACE model.

Many scholars have argued that education is the relevant path to reduce deviance among corporate investigators (e.g., Button *et al.*, 2007a; King, 2023). Theoretical education in corporate investigation focuses on individual learning of important perspectives and aspects when managing fraud examinations in organizational reviews. Empirical education, on the other hand, is focused on group learning activities where the organization facilitates the learning of its members. Empirical education occurs when working in a learning organization focused on lifelong learning among its members (Filstad and Gottschalk, 2013).

6.2 Investigation Compliance Characteristics

Compliance refers to acting in accordance with laws, rules, and regulations for the legal license to operate (Gottschalk, 2025a; Lehman *et al.*, 2020; Teichmann and Wittmann, 2024; Thottoli, 2021). The legal license then refers to compliance with laws, regulations, and rules applicable within the jurisdiction. There are regular criminal laws that all citizens have to follow. For example, corruption is illegal on both the briber's and the bribed's side in many jurisdictions. For a corporate investigation firm to offer a bribe to someone within a client organization to secure an assignment from the client constitutes a criminal offense in the role of briber. For a corporate investigator to accept a bribe from someone within a client organization to influence the outcome of an assignment constitutes a criminal offense in the role of bribed. Corruption is defined as the giving, requesting, receiving, or accepting of an improper advantage related to a position, office, or assignment. In many jurisdictions, the improper advantage does not have to be connected to a specific action or inaction (Artello and Albanese, 2022). Bribery descriptions include "grease in the wheels of commerce" that causes offenders to allocate their resources to the most profitable activities (Cuervo-Cazurra, 2015: 40):

> Corruption is usually seen as sand when it is the government official who demands the bribe, but it is usually seen as grease when it is the manager who offers to pay a bribe to get something that helps the company.

Corporate investigators can violate a number of other legal obligations as well. When they belong to certain professions, they have to follow legal rules related to those professions. For example, attorneys acting as investigators have to adhere to the attorney-client privilege, although an attorney in that role is more like a detective consultant rather than a legal advisor. One of the privileges is secrecy regarding money on client accounts managed by the law firm, preventing transparency and potentially stimulating embezzlement by law firm lawyers, which is sometimes detected (e.g., Gottschalk and Asting, 2020).

Forensic accountants and auditors, as corporate investigators, might demonstrate criminal deviance. They are supposed to be responsible for oversight and guardianship. A lack of oversight and guardianship can become very serious when auditors slide over to the wrong side of the law.

Mohliver (2019: 310) found that some auditors prioritize their clients' interests over their legal obligations by recommending client malfeasance, for example, in terms of illegal stock option backdating:

> The findings suggest that professional experts' involvement in the diffusion of liminal practices is highly responsive to the institutional environment.

Similarly, Chan and Gibbs (2022) found that guardians can become offenders when there is a convergence of motivated offenders, suitable targets, and absent guardianship. The convergence triggers two crime-conducive outcomes. First, it provides motivated offenders access to the target of interest. Second, it reduces offenders' perceived likelihood of being detected.

Another compliance issue is the illegal gathering of information, as reported by Waterson (2023) and discussed by Kapend *et al.* (2024) in the UK. When prosecuted in court, private detective Gavin Burrows denied unlawful information gathering (Allen, 2023). Post office investigator Stephen Bradshaw was grilled over the Horizon scandal in a public inquiry and hearing, where he denied claims of mafia behavior (Seddon and Wright, 2024).

6.3 Investigation Conformity Characteristics

Conformity or conformance refers to meeting and potentially exceeding societal and other informal norms and obligations for the social license to operate (Durand *et al.*, 2019; Gottschalk, 2025a; Hollebeek *et al.*, 2022; Lewis and Carlos, 2022). The social license refers to conformity with norms, values, and guidelines that apply within a society. Conformity by corporate investigators includes being accountable with integrity. Accountability refers to liability, answerability, and blameworthiness (Lewis and Carlos, 2022; Saifer and Zanoni, 2024). Integrity is the quality of acting in accordance with rules that are considered valid and relevant within the context in which the actor operates (Loyens *et al.*, 2022). Conformity can lead to legitimacy, which refers to the acceptance of behavior by corporate investigators. Business activities in the corporate investigation industry are then considered legitimate in the eyes of society (Saenz, 2019).

Some corporate investigators hide their work behind the client-attorney privilege. They prevent transparency by claiming secrecy based on that privilege. Yet, corporate examination work has little or nothing to do with legal work. It is detective work to reconstruct past events and sequence of events. It is knowledge work to assess collected information. Corporate investigators should never assess information in terms of evidence to draw conclusions about criminal liability. They should always stop their assessment before drawing any conclusions regarding criminal codes. Therefore, two conformity issues arise related to the client-attorney privilege. The first is the norm violation of hiding work behind privilege, preventing transparency in society, and the other is crossing the line between their role and the criminal justice system within the jurisdiction.

Of course, some investigations and their resulting investigation reports need to be prevented from disclosure for various reasons. However, the attorney-client privilege is not such an acceptable reason for secrecy. Sensitive personal information about individuals, sensitive business secrets within the client organization, and the requirements of the criminal justice system to protect police and prosecution work are some acceptable reasons for secrecy and disclosure prevention.

For non-conforming corporate investigators, it might be beneficial to hide behind the privilege. Therefore, while accountants and auditors at accounting and auditing firms such as BDO, Deloitte, EY, KPMG, and PwC often conduct the actual investigations, the formal responsibility for each investigation is assigned to a lawyer who is a partner in the firm's legal department, thereby enabling secrecy and a lack of transparency about their work. This is exemplified for PwC by the Pilgaard (2020) investigation in Chapter 5.

In corporate investigations, where someone is accused of wrongdoing within a client organization, there is often a dilemma in protecting both the accuser and the accused. A few years ago, it seemed that the accused was primarily protected, particularly through client management, which influenced the mandate for the investigation. Recently, it seems that the pendulum has swung over to the other side, mainly protecting the accuser. The dilemma occurs, for example, when the accused exercises the right of contradiction. At the stage of contradiction – that is, where the accused responds to accusations in the adversarial proceedings – there is a dispute between the corporate investigator and the accused. Lilli and Sunde (2023) at law firm CMS Kluge served as corporate investigators and believed the accusers and not the accused, as discussed in Chapter 5. The examiners mistakenly returned to the accusers to obtain their comments regarding the contradictory statements offered by the accused. The accused was never invited to a final round of comments. This constitutes a violation of fair and due process in private internal investigations.

Sometimes, corporate investigators can cause miscarriages of justice. Criminal justice refers to the delivery of justice to those accused of committing crime. Doubt should always benefit the accused, and guilt has to be proven beyond any reasonable and sensible doubt to enable conviction by a court of justice. There can be a miscarriage of justice at either end: a guilty person found innocent and an innocent person found guilty. The former outcome of corporate investigations typically emerges when the guilty individual is "too big to fail and too powerful to jail" (Pontell *et al.*, 2014: 1). Then, the corporate investigator applies the attribution mechanism by placing the blame elsewhere. The blame game addresses misleading attributions to others. By successfully engaging in the blame game, people will attribute blame for wrongdoing to another person (Sonnier *et al.*, 2015).

At the other end of the spectrum, individuals considered blameworthy are found guilty of wrongdoing by corporate investigators, especially if such an outcome is desired and expected by the client who pays for the work. Corporate investigators can assist in getting rid of troublesome employees and colleagues by presenting an investigation report in which the selected individual or individuals receive random blame for deviance by someone else.

References

Allen, V. (2023). Private investigator denies 'unlawful information gathering' for Associated Newspapers as High Court releases his full witness statement, *The Daily Mail*, www.dailymail.co.uk, published March 28.

Artello, K. and Albanese, J.S. (2022). Culture of corruption: Prosecutions, persistence, and desistence, *Public Integrity*, 24, 142–161.

Boffey, D. (2024). Post office used threat of jail to persuade accused to keep quiet about Horizon failings, *The Guardian*, www.theguardian.com, published January 11.

Brooks, G., Button, M. and Frimpong, K. (2009). Policing fraud in the private sector: A survey of the FTSE 100 companies in the UK, *International Journal of Police Science & Management*, 11(4), 493–504.

Bruun Hjejle (2018). *Report on the Non-Resident Portfolio at Danske Bank's Estonian branch*, report of investigation, law firm Bruun Hjejle, Copenhagen, Denmark, p. 87.

Button, M. (2020). The "new" private security industry, the private policing of cyberspace and the regulatory questions, *Journal of Contemporary Criminal Justice*, 36(1), 39–55.

Button, M. and Stiernstedt, P. (2017). The evolution of security industry regulation in the European Union, *International Journal of Comparative and Applied Criminal Justice*, 41(4), 245–257.

Button, M. and Stiernstedt, P. (2018). Comparing private security regulation in the European Union, *Policing and Society*, 28(4), 398–414.

Button, M., Frimpong, K., Smith, G. and Johnston, L. (2007a). Professionalizing counter fraud specialists in the UK: Assessing progress and recommendations for reform, *Crime Prevention and Community Safety*, 9, 92–101.

Button, M., Johnston, L., Frimpong, K. and Smith, G. (2007b). New directions in policing fraud: The emergence of the counter fraud specialists in the United Kingdom, *International Journal of the Sociology of Law*, 35, 192–208.

Button, M., Kapend, R. and Stiernsted, P. (2023). Investigative private policing beyond the police: An exploratory study, *Policing and Society*, 33(2), 150–169.

Chan, F. and Gibbs, C. (2022). When guardians become offenders: Understanding guardian capability through the lens of corporate crime, *Criminology*, 60, 321–341.

Cuervo-Cazurra, A. (2015). Corruption in international business, *Journal of World Business*, 51, 35–49.

Dahlkamp, J. and Latsch, G. (2024a). Prozess gegen ehemaligen Biathlon-Weltverbandchef: Uhren, Prostituierte, Trophäenjagden (Process against former biathlon union chief: Watches, prostitutes, trophy hunts), German magazine *Der Spiegel*, www.spiegel.de, published January 12.

Dahlkamp, J. and Latsch, G. (2024b). Blattschuss beim Pinkeln (Leaf shot while peeing), German magazine *Der Spiegel*, number 8, February 17, pp. 84–85.

DiBari, D.D. (2020). *Report of Investigation on Swedbank*, Clifford Chance, Washington, D.C., USA, www.cliffordchance.com, David.dibari@clifford-chance.com, p. 218, March 23.

Filstad, C. and Gottschalk, P. (2013). The police force: To be or not to be a learning organization? In: Örtenblad, A. (editor), *Handbook of Research on the Learning Organization*, pages 179–195, Edward Elgar Publishing, Cheltenham, UK.

Gottschalk, P. (2020). Filling the gap in white-collar crime detection between government and governance: The role of investigative journalists and fraud examiners, *Journal of White Collar and Corporate Crime*, 2(1), 36–46.

Gottschalk, P. (2024). Workplace deviance investigations: A case study of the application of maturity model to a university investigation, *Deviant Behavior*, 45(8), 1081–1094.

Gottschalk, P. (2025a). *Crisis Management – Recovering the Social License by Corporate Conformance*, Oxford University Press, Oxford, UK.

Gottschalk, P. (2025b). *Corruption, Criminal Justice, and Compliance in Sport – The Case of the International Biathlon Union*, Routledge, Abingdon, UK.

Gottschalk, P. and Asting, C. (2020). Entitled to embezzlement? The case of successful executives working for rich heirs, *Deviant Behavior*, 41(3), 269–277.

Hollebeek, L.D., Sprott, D.E., Sigurdsson, V. and Clark, M.K. (2022). Social influence and stakeholder engagement behavior conformity, compliance, and reactance, *Psychology & Marketing*, 39, 90–100.

Kapend, R., Button, M. and Stiernstedt, P. (2024). Private investigations and ethical orientations: A cause for concern? *Journal of Financial Crime*, published first online https://doi.org/10.108/JFC-02-2024-0066.

King, M. (2020). Private investigation into economic crime: Regulation of a multidisciplinary field, *Journal of Applied Security Research*, 16(4), 470–489.

King, M. (2021). Financial fraud investigative interviewing – Corporate investigators' beliefs and practices: A qualitative inquiry, *Journal of Financial Crime*, 28(2), 345–358.

King, M. (2023). A study of interviewing practices by Australian corporate and financial investigators, *Investigative Interviewing: Research and Practice*, 13(1), 111–114.

Lau, M.C. and Flasher, R. (2025). To charge or not to charge: Prosecutorial characteristics and responses to auditor reported findings, *Journal of Forensic Accounting Research*, American Accounting Association, published first online https://doi.org/10.2308/JFAR-2022-022.

Lehman, D.W., Cooil, B. and Ramanujam, R. (2020). The effects of rule complexity on organizational noncompliance and remediation: Evidence from restaurant health inspections, *Journal of Management*, 46(8), 1436–1468.

Lewis, B.W. and Carlos, W.C. (2022). Avoiding the appearance of virtue: Reactivity to corporate social responsibility ratings in an era of shareholder primacy, *Administrative Science Quarterly*, 67(4), 1093–1135.

Lilli, M. and Sunde, L. (2023). Rapport vedrørende påstander om kritikkverdige forhold (Report regarding allegations of objectionable conditions), *CMS Kluge Advokatfirma*, Bryggegata 6, 0250 Oslo, Norway, p. 49.

Loyens, K., Claringbould, I., Heres, L. and Eekeren, F. (2022). The social construction of integrity: A qualitative case study of Dutch football, *Sports in Society*, 25(9), 1714–1733.

Meerts, C. (2020). Corporate investigations: Beyond notions of public-private relations, *Journal of Contemporary Criminal Justice*, 36(1), 86–100.

Meerts, C. (2021). Struggles in cooperation: Public-private relations in the investigation of internal financial crime in the Netherlands, in: Lord, N., Inzelt, E., Huisman, W. and Faria, R. (editors), *European White-Collar Crime: Exploring the Nature of European Realities*, Bristol University Press, Bristol, UK.

Meerts, C. (2023). The private policing of economic crime – Corporate investigations and settlement, *Journal of Economic Criminology*, published first online at https://doi.org/10.1016/j.jeconc.2023.100016.

Mohliver, A. (2019). How misconduct spreads: Auditors' role in the diffusion of stock-option backdating, *Administrative Science Quarterly*, 64(2), 310–336.

Pilgaard, M.S. (2020). *Rema 1000 Torggata: Oppfølging av varsel (Rema 1000 Torg Street: Follow-up of notice)*, PricewaterhouseCoopers, Oslo, Norway, September 25, p. 76.

Pontell, H.N., Black, W.K. and Geis, G. (2014). Too big to fail, too powerful to jail? On the absence of criminal prosecutions after the 2008 financial meltdown, *Crime, Law and Social Change*, 61(1), 1–13.

Saenz, C. (2019). Building legitimacy and trust between a mining company and a community to earn social license to operate: A Peruvian case study, *Corporate Social Responsibility and Environmental Management*, 26(2), 296–306.

Saifer, A. and Zanoni, P. (2024). The political economy of accountability: Philanthropy's 'double dispossession' of racial justice organizations under racial capitalism, *Human Relations*, published first online https://doi.org/10.1177/00187267241303268.

Schneider, S. (2006). Privatizing economic crime enforcement: Exploring the role of private sector investigative agencies in combating money laundering, *Policing & Society*, 16(3), 285–312.

Seddon, S. and Wright, G. (2024). Post office scandal: Investigator denies claims of 'mafia' behavior, *BBC*, www.bbc.com, published January 11.

Sonnier, B.M., Lassar, W.M. and Lassar, S.S. (2015). The influence of source credibility and attribution of blame on juror evaluation of liability of industry specialist auditors, *Journal of Forensic & Investigative Accounting*, 7(1), 1–37.

Taylor, J. (2021). *Final Report of the IBU External Review Commission*, International Biathlon Union, Austria, www.biathlonintegrity.com, jonathan.taylor@twobirds.com, p. 220, January 28.

Teichmann, F.M.J. and Wittmann, C. (2024). Psychology and white-collar crime: Compliance recommendations based on the social and psychological reality dictating perceptions, *Journal of Financial Crime*, 31(2), 408–415.

Thottoli, M.M. (2021). The relevance of compliance audit on companies' compliance with disclosure guidelines of financial statements, *Journal of Investment Compliance*, 22(2), 137–150.

Waterson, J. (2023). Witness in Prince Harry's case against Daily Mail owner unreliable, says lawyers, *The Guardian*, www.theguardian.com, published March 29.

Chapter 7

Case: Sanctions against Russia

Russia attacked and invaded Ukraine in the winter of 2022. Countries such as the United States (US), the United Kingdom (UK), and Canada, as well as multinational organizations such as the European Union, quickly introduced sanctions against Russia, which should represent a penalty for disobeying international law. Western companies that were affected by the sanction regime had to modify or terminate their business activities in and with Russia. This was a matter of compliance.

However, many voiced criticisms of companies that continued their business activities without violating their legal licenses to operate. For example, the Yale School of Management in the US updated on a daily basis a list of companies that had terminated their business in Russia as well as those that remained. The two lists were for a while updated every hour by Professor Jeffrey Sonnenfeld and his research team at the Yale Chief Executive Leadership Institute to reflect new announcements from companies in real time. Some companies on the wrong list quickly informed Yale about their termination of business activities in Russia. This was a matter of conformity.

In May 2023, it was disclosed, exposed, and condemned that Mondelez in the US had continued business operations in Russia. Mondelez International (formerly Kraft Foods) was an American multinational confectionery, food, snacks, and beverage producing company based in Chicago. In Scandinavia, Mondelez owned the major chocolate producers Freia in Norway and Marabou in Sweden. This chapter reviews reactions to the disclosure of Freia's ownership and Mondelez's activities in Russia from the perspective of corporate conformity issues in practice for maintaining the social license to operate.

Generally, sanctions refer to "restrictive policy measures that one or more countries take to limit their relations with a target country in order to persuade that country to change its policies or to address potential violations of international norms and conventions" (Morgan *et al.*, 2023: 3). Gottschalk (2024, 2025) found that economic sanctions tend to cause white-collar and corporate crime. Atiles (2025) studied US unilateral economic and financial sanctions and argued that such sanctions constitute state crime since coercive measures contravene international law and harm the populations of targeted countries.

7.1 Boycotted versus Blacklisted Companies

Mondelez was not on any sanctions lists. Therefore, the company possessed a legal license to operate in Russia. The company was compliant. However, the company was not quite conformant, as the global company seemed to have violated its social license to operate by continuing the business in Russia.

It was Monday, June 12, 2023, when several companies in Norway and elsewhere stopped selling products from chocolate producer Freia. Boycotting companies included airlines such as Scandinavian Airlines System (SAS) and Norwegian hotel chains such as Choice and Classic Hotels, and several others. Many more were considering joining the boycott, sparked by news the previous week that Norwegian chocolate producer Freia was owned by Mondelez, which still had operations in Russia during the war in Ukraine.

The Norwegian newspaper *Aftenposten* addressed the following question: "Should we have Quick Lunch shame now?" It referred to the very popular chocolate brand "Kvikk Lunsj", produced at Freia (Wikan, 2023: 14):

> Suddenly, Freia products were out of favor with large companies such as SAS and Norwegian, the hotel chains Strawberry and Classic Norway Hotels, Elkjøp and Hurtigruten. It was extra painful for the Norwegian chocolate producer when the Norwegian tourist association (DNT) broke ties with Kvikk Lunsj. Freia's chocolate is just one of many

everyday products linked to Ukraine's 'blacklist'. What is going on? And what should Norwegian consumers and companies do?

Wikan (2023) presented five questions and answers regarding the Freia boycott.

(1) Why was Freia boycotted? Freia was a Norwegian company. The chocolate was made at Rodeløkka in Oslo. But Freia's owner, the large American snack company Mondelez International, was on Ukraine's blacklist. The reason was that Mondelez had factories and employees in Russia. They sold their products in Russia and paid taxes to the authorities there. Mondelez had several brands. For example, the company's logo appeared on the Oreo biscuit package. They also made, among other food items, O*Boy and Philadelphia. However, it was important to know one thing: Ukraine's blacklist was not the same as the sanctions regime against Russia. The latter was a regulation Norwegian companies were required to follow.

(2) Which other products were linked to blacklisted companies? Mondelez was not the only company on the blacklist. Several of the others were behind well-known brands that many Norwegians used every day. Procter & Gamble was behind Pampers, Always, Oral-B, Braun, and Gillette. Bonduelle was behind stock canned corn, chick-peas, and green vegetables. Yves Rocher sold cosmetics and perfume in Norway. Xiaomi Corporation was a Chinese electronics manufacturer that made, among other things, mobile phones sold by the electronics chain Elkjøp. And there were many more. If one were to boycott everything, many store shelves would probably become empty. And that could have major consequences. The preference was to have sanctions that harmed Russia but not Norway and Norwegian consumers.

(3) What were other Norwegian companies doing? "It is not very surprising that there are more companies on Ukraine's blacklist, says director of communications at Coop, Bjørn Takle Friis" (Wikan, 2023: 14). The grocery chain Coop was one of several companies currently on the fence. The chain asked the Norwegian authorities for a clarification in principle. This was particularly important, Friis believed, because Freia products were not the only ones linked to the blacklist (Wikan, 2023: 14):

We need that help, and I think consumers need that too, says Friis. – As consumer, should you be ashamed of buying Kvikk Lunsj? Or is there no reason for it? I believe many people wonder about it.

(4) Do you have to have Kvikk Lunsj shame? "No, by no means, said philosopher and BI professor Øyvind Kvalnes. He was an expert in ethics and business. Shame seems to be of little relevance, he added. However, Kvalnes pointed out that many people are concerned about the links between the products they buy in stores and Russia's war in Ukraine. But he believed that companies and organizations have a greater responsibility than consumers. And they should already have been prepared for this situation. The philosopher explained by distinguishing between passive and active ethics. Active ethics involves seeking information when in doubt and deciding on a situation before it arises. Passive ethics involves reluctance to act until you have to when someone else has put the spotlight on the situation (Wikan, 2023: 14):

> I think we are now seeing an example of passive ethics. The companies take a position on things that others draw attention to, instead of actively checking whether any of the suppliers are blacklisted, and then deciding what to do, say Kvalnes. – In such a serious situation as a war, you have a responsibility to take an active position on it. It is an expectation that I think is reasonable for Norwegian companies and actors. So is it right for the companies to boycott Freia? The company follows the Norwegian sanctions. Employees can risk losing their jobs in the worst case scenario. Kvalnes nevertheless answers yes. The reason is the seriousness of the war in Ukraine. He believes the boycott in Norway can help put pressure on Mondelez. – I think this is something that is being noticed, and which can force a revision by the owners as well. I think it is an important move, he says. Not everyone agrees.

(5) Was it immoral not to eat Kvikk Lunsj? Because what about the canned corn from Bonduelle and Pampers diapers from the giant Procter & Gamble? Was it unethical to continue eating Oreo cookies while dropping Kvikk Lunsj? The boycott in Norway might, after all, have major consequences for Freia, while it might hardly be noticed by the major owner, Mondelez. Benedikte Moltumyr Høgberg, a professor at the Department of Public Law at the University of Oslo, was critical. She highlighted two things: Many businesses had

some connection to Russia. This did not only apply to consumer goods. The media had mentioned, for example, that the Norwegian Oil Fund and the bank Nordea had invested several billion kroner in Mondelez. Norway had a system of sanctions that companies were required to follow (Wikan, 2023: 14):

> Initiating private actions against companies that follow the regulations is, I think, questionable, says Høgberg. – Then one must rather have a discussion on whether to expand the sanction regulations through democratic processes. She points out that a boycott carried out by companies and organizations is serious. Boycotts can be illegal and are particularly regulated by the Boycott Act. – But the individual consumer can of course refrain from going to the store and buy Freia's chocolate, says Høgberg.

Law Professor Høgberg and ethics professor Kvalnes do illustrate here the difference between legal license by compliance to boycott and social license by conformity to blacklist. The law professor argued that regulation had to be put in place before companies acted. The ethics professor argued that companies should apply proactive ethics by actively seeking information and making decisions before someone else, like the government, puts the spotlight on the situation.

7.2 Conformity Debate in the Media

One of the commentators in the same newspaper as the above quote, who makes a living by making fun of news, wrote on the same day (Alstadheim, 2023: 15):

> Those who quit Kvikk Lunsj can also kill their robot vacuum cleaner and give up shaving. The banana twist has always been controversial. Some people hate it. Others love it. This weekend it ended up in the firing lane once again. Now because of a boycott campaign. The Elkjøp department store found that the matter was so urgent that the company issued a press release in Saturday. It was illustrated by a picture of the national icon Kvikk Lunsj. Kvikk Lunsj, Twist and other products from Freia will no longer be available for purchase at Elkjøp. Strangely enough, the electronics chain also deals in sweets. The goods from Freia were to be removed "immediately". Why? – We want to take an active

> stance to help influence a positive development in the situation, stated CEO Linda Frid Andresen of Elkjøp Norway.

The background to the conformity debate in the media was that Ukrainian authorities had compiled a blacklist. On it were large international companies that Ukraine believed were contributing to the Russian economy and thus to financing the war. Among them was the Mondelez Group, which owned Freia. Milk chocolate from Freia was at that time still called in marketing “a small piece of Norway”. However, “the product is actually a small piece of an international group” (Alstadheim, 2023: 15). This group also had factories and operations in Russia. The company naturally paid taxes to the Russian state through its operations there. The goods that Mondelez made in Russia were not sold in Norway.

It was Monday, June 12, 2023, when the hotel chain Strawberry, the airline SAS, the cruise line Hurtigruten, and several others announced the removal of Freia products from their minibars, trolleys, and kiosks. The Norwegian Tourist Association severed its long-standing cooperation with Freia, where the milk chocolate was no longer considered a small piece of Norway. The grocery chain Coop asked the government for advice on what it should do. Commentator Alstadheim (2023: 15) wrote:

> If this spreads, the box with 1 kilo King Haakon sweets will also disappear. So what happened at Elkjøp? Yes, Freia was kicked out. But goods from other companies that are on exactly the same Ukrainian list can still be bought at Elkjøp. Procter & Gamble is on Ukraine’s list. The group owns, among other things, Gillette. Elkjøp sells both razors and shaving gel from Gillette. Chinese Xiaomi is also on the list, because the company is heavily involved in the Russian market. Xiaomi produces mobile phones, smart watches and robot vacuum cleaners, among other things. But not even the electric bikes from Xiaomi have been chased out by Elkjøp. Is it likely that the sale of Xiaomi is more important to Elkjøp’s revenues than the sale of chocolate? That should not be overlooked. Freia has done nothing wrong. Not Mondelez either. In any case, not based on the sanction rules the EU has adopted.

It was completely understandable that Ukraine wanted to emphasize the presence of large global companies in Russia. At the same time, the

Ukrainian blacklist was creating trouble for further tightening of the official sanctions. The European Union was working on a 11th package of sanctions. It was directed against attempts to circumvent the measures that had already been adopted. It was important for the sanctions that had already been agreed to be effective. However, organized criminals helped Russia circumvent sanctions, a tradition of state–corporate alignments (Bernat and Whyte, 2020; Rothe, 2020).

Two members of the European Union, Hungary and Greece, were skeptical of further sanctions against Russia. The two countries were reacting to the fact that companies belonging to them had been blacklisted by Ukraine. The two countries demanded that the companies be removed from the list before a new package of sanctions was adopted. Joseph Borrell, the EU foreign policy chief, was trying to resolve the dispute. At the same time, statistics from the EU indicated how random the Ukrainian blacklist can be. It was not the case that all trade with Russia has been stopped (Alstadheim, 2023: 15):

> EU countries still buy some gas from the country. The same applies to nickel, iron, steel and some fertilizers. The import of coal from Russian has virtually disappeared. The import of oil is almost gone. Trade in food is also exempt from the sanctions. Norway has also granted an exception to the port ban so that Russian fishing boats can land fish in three ports in the north.

The sanctions were an attempt to hit where it could hurt. At the same time, the goal was for it to sting as much as possible in Russia as the sanctioned country and as little as possible in Europe as the sanctioning country. For example, there should be as little pain as possible for workers at Rodeløkka in Oslo, where the Freia factory was located. A left-wing politician said it was cool that a boycott campaign emerged organically, including on social media. This could undoubtedly put pressure on large international companies (Alstadheim, 2023: 15):

> At the same time, other companies find themselves in a tussle between Twist and Twitter. Elkjøp's behavior shows how random the result can be. The commitment is understandable. But it resembles mainly posing.

7.3 State for Compliance Not Conformity

Norwegian enterprises considering boycott of other enterprises sought the government for advice. But the government did not want to respond (Tallaksen and Borkamo, 2023: 15):

> The foreign ministry says that it follows EU's sanctions – not the list from Ukrainian authorities.

The debate continued in Norwegian media. Martinsen (2023: 29) at the military defense academy argued:

> While the great majority of western companies have withdrawn, Freia's owner has chosen to stay. That is reason good enough to stay away from the milk roll chocolate.

Stokke (2023: 31), on the other hand, was concerned that Freia was becoming a random victim:

> A fundamental problem with the boycott is that Freia is made a random scapegoat for a challenge that affects Norwegian business and industry widely, without clear guidelines in principle. Which Norwegian company will become the next victim in the boycott bingo?

Some argued that the boycott of Freia would benefit competitors (Venbakken *et al.*, 2023):

> Peggy Simcic Brønn is a professor in the department of communication and culture at BI Norwegian Business School, and researches reputation. Brønn believes that Norwegians are primarily so critical to Freia because the food giant is one of the best known on the market in Norway. – The question is: Who is boycotting? Is the boycott consumer-driven, or are the companies that sell Freia worried about being associated with Mondelez, says Simcic Brønn. (…) – I think Norwegians will eventually find their way back to Freia. Remember that Freia is not just a company, it is part of Norwegian culture. But in the meantime, Mondelez is getting a strong message that their bad behavior cannot be tolerated. (…) Reputation expert Ole Christian Apeland believes the Freia boycott can be good news for the chocolate producer Nidar.

The following day, the major Norwegian business newspaper reported on its front page that there was a complete boycott confusion (Eidesvik and Kirkedam, 2023: 1):

> Customers, businesses and politicians at the parliament are unsure who to respond to the Freia boycott. Sanction expert Tine Elisabeth Vigmostad says there is a big difference between official sanction lists and other blacklists.

A commentator, who believed that she often had the right answer, wrote in the same newspaper (Grinde, 2023: 8): "A short round in the think box before one cashes in on public relation profit is to recommend". A business lawyer called the boycott "naming and shaming" (Borkamo, 2023: 9).

The Norwegian Ministry of Foreign Affairs quickly called a meeting with representatives from business associations, labor unions, retail chains, and other stakeholders making decisions and being affected by potential boycotts of more companies operating in Norway (Noem and Borkamo, 2023: 12):

> Several business actors, including Coop and Freia owner Mondelez, trooped up to the ministry of foreign affairs on Wednesday morning. There they met the state secretaries from the ministry of foreign affairs and the ministry of trade and fisheries. The question of sanctions lists and boycott lists was on the agenda, after Coop asked the minister for trade for a meeting at the weekend. In a press briefing afterwards, state secretary in the ministry of trade, Halvard Ingebrigtsen, was clear that, of course, the decision on boycott rests with companies and private individuals themselves. – We cannot decide on that for anyone, said Ingebrigtsen.

Following the meeting with the ministries, several of the boycotting companies stated that they would continue to do so. Elkjøp, which had been criticized by Alstadheim (2023) and others, dropped its boycott of Freia. Retail chains Coop and Rema never entered into a boycott of Mondelez. Scandinavian Airlines (SAS) continued its boycott, as confirmed by media manager Tonje Sund, who stated that the company related "loyally to the list that Ukrainian authorities have presented" (Noem and Borkamo, 2023: 12):

> We had a thorough review of the whole list – where we detected that Mondelez was included, which for us mainly means Marabou and Freia, says Sund. – So we maintain that decision. For us it is a matter of Mondelez as the owner, and that they have interests in Russia – not single products, she added.

Mondelez's argument for continuing its operations in Russia was not only concern for its 3,000 employees in the country and the 10,000 farms that supplied raw materials. It was also the worry that those who would take over the factories, machines, and recipes left behind could be more supportive of Putin and the Russian war in Ukraine (Noem and Borkamo, 2023). This argument aligns with Bestseller in Denmark, arguing for continued operations in Myanmar controlled by a military junta (Christoffersen and Mikkelsen, 2021). In the end, Bestseller decided to withdraw from Myanmar, leaving hundreds of employees without work and income to support their families (Meixler and Creery, 2022).

The Norwegian Oil Fund, managed by the Norwegian Central Bank, which invests globally almost all the money that derives from oil and gas exploration in the North Sea, had financial investments in Mondelez. The state fund had invested close to USD 1 billion in Mondelez. The fund had no intention of relinquishing its role as a shareholder at Mondelez (Rustad, 2023).

7.4 Some Conformity beyond Compliance

While adhering to the boycott list from government sanctions was a matter of compliance to maintain the corporate license to operate, adhering to the boycott list from Ukrainian officials' blacklisting was a matter of conformity to maintain the social license to operate.

For airline SAS, a special circumstance and trigger for the boycott of products from Freia in Norway and Marabou in Sweden, both owned by Mondelez, was the airline's transport of wounded soldiers from Ukraine. The wounded soldiers were flown by the airline to various hospitals across Europe. SAS crews on the flights had noted the cruel realities of the war. Therefore, SAS continued its boycott of companies blacklisted on Ukraine's "International War Sponsors". It was a matter of corporate social responsibility (Berglihn and Lia, 2023).

Airline Norwegian claimed that it never boycotted Freia; it merely paused the sale of its products for a short while (Nilsen and Borkamo, 2023).

In Sweden, where the boycott of Mondelez began a week before Norway, many companies continued their boycott based on the Ukrainian blacklist, even after learning it differed significantly from the EU's sanction list (Berglihn and Lia, 2023).

During the debate in Norwegian media regarding the potential boycott of Freia based on the blacklist from Ukraine rather than the state sanctions against Russia, an interesting perspective was introduced by the former head of police intelligence, Hedvig Moe. She was now an attorney in a large law firm in Norway, where she provided advice to companies that needed help to understand sanctions and blacklists. She said that "those who thought the Freia case was complicated might find it even more demanding in the future" due to potentially new sanctions and measures against China and other parts of the world (Klevstrand, 2023: 18). The Freia boycott issue did spread from company to company in June 2023. Discussions among Norwegian top executives were heated and could not be resolved by sanction specialists and lawyers giving the green light. The green light simply represented the legal license to operate, not the social license to operate, for confused corporate executives. The attorney warned Norwegian companies against dealing only with what sanction rules prohibited and what was not prohibited. She wanted to sell advice to law firm clients on sanctions and security policies (KLevstrand, 2023: 18):

- — A possible scenario in which China carries out a military action against Taiwan is that Western societies and the United States would react to it. But it will be difficult to agree on sanctions against China, she believes. Moe points out that trade ties between the West and China are far more intertwined than with Russia, and many Western companies are completely dependent on small or large product parts made in China.
- — Then, we might be in a situation where rules are not made against trading with China, but Norwegian businesses should again consider what is wise, not merely what is legal. Security policies are something Norwegian businesses now need to decide on, much more than before. It is no longer possible to separate business from security politics.

— We will see more cases like the Freia case, and even more nuances and shades. And when you don't have sanction rules at the bottom, it becomes even more complicated to make these assessments, she says.

Additional expectations from shareholders, employees, and the public were on top of legal regulations. These stakeholders expected that corporate executives prepare themselves for nuances and shades when they involved their companies in global trade (Klevstrand, 2023).

The Ukrainian blacklist was frequently updated. The list labeled "War & Sanctions" can be found on the website www.sanctions.nazk.gov.ua/en/boycott, listing international sponsors of war. The ranking of countries as sponsors of war began in August 2023, with China, followed by Greece, the US, France, Italy, and the UK. The entities listed started with Philip Morris International, Japan Tobacco International, and Alibaba Group Holding Company Limited. The first listed, Philip Morris International acquired the company Swedish Match in Sweden in the fall of 2022. This was detected by the Ukrainian blacklist, which caused the airline SAS to terminate Swedish Match products, in addition to Mondelez products (Bach, 2023).

References

Alstadheim, K.B. (2023). Et lite stykke Norge i skuddlinjen (A small piece of Norway in the firing line), daily Norwegian newspaper *Aftenposten*, Tuesday, June 13, p. 15.

Atiles, J. (2025). Economic sanctions as state crime: Empire, law and the United States' economic warfare in Latin America, *British Journal of Criminology*, published first online https://doi.org/10.1093/bjc/azaf003.

Bach, D. (2023). Ukraina setter tobakksgigant på svarteliste – SAS går i dialog med charteroperatører (Ukraine puts tobacco giant on blacklist – SAS enters into dialogue with charter operators), web-based Norwegian business newspaper E24, www.e24.no, published August 25.

Berglihn, H. and Lia, L.M. (2023). Slik startet Freia-boikotten (That is how the boycott started), daily Norwegian business newspaper *Dagens Næringsliv*, Friday, June 16, pp. 8–9.

Bernat, I. and Whyte, D. (2020). State-corporate crimes, in Rorie, M.L. (editor), *The Handbook of White-Collar Crime*, Wiley & Sons, Hoboken, NJ, chapter 9, pp. 191–208.

Borkamo, B. (2023). Kaller boikottliste "Naming and shaming" (Labels the boycott list "Naming and shaming"), daily Norwegian business newspaper *Dagens Næringsliv*, Wednesday, June 14, p. 9.

Christoffersen, J. and Mikkelsen, M.S. (2021). *Redegjørelse: Bestseller A/S' samfundsansvar i Myanmar (Statement: Bestseller Ltd.'s Social Responsibility in Myanmar)*, law firm Offersen Christoffersen, Copenhagen, Denmark, 122 p., May 10.

Eidesvik, A. and Kirkedam, M. (2023). –Hvis vi først skal boikotte, må vi boikotte ordentlig (If we first are to boycott, we must boycott substantially), daily Norwegian business newspaper *Dagens Næringsliv*, Wednesday, June 14, pp. 1 and 4–7.

Gottschalk, P. (2024). How convenient is deviance to circumvent and evasion sanctions against Russia? The case of alleged economic crime in a Norwegian seafood company, *Journal of Economic Criminology*, 3, 1–8.

Gottschalk, P. (2025). When economic sanctions cause white-collar and corporate crime: The case of hidden Russian ownership revealed by a Norwegian insurance firm, *Deviant Behavior*, 46(1), 101–110.

Grinde, E. (2023). NHO, Virke og alle barna i barnehagen (som ikke får sjokolade) (Business association, trade association and all children in kindergarten (who do not get chocolate)), daily Norwegian business newspaper *Dagens Næringsliv*, Wednesday, June 14, p. 8.

Klevstrand, A. (2023). — De som syntes Freia-saken var vrien, kan få det enda mer krevende fremover (Those who thought the Freia case was difficult may find it even more demanding in the future), daily Norwegian business newspaper *Dagens Næringsliv*, Monday, June 26, pp. 18–19.

Martinsen, K.D. (2023). Mondelez, Putin og norsk navlebeskuelse (Mondelez, Putin and Norwegian navel examination), daily Norwegian business newspaper *Dagens Næringsliv*, Tuesday, June 13, p. 29.

Meixler, E. and Creery, J. (2022). EU targets Myanmar's lucrative energy sector in latest sanctions, *Financial Times*, www.ft.com, published February 22.

Morgan, T.C., Syropoulos, C. and Yotov, Y.V. (2023). Economic sanctions: Evolution, consequences, and challenges, *Journal of Economic Perspectives*, 37(1), 3–30.

Nilsen, M. and Borkamo, B. (2023). – Vi boikottet ikke, vi pauset salget midlertidig (We did not boycott, we paused sales temporarily), daily Norwegian business newspaper *Dagens Næringsliv*, Friday, June 16, p. 9.

Noem, M. and Borkamo, B. (2023). – At vi trekker oss ut av Russland, vil hjelpe Putin langt mer enn om vi forblir der (– That we withdraw from Russia will help Putin much more than if we remain there), daily Norwegian business newspaper *Dagens Næringsliv*, Thursday, June 15, pp. 12–13.

Rothe, D.L. (2020). Moving beyond abstract typologies? Overview of state and state-corporate crime, *Journal of White Collar and Corporate Crime*, 1(1), 7–15.

Rustad, M.E. (2023). Oljefondet og Nordea har investert milliarder i Mondelez (The oil fund and Nordea have invested billions in Mondelez), Norwegian web-based business newspaper *E24*, www.e24.no, published June 11.

Stokke, O.M. (2023). Boikottbingoens tilfeldige ofre – hvorfor Freia, men ikke Friele? (The boycott bingo's random victims – why Freia, but not Friele?), daily Norwegian business newspaper *Dagens Næringsliv*, Tuesday, June 13, p. 31.

Tallaksen, S. and Borkamo, B. (2023). Vil ikke gi boikott-svar (Will not give boycott answer), daily Norwegian business newspaper *Dagens Næringsliv*, Tuesday, June 13, pp. 14–15.

Venbakken, K., Barka, E.H.T. and Andersen, E. (2023). Tror Freia-smellen kan gagne konkurrent: – Blir en bra sommer (Believe the Freia bang could benefit the competitor: – Will be a good summer), web-based Norwegian newspaper *Nettavisen*, www.nettavisen.no, published June 13.

Wikan, V.S. (2023). Bør vi ha Kvikk Lunsj-skam nå? (Should we have Kvikk Lunsj shame now?), daily Norwegian newspaper *Aftenposten*, Tuesday, June 13, pp. 14–15.

Chapter 8

Case: Sanctions against Myanmar

The Danish garment producer Bestseller did not violate the legal license to operate, as its manufacturing activities were not subject to sanctions against the military junta in Myanmar. An investigative report by a law firm concluded that the company was indeed compliant. However, negative reactions continued against the company. Eventually, Bestseller withdrew from Myanmar to demonstrate conformity in order to regain and maintain the company's social license to operate.

This case study applies the perspective of social license to operate. The perspective of social license suggests that legal and social obligations and expectations represent separate but interacting issues for assessing how business conduct aligns with norms in the community. While each business enterprise serves a number of purposes in the community, such as employment and goods and services, business conduct has to meet both legal and social requirements to operate. The community does not exist to serve the business enterprise. Rather, each corporate entity exists to serve the community with benefits without violating the legal and social licenses. The social license to operate can be part of a bottom-up as well as an outside-in effort to enhance the social control of business activity. Business enterprises attempt to respond by indicating that their activities are not only legally legitimate but also socially responsible. The expression is often used when a company's activities may face disapproval – especially if such disapproval could result in resistance that harms their business interests.

The Danish law firm Offersen Christoffersen was commissioned to assess whether the company Bestseller had economic relations with the military junta in Myanmar in violation of the Danish Ministry of Foreign Affairs' or the EU's guidelines and rules for sanctions. The law firm was also supposed to assess whether Bestseller's due diligence in Myanmar lived up to international standards of corporate social responsibility (Christoffersen and Mikkelsen, 2021).

Bestseller had 2,700 branded chain stores across 38 markets worldwide, and its products were sold in 15,000 multi-brand and department stores. Bestseller seemed to violate its social license to operate when it placed orders in Myanmar after the military coup in the country (Reed, 2022):

> In garments, multinational companies such as H&M, Bestseller and Primark brought in supply-chain investors and created jobs, mostly women, during Myanmar's decade of democratic transition, which ended with a coup. While some have suspended their Myanmar operations, others are quietly still buying.

Bestseller faced serious criticism (Einarsdottir, 2021; Thomsen, 2021), including negative comments from the Danish foreign minister (Ritzau, 2021) and the fashion industry (Einarsdottir, 2021). A report by the United Nations showed that companies producing clothes in Myanmar had financial ties to the military.

The military in Myanmar carried out a coup on February 1, 2021, and established a junta of generals to rule the country. In 2022, the junta executed four democracy activists (Nystuen, 2022). The European Union (EU) imposed sanctions on the junta on March 22 and April 19, 2021. The sanctions were implemented to harm military financial interests in the country and targeted companies having financial relations with the junta. Bestseller has since 2014 produced clothes at several factories in Myanmar.

Generally, as mentioned in the previous chapter, sanctions refer to "restrictive policy measures that one or more countries take to limit their relations with a target country in order to persuade that country to change its policies or to address potential violations of international norms and conventions" (Morgan *et al.*, 2023: 3). Gottschalk (2024, 2025) found that economic sanctions tend to cause white-collar and corporate crime. Atiles (2025) studied US unilateral economic and financial sanctions and argued that such sanctions constitute state crime since coercive measures contravene international law and harm the populations of targeted countries.

8.1 Challenging the Social License

The foreign minister of Denmark, Jeppe Kofod, was upset over Bestseller's use of factories in Myanmar (Ritzau, 2021):

> The military is in power in Myanmar. According to the UN report, factories that Bestseller uses are effectively owned by the military. Two of the factories used by Danish clothing giant Bestseller in Myanmar in recent years are cooperating with the military in the country, according to a UN report. And this could have consequences, Denmark's foreign minister Jeppe Kofod told the newspaper. He is greatly exasperated by the cooperation.
>
> I would like to make it quite clear that I think it is highly problematic if Bestseller chooses to have clothes produced in factories controlled by the military dictatorship in Myanmar, according to the UN, he told the newspaper.

Bestseller faced serious criticism from the clothing and fashion industry, which could harm the company's outlets and brands (Einarsdottir, 2021):

> Bestseller receives criticism for alleged military connections in crisis-stricken Myanmar. The Danish fashion giant Bestseller is once again in bad weather. This time it is due to their connections in crisis-hit Myanmar. Bestseller, which owns about twenty fashion brands such as Vero Moda, Only and Jack & Jones, produces at three factories in the industrial zone Ngwe Pinlae outside the city of Yangon. A report from 2019 to the UN Human Rights Council points out that the zone is controlled by the industrial conglomerate Myanmar Economic Holdings Limited (MEHL). Their owners consist of the military and individuals in the military leadership, among them chief of staff Min Aung Hlaing who is mainly responsible for the recent bloody attacks on civilians in the country where over 700 people have been killed, writes Fashion Forum.

Because of the criticism, Bestseller was "among the companies that froze orders from the south-east Asian country because of human rights concerns and civil unrest" (Reed and Nilsson, 2021). The EU targeted Myanmar's lucrative energy sector with its sanctions, pressured companies to divest from the country, and sought to cut off indirect funding for the junta. The EU imposed "sanctions against almost two dozen Myanmar government and military officials as well as a state-backed oil and gas group" (Meixler and Creery, 2022). Nevertheless, the Danish company wanted to resume its business in Myanmar again (Reed and Nilsson, 2021):

> Bestseller, which describes itself as a champion of sustainable development and whose Myanmar suppliers have about 48,000 workers, concluded that the three factories were not on military-owned land, and it had not violated EU sanctions. The Danish group also said it had 'started to resume business in Myanmar again'.

To legitimize a resumption of its business in Myanmar again, Bestseller argued that its business did not benefit the military junta (Reed and Nilsson, 2021):

> Proceeds from the garment industry for the most part do not directly benefit the country's military, unlike industries such as gemstones, timber, and oil and gas. However, Bestseller commissioned an independent investigation into its business in the country to investigate the status of three of its factories in an industrial zone linked to Myanmar Economic Holdings, a military-controlled conglomerate that has been placed under sanctions by the US, EU and UK since the coup.

Surprisingly, Bestseller's response to the threat of losing the company's social license to operate was to commission an investigation primarily into the legal license to operate by lawyers as examiners.

8.2 Bestseller's Convenience Themes

Assuming the allegations against the company were correct, it is possible to identify convenience themes for the offender, as illustrated in Figure 8.1. There was a corporate threat against the supply of quality goods at low prices from Myanmar. At the same time, the possibility of continued supply would ensure more profits. The company had access to resources to continue its business in Myanmar, and the lack of oversight and guardianship by the international community created a chaotic situation. It was a rational choice for the company to continue its business in

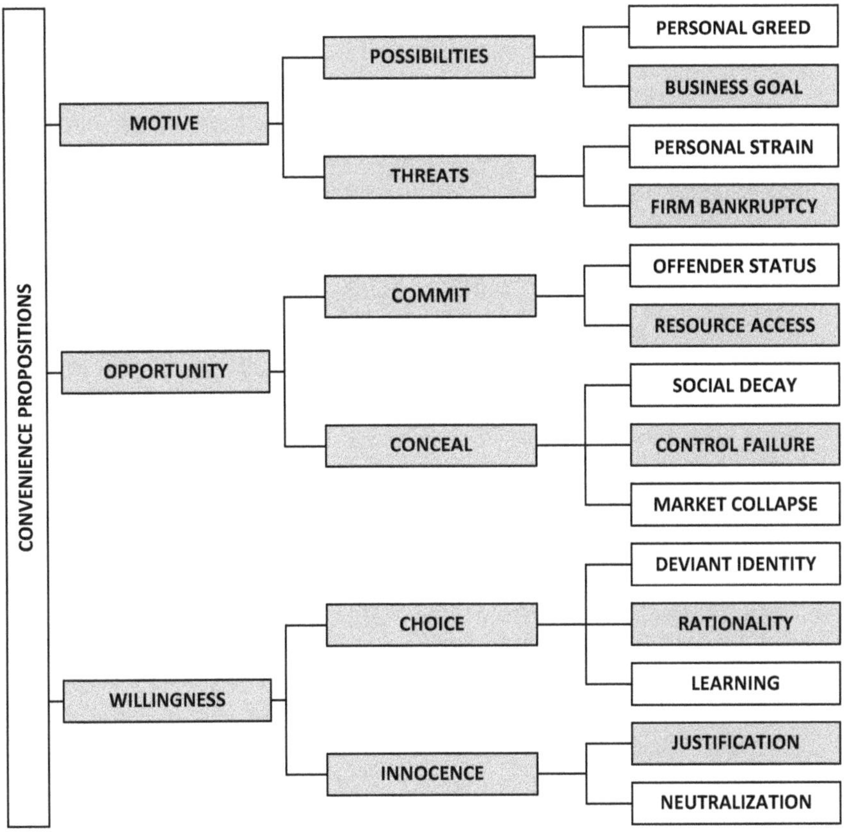

Figure 8.1. Convenience themes in the case of the Danish company.

Myanmar, which they justified by the employment they provided to thousands of poor people in the country.

The founder of Bestseller was Troels Holch Povlsen, and his son, Anders Holch Povlsen, developed the business into 2,700 retail stores and 15,000 retail customers. The number of employees was 17,000 at Bestseller, headquartered in Brande, Denmark. The son became a billionaire and remained CEO and sole owner of the international retail clothing chain, which was a privately held, family-owned company. In a statement, Anders Holch Povlsen said, “we cannot imagine anything worse than if our company, in any way possible, should contribute to the situation Myanmar now finds itself in. Our work in the country to date has been about the exact opposite – contributing positively to the country's development, both economically and politically" (Larsen, 2021). He argued that continuing operations in Myanmar would help poor people, where almost half of the population lives below the poverty line. He claimed that it would cause serious harm to the population if international businesses had to withdraw from Myanmar. He argued that corporate social responsibility implies staying in Myanmar, while critics argued that the only responsible course of action would be to close down business in Myanmar as long as a military clique was in power in the country.

This CEO's reasoning is in line with the motive of social concern for others. Agnew (2014) introduced the motive of social concern for wrongdoing, where there is a desire to help others, and thus moving beyond the assumption of simple self-interest. However, as argued by Paternoster *et al.* (2018), helping others can be a self-interested, rational action that claims social concern.

The CEO's reasoning for the motive of corporate possibilities may also be rooted in the historical tradition of reputational benefits associated with being an employer in Myanmar. When the previous military dictatorship collapsed and Aung San Suu Kyi was elected president of the country, being an employer of workers resulted in improved corporate reputation as part of the Myanmar "fairytale" (Mortensen *et al.*, 2019). With the Nobel Peace Prize winner Kyi in front as president of Myanmar, Bestseller and other companies contributed to raising the standard of living in the country. By establishing factories in Myanmar with very low wages for employees, Bestseller and others could claim to have contributed to the economic development of local communities. At the same time, the companies were making substantial profits from the sale of garments on markets in Europe. By withdrawing from production in Myanmar, Bestseller faced the threat of significant reduction in profits and potential economic losses in the clothing business, as indicated in Figure 8.1.

In the opportunity structure, Bestseller management had access to resources to continue operations in Myanmar, as indicated in Figure 8.1. The company also had the opportunity to conceal potential links to the junta by avoiding direct trade with garment factories. Instead, Bestseller conducted business with local vendors that had links to the factories. In the principal-agent perspective of detachment (Bosse and Phillips, 2016), Bestseller, as the principal, appeared detached from the factories, as agents, that were producing clothes for the company.

The innocent justification might rely on an argument that many other foreign companies operated the same business structure as Bestseller's in Myanmar. Furthermore, the argument that employing workers could help secure a minimum standard of living for them may also be used to justify continued operations in Myanmar, despite the country's junta dictatorship.

8.3 The Fraud Investigation Report

The mandate for the examiners required them to conduct a review of whether Bestseller had lived up to the highest international standards for corporate social responsibility, including the United Nations' guidelines for human rights and business and the OECD's guidelines for multinational enterprises. The other part of the mandate asked examiners to review whether Bestseller had economic relationships with the military and thus had acted in violation of the rules of the Danish foreign ministry and the EU.

The examiners argued that discontinuing activities in Myanmar would be a breach of Bestseller's corporate social responsibility (Christoffersen and Mikkelsen, 2021: 120):

> Myanmar's situation is bleak, not just politically but also economically. In case many international companies decide to halt their activities in Myanmar, it would cause an economic meltdown and lead to widespread and serious poverty and famine. It is therefore, in our view, in clear breach of Bestseller's corporate social responsibility, should they decide not to continue with their economic and social activities in Myanmar. It is therefore our recommendation, that Bestseller as quickly as possible resume their activities in Myanmar.

One of the main questions that the examiners were commissioned to answer was whether Bestseller had economic relations with the military in Myanmar, given that three of the 30 factories, from which Bestseller sourced products, were located in the Ngwe Pinlae industrial zone. Based on the review, the examiners did not believe there were reasonable grounds to assume that the three factories were located on plots of land owned, directly or indirectly, by the military. Neither did the examiners believe there were reasonable grounds to assume that the three factories had paid administrative fees, directly or indirectly, to the military. Based on the volatile situation in Myanmar, the examiners recommended that Bestseller continue to exercise considerable due diligence in order to avoid breaching the EU sanctions.

Another main question addressed by the examiners was whether Bestseller had acceptable standards in its corporate social responsibility (Christoffersen and Mikkelsen, 2021: 121):

> We are clearly of the opinion that there is no doubt that Bestseller lived up to their corporate social responsibility in accordance with the highest international standards in relation to their activities in Myanmar.

A third main question was whether Bestseller, in the case of its economic relations with the military, was in breach of Danish or EU guidelines and rules. The examiners found that there were no reasonable grounds to assume that Bestseller had any economic relations with the military in Myanmar as a result of their activities in the Ngwe Pinlae

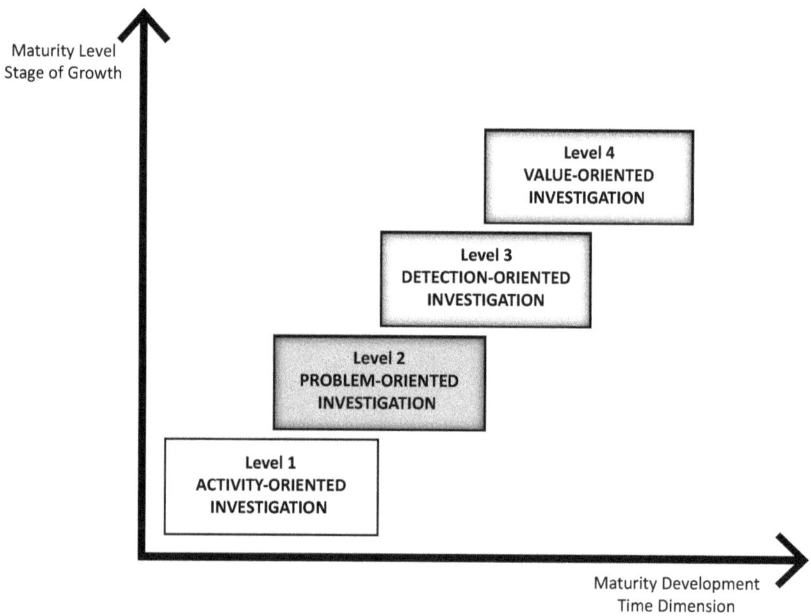

Figure 8.2. Maturity of investigations by Christoffersen and Mikkelsen (2021).

industrial zone. They found no evidence of breaches of the sanctions from the EU.

The conclusions drawn by the examiners were based on various documents from Bestseller, including emails, minutes of meetings, and contracts. They interviewed a number of people, and some interviewees had to remain anonymous because of safety issues. Some relevant information sources never responded to requests from the examiners. The investigation is assigned a maturity level of 2, as shown in Figure 8.2.

8.4 Regaining the Social License

The investigation by Christoffersen and Mikkelsen (2021) was an attempt to regain not only the legal license to operate but also the social license to operate in Myanmar. The main argument for Bestseller to continue its business in the country, which had been occupied by a military dictatorship, was concerned with the avoidance of poverty. The firm claimed that 48,000 people in Myanmar were dependent on new orders of clothing from Bestseller. The story was told that not only employees would suffer but also their families. Furthermore, the firm claimed that its continued business activities in Myanmar in no way would benefit the military junta. Investigators strongly recommended that Bestseller place new orders when their report was released on May 10, 2021.

However, on August 27, 2021, Bestseller announced that it had already stopped its business in Myanmar and that it would not place any new orders (Bestseller, 2021):

> Following the announcement from IndustryALL Global Union and their Myanmar affiliate, the Industrial Workers Federation of Myanmar (IWEM), Bestseller will not place new orders in the country until an impact assessment and dialogue with experts, NGOs, trade unions and other relevant stakeholders with a clear focus on the wellbeing of garment workers in Myanmar has been conducted.

The report by Christoffersen and Mikkelsen (2021) was obviously not sufficient to regain the social license since global and local unions remained skeptical of business activities in Myanmar. The only relevant attempt to regain the license seemed to be through not placing new orders in Myanmar. The argument that poor workers and their families would suffer income loss contradicted the argument that the well-being of garment workers in the country was not guaranteed and that the military junta would benefit from Bestseller's business in the country (Thomsen, 2021).

Furthermore, while stakeholders felt sorry for citizens in Myanmar who suffered under the boycott, they also knew that there are always innocent victims of various sanctions. For example, when hospital employees go on strike to gain higher wages, patients waiting in line for treatment become innocent victims. Therefore, it may not come as a surprise that the innocent-victim approach suggested by the investigators did not work for Bestseller to regain the social license to operate in Myanmar.

The attempts to regain the social license by Bestseller management can be studied in terms of the factors that are needed to earn it, as suggested by Saenz (2019) and Sale (2021), and illustrated in Table 8.1.

Table 8.1. Attempts to regain the social license by Bestseller executives.

Social Legitimacy	Violation	Correction
Pragmatic legitimacy	Supporting business benefitting military junta	Withdraw from further business that could benefit the military junta in Myanmar
Moral legitimacy	Military junta hurting innocent civilians	Keep readiness to return to business in Myanmar if social license granted by local unions
Cognitive legitimacy	Profiting from poor people in the country	Keep readiness to return to business in Myanmar if acceptable to garment industry
Trust Vulnerability	**Violation**	**Correction**
Risk tolerance	Ignorance of transition from democracy to dictatorship	Alignment with other corporations and national guidelines
Adjustment level	Military junta's power regulation of business conduct	Home country's guidelines for business abroad
Relative power	Retail customers in chain stores reacted to misconduct	Avoidance of garments marked "Made in Myanmar"

References

Agnew, R. (2014). Social concern and crime: Moving beyond the assumption of simple self-interest, *Criminology*, 52(1), 1–32.

Atiles, J. (2025). Economic sanctions as state crime: Empire, law and the United States' economic warfare in Latin America, *British Journal of Criminology*, published first online https://doi.org/10.1093/bjc/azaf003.

Bestseller (2021). *Not Placing New Orders in Myanmar*, Bestseller, www.bestseller.com, published August 27.

Bosse, D.A. and Phillips, R.A. (2016). Agency theory and bounded self-interest, *Academy of Management Review*, 41(2), 276–297.

Christoffersen, J. and Mikkelsen, M.S. (2021). *Redegjørelse: Bestseller A/S' samfundsansvar i Myanmar* (*Statement: Bestseller Ltd.'s Social Responsibility in Myanmar*), law firm Offersen Christoffersen, Copenhagen, Denmark, 122 p., May 10.

Einarsdottir, I.E. (2021). Bestseller får kritikk for påståtte militærforbindelser i kriserammede Myanmar (Bestseller receives criticism for alleged military connections in crisis-stricken Myanmar), Fashion industry magazine *Melk & Honning*, www.melkoghonning.no, published April 20.

Gottschalk, P. (2024). How convenient is deviance to circumvent and evasion sanctions against Russia? The case of alleged economic crime in a Norwegian seafood company, *Journal of Economic Criminology*, 3, 1–8.

Gottschalk, P. (2025). When economic sanctions cause white-collar and corporate crime: The case of hidden Russian ownership revealed by a Norwegian insurance firm, *Deviant Behavior*, 46(1), 101–110.

Larsen, M. (2021). Danish company Bestseller urges EU to take action on Myanmar, *ScandAsia*, Nordic News and Business Promotion in Asia, www.scandasia.com, published April 21.

Meixler, E. and Creery, J. (2022). EU targets Myanmar's lucrative energy sector in latest sanctions, *The Financial Times*, www.ft.com, published February 22.

Morgan, T.C., Syropoulos, C. and Yotov, Y.V. (2023). Economic sanctions: Evolution, consequences, and challenges, *Journal of Economic Perspectives*, 37(1), 3–30.

Mortensen, N.H., Danwatch, K.L.H., Myanmar Now, Cha, P.T. and Frontier. (2019). Baksiden av eventyret om "Made in Myanmar" (The flip side of the fairytale about "Made in Myanmar"), Norwegian foreign aid magazine *Bistandsaktuelt,* www.bistandsaktuelt.no, published April 29.

Nystuen, M.M. (2022). Demokratiforkjempere henrettet av Myanmars militærjunta (Pro-democracy activists executed by Myanmar's military junta), daily Norwegian newspaper *Aftenposten*, Tuesday, July 26, p. 10.

Paternoster, R., Jaynes, C.M. and Wilson, T. (2018). Rational choice theory and interest in the "fortune of others", *Journal of Research in Crime and Delinquency*, 54(6), 847–868.

Reed, J. (2022). Stay or go: The dilemma for multinationals in Myanmar, *Financial Times*, www.ft.com, published January 25.

Reed, J. and Nilsson, P. (2021). H&M and Primark resume Myanmar orders for first time since coup, *Financial Times*, www.ft.com, published May 21.

Ritzau (2021). Kofod fortørnet over Bestsellers brug af fabrikker i Myanmar (Kofod upset over Bestseller's use of factories in Myanmar), Danish broadcasting *TV2*, www.nyheder.tv2.dk, published April 18.

Saenz, C. (2019). Building legitimacy and trust between a mining company and a community to earn social license to operate: A Peruvian case study, *Corporate Social Responsibility and Environmental Management*, 26(2), 296–306.

Sale, H.A. (2021). The corporate purpose of social license, *Sothern California Law Review*, 94(4), 785–842.

Thomsen, C.B. (2021). Dansk tøjgigant vil ikke støtte brutalt militær og trækker sig ud af Myanmar – i hver fald for en periode (Danish clothing giant will not suport brutal military and withdraws out of Myanmar – at least for a period of time), Danish daily newspaper *Politiken*, www.politiken.dk, published September 16.

Chapter 9

Case: Member Revolt in Housing

A social housing company in Norway did not violate its legal license when it entered the luxury and rental markets. However, the norm of building and managing ordinary housing for ordinary people had been violated. A member revolt in the cooperative organization of the company led to the termination of luxury and rental apartments in the future. The termination was necessary to regain the social license to operate by conformity.

Crime is usually defined as a violation of the law. If there is no law sanctioning an offense, then it follows that the action is not a crime. However, in criminology, an offense might be labeled a crime and an offender might be labeled an offender even if there are no sanctions according to statutes in laws. In criminology, an act can qualify for the label of crime if it satisfies two requirements. First, people think it is wrong to do it. Second, people believe that if someone does it, the person or entity should be punished. The difference between legal and social definitions of crime can be explained by the fact that laws do not always cover behaviors that people consider wrong and deserving of punishment. This is in line with the two perspectives of compliance versus conformity, where compliance refers to legal issues while conformity refers to social issues. Economic crime can occur even when no law is violated as long as people think it is wrong and believe it should be punished. People in this setting include everyone, but with an emphasis on those who are influenced by or influence the situation. Those being influenced by the actor and those influencing the actor are labeled "stakeholders". Stakeholders have a special role related to conformity. If they believe that an observed action constitutes wrongdoing and that the wrongdoing should be punished, then the wrongdoing qualifies for the label "crime".

Generally, stakeholders are people and entities influenced by or influencing corporate business (Carnahan *et al.*, 2017; Davidson *et al.*, 2019; Haack *et al.*, 2021; Jardine *et al.*, 2020; Sajko *et al.*, 2021; Sorour *et al.*, 2021). As argued by Uygur and Napier (2023: 1), "stakeholders are the agents or performers of social control".

With this explicit expansion of the term "crime" from compliance to conformity, the following case study is concerned with economic crime. A social housing company began constructing non-social and rental housing, which contributed to a lack of conformity and thus crime. The company violated its social license to operate, as stakeholders, in the role of being members of the social housing cooperative, reacted negatively to non-social and rental housing since such developments were in conflict with the social housing mission of the company. When the deviance was investigated, lawyers found that compliance was in place because no legal statutes had been broken. However, when questions regarding conformity for the social license to operate were raised, the stakeholders expressed strong criticism of the recent developments and labeled them economic crime.

While this chapter begins by describing and discussing executive deviance causing economic crime from a criminological perspective, it continues by emphasizing how executives can restore social license by conformity. Actions to regain the social license are discussed both in terms of a literature review and in terms of interviews with stakeholders conducted by business school students Asfaldo and Nilsson (2023).

9.1 Criminal Conformity Deviance

Conformity deviance is here labeled a crime, as discussed above. Specifically, the Norwegian housing company Obos deviated from its mission and vision of social housing, meaning ordinary housing for ordinary people. Luxury apartments that Obos management started to build were not affordable to ordinary people. Housing for rent was profitable for investors taking over the apartment blocks from Obos, but it did not help solve the housing shortage for ordinary people in Oslo, the capital of

Norway. Through its non-conformity, the company violated its social license to operate (Larsen, 2021; Lorch-Falch *et al.*, 2021; Sørgjeld, 2021).

The social license refers to the ongoing acceptance of a company's or an industry's standard business practices and operating procedures by its employees and other stakeholders, as well as various interest groups in society. Social license is granted, created, and maintained gradually over time as a company builds trust with the community in which it operates. In order to protect a social license, the company must operate responsibly in accordance with community expectations. The company may have to do the right things first and then be seen as doing the right things in order to act like good corporate citizens.

Demuijnck and Fasterling (2016) defined social license to operate as a contractarian basis for the legitimacy of a company's specific activities or projects. From a normative perspective, the concept is closely related to social contract theory and has a political dimension. Business enterprises invoke the social license to operate to indicate that their activities are considered legitimate in the eyes of society generally and stakeholders particularly. The expression is often used in the context of possible disapproval of their activities, when such disapproval may result in resistance that could harm business interests (Morrison, 2014). In such situations, enterprises might acknowledge that their social license is under pressure, deteriorating, or even lost. This situation may result in a policy or change of policy aimed at overcoming the disapproval and resulting harm and damage. Sometimes, the harm and damage from disapproval can be more serious than the harm and damage from violating laws and regulations.

In this context, social license refers to the acceptance and approval by stakeholders and local communities of the organization's activities. The social license is relevant to virtually any kind of activity that might stir up controversy and hinder rather than enable it (Morrison, 2014). Organizations holding a social license may not recognize that they possess one. However, when a social license is broken, the situation typically becomes obvious to everyone involved, and both human and economic costs represent harm that might be irreparable. The social license can be moral or pragmatic (Demuijnck and Fasterling, 2016). From an ethical viewpoint, it is preferable that corporate activities with significant social or environmental impacts are broadly accepted or even acclaimed by society as a whole and by the communities that are impacted in particular. It is obviously preferable that the social license be uncontroversial among stakeholders and local communities.

Morrison (2014) emphasized that the social license relates to what an organization does, not what it is. He referred to social license as the sum of expectations held between an organization and relevant social groups in relation to a specific activity or set of activities. He and other scholars argue that the social license is not primarily a moral or ethical ideal, but rather a smart thing to gain and sustain in order to secure the survival and functioning of organizational activities. Organizational theorists have long argued that legitimacy – understood as conformity with social norms, values, and expectations – enables organizational survival and enhances performance (Meyer and Rowan, 1977).

9.2 Obos Deviance Member Revolt

Obos is the largest housing developer and housing association organization in Norway, with over 500,000 members owning homes it has built. Established in 1929 by Martin Strandli and Jacob Christie Kielland, Obos was created to promote cooperative housing development inspired by a Swedish model. The organization's unique structure enables the cooperative to build homes for its members, where each housing project operates as an independent subsidiary owned by the residents, with the parent corporation in charge of ongoing housing construction. In 1935, Obos changed its name and formed a partnership with the municipality of Oslo to become the city's home-building agency. The partnership allowed Obos to play an essential role in developing Oslo's social housing market, including apartments, and led to the creation of several significant housing areas covering parts of Oslo. Today, Obos has expanded beyond Oslo and developed housing projects in other cities across Norway.

Obos' primary goal is to provide affordable housing and benefits to its members. In addition to property development and sales, Obos engages in real estate brokerage, planning and construction management, property management for other apartment buildings, savings and loans, insurance, and property leasing. Obos also offers financial assistance to its members, such as low-interest loans, to help them purchase homes instead of renting them. Members play an important role in Obos' formal decision-making processes, where they have the right to vote at the annual meeting and elect the board of directors. Members' participation in the organization's major policies is an essential aspect of Obos' cooperative principles.

The power to grant or withhold a social license to operate based on conformity or lack of conformity at Obos is vested in its members, who serve as the source of that authority. The member revolt was sparked by concerns about the cooperative's governance and a desire for greater member involvement in decision-making processes. One of the primary issues that fueled the revolt was the controversial Ulven transaction of 2017, which involved the sale of a large plot of land in Oslo. The land was sold by Obos management to a private property developer. Some members of Obos criticized the sale, arguing that the price was too low and that the cooperative had not consulted with its members before making the decision. Furthermore, there was suspicion of family and other kinds of ties on both sides of the table when the deal was signed. The controversy led to protests and calls for greater transparency and member involvement in the decision-making processes of the cooperative.

When Obos management prioritized a residential quarter for rich people in Oslo, it was considered a serious violation of the social license and an economic crime in the sense of fraud against its members (Holm, 2021; Jacobsen, 2020; Lorch-Falch and Tomter, 2021). Top apartments were priced in 2020 at the equivalent of USD 10 million, which was hardly affordable for most members. The most expensive apartments ended up being sold to non-members, which was considered a serious violation of the cooperative's premise.

Following up on these concerns, a Facebook group was created in 2019 with a title suggesting a member-managed Obos. The group aimed to promote democratic processes and transparency within Obos and has been critical of the cooperative's leadership. The growing group called for the establishment of a member council with greater authority, the introduction of online voting rather than requiring attendance at the annual meeting, and increased transparency in decision-making processes. The Facebook group gained increasing support from members of Obos and became instrumental in promoting discussions about the need for more fair and democratic processes within the cooperative to continue on the main avenue of building and administering ordinary homes for ordinary people. However, the group also faced criticism from some members who felt it was too confrontational and that it did not represent the views of all Obos members.

Thomson and Boutilier (2011) proposed a cumulative pyramid model of social license that emphasizes the independence and varying degrees of importance of three components: legitimacy, credibility, and trust. According to the model, a company must establish legitimacy with its local stakeholders. The next step is to build credibility, which involves demonstrating that the company has the necessary expertise, experience, and resources to deliver on its premises. Credibility is built over time through consistent and reliable performance, as well as by demonstrating a genuine commitment to fulfilling the company's obligations. Legitimacy is essential for starting in a community, while credibility surpasses it in importance for building trust and lasting relationships. Trust, the cornerstone of the pyramid, signifies the highest level of engagement and commitment between a company and the local community. Trust implies that vulnerability is accepted based on positive expectations of the motives and actions of the entity.

Asfaldo and Nilsson (2023) found that Obos had violated legitimacy, credibility, and trust. In terms of legitimacy, despite priding itself on providing pleasant and affordable housing for its cooperative members, the criticized decisions contradicted these foundational principles. The sale of two residential buildings to a profit-oriented landlord, whose primary goal was to generate financial returns by renting out the housing units, directly conflicted with the cooperative's social responsibility to offer affordable housing options for ordinary individuals.

The deviation from Obos' cooperative values and the prioritization of profit over members' well-being had a profound negative impact on the organization's legitimacy. The legitimacy was violated since recent management decisions did not align with the declared mission, values, and social expectations. When an organization deviates from its stated purpose and core values, as evidenced by Obos management's focus on profit generation over affordable housing provision, then the deviance violates the legitimacy of the foundation. The specific example of luxury apartments on Middelthunet illustrated the disconnect between management priorities and Obos' commitment to providing affordable housing to ordinary people. Attempting to sell a penthouse apartment at an exorbitant price of NOK 95 million (about USD 9.5 million) in 2021 not only generated resentment among less affluent members but also raised concerns about the erosion of the traditional Obos spirit (Skjerven, 2023):

> This is Oslo's new disgrace. The penthouses are among the most expensive on the market in Oslo, sold for up to 52 million. In other words, it is

> not about a project that contributes to solving Oslo's housing problem, and has little to do with Obos' policy of creating housing for most people.

In an interview with Asfaldo and Nilsson (2023: 38), Fabian Stang, the former mayor of Oslo from the Conservative Party, pointed out:

> "When Obos now puts up and apartment of 400 square meters for nearly 100 million, the company has completely abandoned its role as a social developer, which we politicians assumed they were created for." These words underscore the abandonment of Obos' responsibility as a social developer. Stang also proposed an alternative approach, suggesting that the apartment could have been transformed into five separate units, each measuring 80 square meters, to meet the housing needs of loyal members at an affordable price, aligning with cooperative principles.

Asfaldo and Nilsson (2023) found that Obos had violated its credibility, as the sale to a landlord was conducted "off market" without considering other bidders. This raised concerns about transparency and fairness in the decision-making process. There was also a concern regarding conflicts of interest, as the parties involved in the transaction were familiar with each other. The apartment buildings were sold to the rental company in a secretive, off-market transaction with only one bidder, which was contrary to the role of the social democratic giant as described by a journalist at the Norwegian Broadcasting Corporation (NRK) (Johnsen, 2021):

> NRK has continuously exposed that the old social democratic giant has sold apartments in Ulven to a rental company. The sale was conducted in secrecy, so-called off market, with only one bidder. This raises speculation about the integrity of CEO Siraj and the attitudes of the cooperation Obos. Isn't Obos meant to serve its members, to provide people with a roof over their head in owned homes?

The sale of apartments at a significantly undervalued price per square meter, as critics argued, did not only result in financial losses for Obos but also raised concerns about potential favoritism and biased decision-making. One concern was that personal relationships and interests might have determined the outcome, disregarding the cooperative's best interests and compromising its credibility. A former mayor of Oslo, Fabian Stang, claimed (Asfaldo and Nilsson, 2023: 40):

> The profits are kept far away from the owners that are the members. The money is not spent on a careful price reduction on new apartments, which would result in a fall in prices throughout the market. They are used for constantly new activities, further and further away from the basic idea. Numerous members now realize that Obos, which they believed was theirs, has transformed into a profit-driven entity.

Asfaldo and Nilsson (2023: 40) found that the actions leading up to the general assembly in 2021 contributed to the erosion of credibility:

> CEO Daniel Siraj's messages to employees, encouraging them to register as candidates, sparked skepticism among some individuals. This move was viewed by some as an attempt to sway the results in favor of the company's interests or specific agendas, rather than ensuring a fair and impartial decision-making process. As Stephansen (2021) highlights, there have been attempts to influence the general meeting by asking directors and other employees to join Obos as housing seekers in order to secure a majority against the troublesome members – or owners, as they actually are.

Thomson and Boutilier (2011) proposed a cumulative pyramid model of legitimacy, credibility, and trust. Regarding trust, a violation occurred because the cooperative housing association was entrusted with the responsibility of providing affordable housing and protecting the interests of its members (Asfaldo and Nilsson, 2023: 42):

> Right in front of the nose of members waiting neatly in line, ready-to-move-in apartments were sold to a rental investor. The board let the sun be shining on them in a report they ordered, which said the sale did not violate the law or the statutes of the cooperative.

The violation of trust did not only cause vulnerability among current members who were either in line for their first cooperative apartments or looking to move within the cooperative housing. The violation also caused potential members to reconsider whether they would join the cooperative and sign up, knowing they could not rely on management to provide them with suitable housing. Members and potential members were questioning whether management actions aligned with the members' best interests and whether the organization can be relied upon to fulfill its obligation as a professional provider of affordable housing.

In response to all the criticism leading to a member revolt on Facebook and other channels, Obos leadership recruited lawyers at audit firm KPMG (2021) to investigate the allegations. However, the corporate investigators only considered legal issues, including formal articles of association for the cooperative, where they found no violations. The investigators did not review conformity violations that had caused harm to the company's social license to operate.

During the spring of 2021, Obos management, member representatives, local politicians, and the board of directors held several meetings and discussions. This communication approach aligns with the recommendations of Rooney *et al.* (2014) regarding social license negotiations. However, Obos primarily communicated with its members through member representatives, the media, and social networks, which contradicts Saenz's (2019) suggestion of direct communication with the masses. Later that spring, Obos management implemented Saenz's (2019) proposed communication strategy by holding several member meetings publicly.

9.3 Social License Recovery Measures

According to Durand *et al.* (2019), rather than coming up with their own plans to deal with the stress, businesses should instead adapt by trying to accommodate the requirements of various stakeholders. The process of organizational adaptation is ambiguous (Cui *et al.*, 2016). One might define adaptation as the process by which members of an organization consciously make decisions that result in observable behaviors, with the intention of closing the gap that exists between their organization and the institutional and economic environment in which it operates (Demuijnck and Fasterling, 2016). It is, therefore, not a matter of active strategy but rather a matter of passive adaptation. This might seem strange to business scholars who typically argue that for every challenge, the business needs a strategy. Here, it is argued that strategy might not be the relevant response, as it can easily miss a moving target. Institutional conformity adaptation and compliance to normative pressures are stronger than "the more traditional list of strategic responses to institutional pressures" (Durand *et al.*, 2019: 314). This is in line with research by Bundy and

Pfarrer (2015) and Gottschalk and Benson (2020), who suggest a dynamic response as stakeholders and others in the community express their concerns and disapproval. To restore the social license, there has to be a continuous alignment between changes in external expectations and internal responses.

Both compliance (alignment with rules) and conformity (alignment with norms) are important institutional theory perspectives. Compliance refers to meeting legal and other formal obligations, while conformity refers to meeting and potentially exceeding societal and other informal norms and obligations (Durand *et al.*, 2019: 300):

> (…) we posit that conformity characterizes voluntary actions that constitute a response to social and normative expectations not (yet) codified in standards and law, while compliance relates to formal mandatory regulations that typically enact only minimal conditions of institutional acceptability.

Durand *et al.* (2019) built their argument of adaptation rather than strategy on institutional theory, emphasizing conformity, which refers to meeting and potentially exceeding societal and other informal norms and obligations. They made a distinction between the willingness and ability of organizations to respond to normative pressures. The willingness derives from the salience of an issue, which refers to the extent to which it resonates with and is prioritized by management. The ability refers to available resources and capabilities that lead to an assessment of whether to take or not take action on the issue.

Durand *et al.* (2019) also made a distinction between symbolic and substantive conformity. Symbolic conformity occurs in business activities that create an impression of meeting or exceeding norms and obligations without actually fulfilling them. Substantive conformity, on the other hand, is present when corporate processes meet the desired and required specifications indicated by stakeholders. Typically, substantive conformity requires resource mobilization and organizational change, which is not needed in the case of symbolic conformity (Eberl *et al.*, 2015; Nardi, 2022).

According to Haines *et al.* (2022), there may be a window of opportunity for securing the social license by constructing more meaningful rules governing commercial activity. The social license to operate is one component that could be used in a bottom-up initiative to improve social control of business activities. It is necessary to invest meaning in terms such as "social license" in order for it to be able to represent more expansive systems of accountability surrounding corporate conduct within the context of a democratic society (Panda and Sangle, 2019; Sanger *et al.*, 2017). Companies may recover the social license by implementing and communicating meaningful rules for accountability and integrity (Melé and Armengou, 2016). Business integrity is the quality of acting in accordance with moral values, norms, and rules that are considered valid and relevant within the context in which the actor operates (Loyens *et al.*, 2022). Integrity refers to taking responsibility for one's self-representation and commitments (Gardiner *et al.*, 2017).

Haines *et al.* (2022: 184) examined "how social control in the form of community pressure might be used to control corporate harm and shape business conduct in a more socially responsible direction". Stakeholders can return the social license to operate to the company if they find it trustworthy. Haines *et al.* (2022: 189) referred to cooperation:

> When a social license is understood as the development of trust, reciprocity and problem-solving between the community and the company, the aim of the social license is one of cooperation moving towards a shared goal.

The content of a social license is permission for business activity when requirements outlined in stakeholder communications have been met (Haines *et al.*, 2022: 186):

> This social permission and the currency of the term provide a potentially important enabler for communities to control the activities of the business in their midst and reduce associated harms. At the same time, the absence of a clear institutional authority underpinning the social license means that its legitimacy as a business requirement can be challenged. The centrally social character of the social license also means that tensions around what is and what is not socially desirable business conduct often emerge simultaneously and can settle on the same activity. Legal and regulatory regimes are ordered around specific harms. A relatively straightforward orientation to hold a business to account for specific harm under the law (safety, environmental damage, fraud) from a social

> license orientation becomes a multi-faceted struggle over what is desirable, what is undesirable and who has the right to decide whether the business activity should or should not proceed.

According to Sale (2021), the social license of an organization can be reclaimed when its board of directors pursues governance models that anticipate and respond to the concerns of its stakeholders. According to Saenz (2019), regaining a company's social license requires a high level of trusting relationships between the company and the community. According to Rooney *et al.* (2014), recovering the social license will occur in a complex series of negotiations with stakeholders in the community, where various stakeholders contribute to a continuous debate (Beukel and Geuns, 2019) and exchange information to influence business practices (Baba *et al.*, 2021; Hurst *et al.*, 2020).

Table 9.1 summarizes recovery recommendations in the research literature by focusing on whether each recommendation relates to legitimacy, credibility, or trust. These three components were defined in a pyramid model by Thomson and Boutilier (2011) and were also characterized

Table 9.1. How management can regain the social license.

Author	Message	Stage	Concern
Baba *et al.* (2021)	Let various stakeholders contribute in a continuous exchange to influence business practice	3	Trust (identity)
Berghoff (2018)	Avoid participating in markets that have the potential to foster what is harmful to society and even illegal	1	Legitimacy (acceptance)
Beukel and Geuns (2019)	Engage in a constructive debate to explore options for long-term continuation of business activities	2	Credibility (approval)
Cui *et al.* (2016)	Engage in socially acceptable practices depending on the needs of the local community	2	Credibility (approval)
Demuijnck and Fasterling (2016)	Conform to social norms, values and expectations to achieve legitimacy among stakeholders	1	Legitimacy (acceptance)
Durand *et al.* (2019)	Adapt to the demands and expectations of stakeholders rather than develop own strategies	2	Credibility (approval)

Table 9.1. (*Continued*)

Author	Message	Stage	Concern
Eberl *et al.* (2015)	Avoid formal control mechanisms that represent window dressing approaches and introduce cultural change instead	1	Legitimacy (acceptance)
Haines *et al.* (2022)	Develop more expansive systems of accountability surrounding corporate conduct for executives	1	Legitimacy (acceptance)
Hurst *et al.* (2020)	Meet the demands and expectations held by local stakeholders and broader society in business practice	2	Credibility (approval)
Melé and Armengou (2016)	Convince stakeholders and the general public of the ethical acceptability of business activities	1	Legitimacy (acceptance)
Panda and Sangle (2019)	Listen to social media and non-government organizations to identify stakeholder demands	3	Trust (identity)
Rooney *et al.* (2014)	Negotiate with stakeholders by giving communities a voice and listen to it and act on it	3	Trust (identity)
Saenz (2019)	Listen to community concerns and spread awareness about the company as to what it is actually doing	3	Trust (identity)
Sale (2021)	Pursue governance models that anticipate and respond to stakeholder concerns ahead of potential negative reactions	2	Credibility (approval)
Sanger *et al.* (2017)	Avoid inappropriate guidance to subordinates on what constitutes acceptable conduct in management practice	1	Legitimacy (acceptance)

as three stages of social license by Sale (2021), starting with legitimacy (acceptance), moving to credibility (approval), and ending at trust (identity).

Legitimacy refers to a belief that a business has the basic right to operate. Legitimacy is an assessment of the appropriateness of an entity's actions (Bundy and Pfarrer, 2015; Fitzgibbon and Lea, 2018). Legitimacy implies that the company and its activities are reasonable and acceptable. According to Demuijnck and Fasterling (2016: 678), legitimacy "refers to the congruence between social values associated with or implied by activities and the norms and acceptable behavior in the larger social system". Legitimacy implies that activities are neutral or desirable, proper and uncontroversial, and appropriate within a socially constructed space of norms, values, and beliefs (Baba *et al.*, 2021; Demuijnck and Fasterling, 2016; Hurst *et al.*, 2020; Saenz, 2019).

Credibility refers to the quality of being believed in (Gomulya and Mishina, 2017). It is a matter of gaining approval from local communities, society, and stakeholders of a business enterprise's activities (Demuijnck and Fasterling, 2016). Credibility builds on approval of stakeholders (Sale, 2021: 825):

> Credibility requires the prior existence of legitimacy. Here, however, the focus is on the company working with stakeholders to achieve more than just tacit approval. Instead, the company builds a relationship that involves initial trust and stakeholder voice in operations. Credibility, like legitimacy, requires action and interaction above the legally required line. For credibility to exist, the entity and the project must be 'believable', and the entity's promises must be both realistic and achievable. Put differently, before an entity can earn credibility, the stakeholders must perceive it to be honest. In addition to honest and open communication, credibility requires deliverables. The company must have certain characteristics, and the community must believe it has them.

Trust implies that vulnerability is accepted based on positive expectations of the motives and actions of the entity. Kim *et al.* (2009: 401) defined trust as "a psychological state comprising the intention to accept vulnerability based on positive expectations of the intentions or behavior of another". The positive expectations can relate to what another does, how they do it, and when they do it. The positive expectations can relate to the reaction of another, where it is expected that the reaction will be understandable, acceptable, and favorable. Vulnerability refers to "an affective openness to facing uncomfortable truths", allegations, damage, and harm, where vulnerability is "the realization of the possibility of being harmed emotionally, socially, or materially", and vulnerability includes "opening oneself up to doubt, confusion, and skepticism" (Endrissat and Lüthy, 2025: 6). A person or organization is vulnerable "if, as a result of their situation or circumstances, they are unable to take care of or protect themselves or others from harm or exploitation" (Brown *et al.*, 2025: 20). Vulnerability implies that trust can be easily violated without detection or correction of deviant behavior, potentially causing harm to the trustee. Trust is thus associated with dependence and risk (Chan *et al.*, 2022: 306):

> The trustor depends on something or someone (the trustee or object of trust), and there is a possibility that expectations or hopes will not be satisfied, and that things will go wrong. Trust is not absolute, but conditional and contextual.

Sale (2021) referred to the stage of trust as a transition from acceptance and approval to a state where stakeholders identify with the entity. Stakeholders have confidence that entity actions will be favorable or at least neutral to the community's interests. At this stage of trust, interests of the company and the community seem aligned.

A quick assessment in Table 9.1 indicates that of the 15 recommendations regarding how management can regain the social license, six recommendations are concerned with legitimacy (acceptance), five recommendations are concerned with credibility (approval), and four recommendations are concerned with trust (identity).

9.4 Student Interviews with Stakeholders

Graduate business students interviewed seven stakeholders who were all members of the Obos cooperative (Asfaldo and Nilsson, 2023). Some were resident members, while others were non-resident members. Three respondents were on the member representative board at Obos. The interviews represented qualitative research (Bell *et al.*, 2022), where interviewees were identified successively using the snowball method. The snowball method is a non-probability sampling technique that involves using referrals from current study participants to recruit additional participants (Biernacki and Waldorf, 1981). By using this method, the students were able to move beyond those who denied participation in the research and reach new participants who might have been difficult to identify otherwise. To allow respondents to interpret events and actions in their own words, student interviewers used open-ended questions (Bryman and Bell, 2022; Davies and Francis, 2018).

Thematic analysis is a method that aims to identify, analyze, synthesize, and interpret themes that emerge from qualitative data (Braun and Clarke, 2012). The purpose of thematic analysis is to identify common issues. The first theme is respondents' perceptions regarding issues in the member revolt. The theme was to identify the specifics of the member revolt in terms of issues. One issue was the sale of a building quarter to the private rental enterprise. A second issue was the sale of luxury apartments to wealthy individuals at an exclusive downtown location in Oslo. Obos was meant for the ownership of ordinary housing for ordinary people, not homes for renting or wealthy people. A third issue, following somewhat from the first two, was Obos becoming too capitalistic, raising questions about its management and how corporate decision-making allocated resources. A fourth issue, following again to some extent from the previous one, was the continued preference for an organization with a social democratic ideology:

> A case led by someone who disagreed with how Obos manages its resources, especially the case of Middelthunet. Obos was becoming too capitalist, which raised questions about how it was being managed and its resource management. Members wanted a different type of organization with a social democratic ideology (Respondent #1).

The member democracy was thus put on the agenda. It was a wake-up call directed at Obos top management. It was questioning who controls Obos, what mandate the board and management have, and why members are not being listened to. Furthermore, many criticized that Obos employees, who were also members and residents, entered into the member representatives' council and the board, which critics believe is wrong since it implies a double or even triple role in decision-making processes. The member revolt centered on how members with various grievances and concerns could come together and voice their demands, thereby challenging the existing power structure within Obos. The first theme from this thematic analysis is thus the skepticism and criticism of recent top management decisions, leading to a revolt regarding the lack of member democracy in influencing organizational practices.

The second theme is respondents' perceptions regarding issues addressing how Obos has evolved in recent years. An issue is the reduced focus on building homes for ordinary people in ordinary neighborhoods compared to the past, when Obos first began addressing the housing shortage in the capital:

> Focuses less on building homes for ordinary people in ordinary neighborhoods than they did when they first started out their business in Oslo (Respondent #7).

Another issue is Obos going from being a capital investment company to a market-driven company due to poor management processes. The society may have changed more than Obos, as politicians in the municipality of Oslo reduced their emphasis on the construction of social housing. In recent years, Obos has expanded beyond Oslo in Norway and even into Sweden. The original purpose of Obos is changing, and it is difficult for members to have a say in a cooperative that is expanding so rapidly. Obos reputation has declined. The representative assembly has changed in recent years, as members and leaders were replaced. Recently, there has been a desire to use the representative assembly more in cooperative decision-making. The second theme from this thematic analysis is thus a change characterized by market orientation and business expansion, combined with selective member representation in decision-making forums.

The third theme is respondents' perceptions regarding issues addressing how the governance of Obos has changed in recent years. Governance refers to the act of directing behaviors in business conduct through rule-making, enforcement, and sanctioning (Kourula *et al.*, 2019). A stable board with minimal changes in leadership suggests that major changes are unlikely. However, they have been more open and engaged in dialogue with the members, opening up about what they are doing. At the same time, it can be seen as a show for the gallery and window dressing. Window dressing is the act or the instance of making something appear better than it actually is (Desai, 2016). The issue is the lack of change in governance, and the observed small increments of change may be symbolic rather than substantial in nature. There have not been many changes in governance, but political bodies have gained somewhat more influence. Committees have been established to help decide on the allocation of funds. The list of those who are part of the member panel consists of older individuals in high positions. It is not very representative, as it includes only well-established individuals. Governance has become more professionalized, creating a larger gap between management bodies and individual members. Some board members and executives were controversial due to a lack of knowledge and contact:

> They do not understand the board's responsibility and position. I understand more about the role of a chairman than the chairman does himself (Respondent #6).

There is an increasing lack of democracy and a lack of interest in fulfilling the members' preferences. The third theme from this thematic analysis is thus the lack of change in governance, creating an increased distance between the idea of the cooperative and its practice.

The fourth theme is whether respondents gained more or less influence on the business in their roles. Four out of seven respondents said no, and three said yes. The no-responders argued that management and the board ultimately make all the decisions anyway. Everything else is a bit of a show. There is no feeling of influence, as no one knows what happens at board meetings, and no one outside has any influence. A regular member certainly has less influence than in earlier times. It is possible to speak up, but nobody really listens. The yes-responders found that being members of certain committees or other bodies, not merely being regular members of Obos, opened up opportunities for them to be heard:

> Yes, have gained more influence by being part of the representative assembly and experience being heard (Respondent #4).

Obos management did not ask for feedback. The fourth theme from this thematic analysis is thus that regular members have even less influence than in the past, and some newly appointed members on committees or assemblies felt they had slightly more influence than before. In addition, the member revolt gave some members an opportunity to be seen and heard.

The fifth theme is how Obos responded to the criticism. One issue was the involvement of external consultants to evaluate potential violations of Obos bylaws and to review democratic principles. Those external reports seemed to satisfy the executives rather than the rebels. Another issue was a number of online meetings where people could speak up, but there were no dialogue options. There were only cosmetic changes to activities and changes that did not alter their structures:

> They have made cosmetic changes and changes that do not alter the structures, for example, initiating a dialogue option without any possibility for discussion. One gets empty answers from the management (Respondent #2).

Symbolically, Obos leadership showed a willingness to be more open and engage in dialogue. They invited members to general meetings and other types of online and offline meetings. They shared more information. They looked into other channels they could use to communicate, such as using more electronic newsletters. However, they dismissed all questions that were raised. They established a democracy committee with lawyers without any background in organizations, who failed to understand that the member revolt was about conformity rather than compliance. The fifth theme from this thematic analysis is thus that Obos responded by opening up a number of communication channels and hiring consultants to review the situation but remained in control of messaging by preventing discussion. However, it was expected that Obos would cease actions that triggered the member revolt, such as selling apartment buildings to rental firms and constructing apartment blocks that only rich people can afford.

The sixth and final theme to be presented here is what respondents think Obos should do to regain the social license to operate. One issue is to admit mistakes if Obos leadership agrees that they have made mistakes. They might admit that selling for hiring was a mistake; they might admit that selling to wealthy individuals was a mistake; they might admit that hiring lawyers to review compliance was a mistake; and they might admit that recruiting employees as members into core committees was a mistake:

> Say that they have done wrong with the luxury homes (Middelthunet) and take responsibility (social responsibility). Without Obos, there would be no shared responsibility (Respondent #3).

Another issue was the shift in business orientation. Rather than becoming more capitalistic and market-driven, Obos should take the lead in building for the future where energy efficiency, smart cities, good urban areas, and sustainable housing should be on the agenda. As a major player, many will then listen to Obos management, and others will be forced to adopt similar models and ways of thinking. Members could then be proud of their membership, and new members would be gained. A third issue was the roles of various people. Board members should not be in charge of the Obos magazine, which completely lacks critical views on business activities. Instead, there should be a professional editorial board. The election committee should not be in charge of recommending members to various committees, and it should not be electing members to itself. Management and their families should not serve as delegates. Board members should not be allowed to vote in the general assembly since they obviously vote in favor of their own proposals. This is a problem when very few members turn out at assembly meetings. The sixth theme from this thematic analysis is thus role adjustments by admitting mistakes in the previous set of roles.

9.5 Internal Investigation Outcome

Fraud examiners from KPMG (2021) found that there was a close relationship between chief executive officer (CEO) Siraj and Quality Living Residential (QLR) executive Schumann. The tone was cordial. They had extensive contact regarding various business matters. Siraj never considered his impartiality because he thought his relationship with Schumann was exclusively businesslike. The board of directors at Obos had no knowledge of the nature and extent of the relationship, but Siraj informed the board during its November 2018 meeting that Schumann served as chairman of the board of a rental fund set up by a financing fund. Siraj and Schumann confirmed with the examiners that they have known each other as industry colleagues for about 10 years. They have been active in the housing policy debate in politics, participated together on municipal committees, and met each other in various industry contexts. On two occasions, they participated together in television programs by the Norwegian public broadcaster NRK. Siraj had used the terms "good friend" and "good buddy" to refer to Schumann on social media. They had never visited each other privately, participated in leisure activities together, or had social contact of a private nature. They have never conducted private business together, exchanged gifts, or covered expenses among themselves or their respective family members. Siraj did not consider his relationship with Schumann to be a private friendship.

Based on these statements of facts as described by KPMG (2021), fraud examiners found that Siraj's impartiality was adequate. They found no information that Siraj had acted unfavorably toward Obos and favorably toward Schumann and QLR. They found no evidence of either infidelity or corruption. The relationship did not constitute a conflict of interest, according to Obos' ethical guidelines. There were circumstances that could be perceived externally as the relationship also being of a private nature, but according to the ethical guidelines, examiners found that there was no evidence suitable for weakening confidence in the CEO's impartiality.

The above conclusion relates to the second part of the investigation mandate, which was concerned with questions about the relationship between the CEO of Obos and the purchasing representative from QLR.

This second part also questioned the relationship between the executive director of housing development and his uncle and cousin who invested in QLR (KPMG, 2021: 5):

> Executive vice president housing development heads the housing development division and has been a board member of Ulven Housing in the period from November 22, 2017 to April 29, 2020. He is a board member of Obos New Homes and other Obos companies. During the period as a board member of Ulven Housing, the executive vice president was involved in the case processing of the Ulven transaction. KPMG has evidence that the executive vice president of housing development was contacted by telephone by his wealth advisor on September 4, 2020 in connection with the Ulven transaction. The wealth advisor is also an advisor to the family branch that invested in QLR. In the conversation, the executive vice president became aware that the investment company of the uncle and cousin was considering investing in QLR (...) The audio log of this telephone conversation has been reviewed by the external auditor. KPMG is told that the content does not deal with information that was not otherwise publicly known.

As in the case of the CEO, fraud examiners concluded that they found no evidence suggesting the housing executive acted in favor of anyone but the employer, Obos. The executive did not act in favor of the investor family or in his own self-interest. There was no basis found for suggesting insider trading, infidelity, or corruption.

The first part of the investigation mandate was concerned with Obos on the occasion of the development at Ulven, Oslo, where two apartment blocks containing a total of 182 apartments were sold to the private rental company QLR for NOK 936 million. In retrospect, criticism was leveled at Obos from various quarters. The criticism was mainly related to whether the sale fulfills Obos' purpose as a housing association and the members' interests as such. KPMG (2021) concluded that the transaction with QLR did not violate any rules and regulations at Obos.

9.6 Assessment of Offender Convenience

Daniel Kjørberg Siraj was appointed chief executive officer at Obos in 2017. His predecessor, Martin Mæland, held the CEO position for 34 years since 1983. He was a social democrat who had a loyal approach to the vision and mission of Obos as a construction cooperative building ordinary homes for ordinary people. Lars Buer, who held the board chair position, was a trade unionist also committed to the social democracy of Obos, as a member organization for ordinary people.

After four years as CEO at Obos, Daniel Kjørberg Siraj became the main target of a membership revolt, as exemplified by Stang's (2021) article. The revolt included demonstrations in front of Obos headquarters with the demand from members stating on posters that Obos is ours (Sørgjeld, 2021).

In 2021, less than 20 percent of Obos' revenues came from housing. CEO Siraj did not think that was a problem. He was proud of all the large-scale prestige projects that he had launched. One of them was a massive construction effort to build a completely new city district. Some observers labeled it megalomania (Lundgaard and Sørgjeld, 2021).

CEO Siraj sold an entire block of apartments to an investor who was to profit from rental arrangements. This was in conflict with the basic idea of Obos to provide ownership of ordinary homes to ordinary people. The idea of home ownership is rooted in the Norwegian tradition, where very few rent their homes. However, CEO Siraj preferred to sell the block to investor Baard Schumann, with whom he had a cordial tone (Lorch-Falch and Tomter, 2021).

The primary theme regarding motive convenience was corporate gain to make Obos even more profitable, as illustrated in Figure 9.1. In many organizations, the ends justify the means (Campbell and Göritz, 2014). If the ends, in terms of ambitions and goals, are difficult to realize and achieve in normal ways, deviant means represent an alternative within many organizations (Jonnergård *et al.*, 2010). Among most executives, it is an obvious necessity to achieve goals and objectives, while it is an obvious catastrophe to fail to achieve goals and objectives. Welsh and Ordonez (2014) found that high-performance goals can cause unethical behavior. Dodge (2009: 15) argues that intense rivalry compels executives within the organization to commit wrongdoing to attain goals:

> The competitive environment generates pressures on the organization to violate the law in order to attain goals.

Individual executives would like to be successful, and they would like their workplace to be successful. Being associated with a successful business is important to the identity of many executives. They explore and

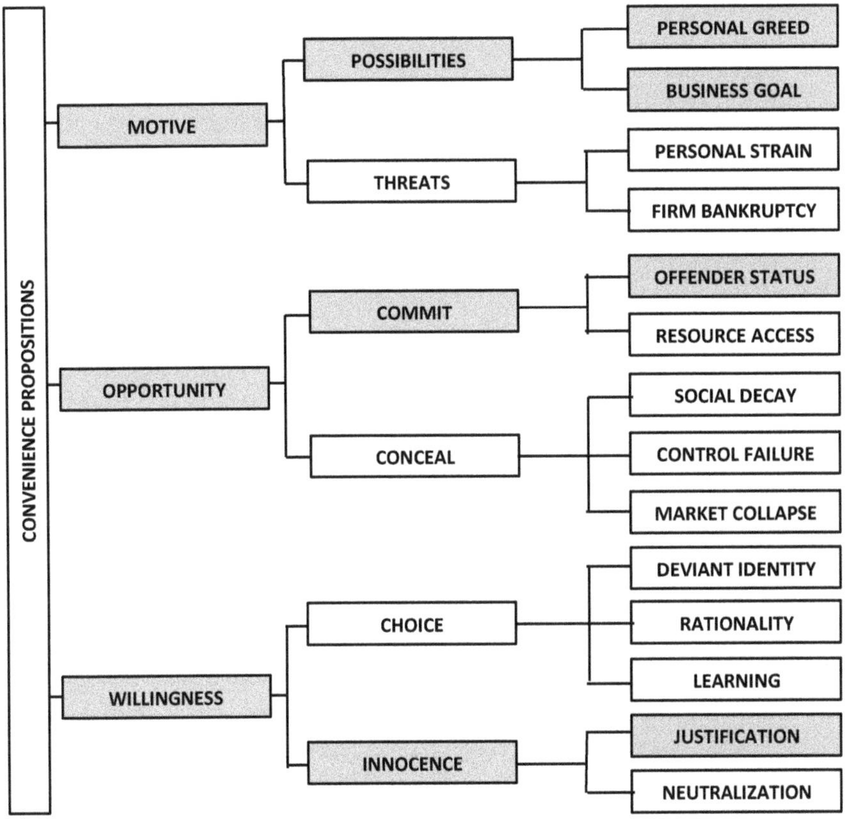

Figure 9.1. Convenience themes in the case of Obos.

exploit attractive corporate economic possibilities in both legal and illegal ways, so that their organization can emerge just as successful, or even more successful, than other organizations. Profit orientation becomes stronger in goal-oriented organizations whose aim tends to be an ambitious financial bottom line.

It seems that Siraj, at an individual level, wanted to climb in the hierarchy of needs toward fame and admiration. Maslow (1943) developed a hierarchy of human needs. The needs start at the bottom with physiological needs, the need for security, social needs, and the need for respect and self-realization. When basic needs such as food and shelter are satisfied, a person moves up the pyramid to satisfy needs for safety and control over their life situation. Further up the pyramid, the person strives for status, recognition, and self-respect. While street crime is often concerned with lower levels, white-collar crime is often concerned with upper levels in terms of status and success.

Concern for others is sometimes a motive for executive wrongdoing (Agnew, 2014). Helping others can be a self-interested, rational action that claims to express social concern (Paternoster *et al.*, 2018). In the portrait interview with Siraj, he claims concern for others through his membership in the Pentecostal congregation (Mauno, 2017). He might have satisfied his desire to help others as a social concern.

Agnew (2014) suggested that economic wrongdoing can be committed when individuals think more of others than of themselves. An entrepreneur can commit financial crimes to ensure that all employees have a job where they can return. A trusted employee can pay bribes to ensure that the company secures new orders and survives. An executive may commit embezzlement to be able to help his adult children recover after personal bankruptcy. Agnew (2014) argued that social concern consists of four elements: (1) individuals care about the welfare of others; (2) they want close ties with others; (3) they are likely to follow moral guidelines, such as innocent people should not suffer harm; and (4) they tend to seek confirmation through other people's actions and norms. That a person puts others before oneself will initially lead to less crime. However, economic crime may be committed where the welfare of others and their success is the motive.

Several executives objected to the sale of the Ulven block to the investor Schumann, who wanted to rent out apartments. One of them was chief housing officer Arne Baumann, who sees himself as a housing provider for members. But the housing director explained that he was loyal to the chief executive (Lorch-Falch and Tomter, 2021):

> Housing director Arne Baumann sees himself as someone who builds homes for the members. According to KPMG, he said that it "tears in the heart of the home builder" to sell a plot in central Oslo to external investors who will rent out. But the director of housing also explained that he was loyal to the CEO.
>
> When the agreement was entered into in May last year, Schumann was given a deadline of October 1, 2020 to put money in place. The money did not appear within the deadline. At the time, both housing director Arne Baumann and director of commercial real estate, Nils

> Bøhler, thought that Obos should turn around to sell to members. Siraj instead gave an extended deadline to get the agreement realized.

Similarly, the board did not react to Siraj's deviance, and chair Roar Engeland, in his account, expressed support for the decision, although it led to fewer homes for members (Lorch-Falch and Tomter, 2021):

> Like Siraj, he saw that the sale could provide almost one billion in cash. Money Siraj could spin to get plots for more homes that Schumann bought. However, in the short term, the sale means that there will be fewer homes for the members.

The status of CEO Siraj can explain his ignorance of negative reactions to his business model, rather than the membership model of the cooperative Obos. Status as a convenience theme in the organizational dimension is illustrated in Figure 9.1. Status is an individual's social rank within a formal or informal hierarchy or the person's relative standing along a valued social dimension. Status is the extent to which an individual is respected and admired by others, and it is the outcome of a subjective assessment process (McClean *et al.*, 2018). High-status individuals enjoy greater respect and deference from, as well as power and influence over, those positioned lower in the social hierarchy (Kakkar *et al.*, 2020: 532):

> Status is a property that rests in the eyes of others and is conferred to individuals who are deemed to have a higher rank or social standing in a pecking order based on a mutually valued set of social attributes. Higher social status or rank grants its holder a host of tangible benefits in both professional and personal domains. For instance, high-status actors are sought by groups for advice, are paid higher, receive unsolicited help, and are credited disproportionately in joint tasks. In innumerable ways, our social ecosystem consistently rewards those with high status.

Especially, individuals with high status based on prestige rather than dominance tend to be excused for whatever wrongdoing they commit. Individuals who attain and maintain high rank by behaving in ways that are assertive, controlling, and intimidating are characterized as dominant.

Individuals who attain and maintain high rank through their skills, knowledge, expertise, and willingness to share them with others are characterized as prestigious (Kakkar *et al.*, 2020).

CEO Siraj does not believe that his business model deviates from the social model (Mauno, 2017):

> — Do you ever get tired of being confronted with the glossy image of the old, social democratic project Obos – those who built apartments for ordinary people in housing need?
> — No, I'm never tired of that story. I think it's a proud story Obos has, and I still like to think that we take social responsibility by building as many homes as possible and start projects that we may not make as much money on, but that help young home buyers, says Siraj.
>
> By the way, I was called "an anti-social housing shark" in an editorial in your newspaper. I still remember that. Ha-ha-ha! He laughs.

At the annual general meeting on June 22, 2021, CEO Siraj said he was sorry, as a response to a request from member Starrfelt that he should step down from his position as chief executive (Lorch-Falch *et al.*, 2021):

> Everyone gets to express their opinions. That's how member democracy works. As a top manager, you have to endure different views on the job you do, Siraj told us before the meeting. Starrfelt took the floor and asked everyone to think about whether Siraj should continue to steer the ship. -I do not believe that the CEO has the right expertise, or the deep-seated commitment needed to renew Obos to become a strong, member-driven organization that engages, listens, and delivers, he said.

The willingness to build houses for the rich and mighty seemed based on the belief that if Obos made money on the rich and mighty, then there would be even greater funding for ordinary homes for ordinary people. In the annual report for Obos for 2020, CEO Siraj wrote that he would help young people into their own first homes by sharing space and saving money:

> Obos is more than building homes and making money. One of the biggest innovations is the brand-new home purchase model Bostart and Deleie, which open the way into the housing market for many who would otherwise be left out. An absolutely important task for Obos is the

> major social mission associated with contributing to life between the houses. NOK 567 million have been returned in the five-year period, both to members and living environments in the form of support for sports, culture, local activities, and social meeting places.

CEO Siraj justified his actions, illustrating the convenience theme along the willingness dimension. In a justification, the actor admits responsibility for the act in question while denying its pejorative and negative content. Justifications differ from denials, excuses, or admissions. In a denial, the actor either disavows that anything untoward happened or denies responsibility for whatever it is that happened. In an excuse, the actor admits that the act in question was wrong but denies full responsibility for it. In an admission, reference is made to the wrongdoer by name as having engaged in the wrongdoing.

In the student thesis by Asfaldo and Nilsson (2023), they made the following four recommendations to Obos management: admit mistakes and apologize, facilitate communication, make changes in the representative assembly, and prioritize internal work over media. The stakeholders of Obos were seeking an apology rather than a justification for the actions taken. According to Bundy and Pfarrer's (2015) definition of apology, it would be essential for Obos management to acknowledge their mistakes, express remorse, and accept responsibility for the negative consequences resulting from the situation. An apology is an act of expressing regret, remorse, or sorrow for having insulted, failed, injured, harmed, or wronged another.

The recommendation to facilitate communication stems from a rich body of scholarly works, including the contributions of Baba *et al.* (2021), Beukel and Geuns (2019), and Rooney *et al.* (2014). These sources underscore the imperative for organizations to engage in open and honest dialogue, listen attentively to stakeholders, and provide transparent and clear information. Insights gathered from the interviews by Asfaldo and Nilsson (2023) with Obos stakeholders made it evident that members desire more open and meaningful communication from the organization. Interviewees expressed a strong desire for genuine answers, active involvement in decision-making, and a transparent exchange of information.

A change in the representative assembly could lead to greater diversity. Baba *et al.* (2021) support this notion, stating that a diverse representative assembly brings forth a broad range of perspectives, experiences, and knowledge, resulting in better decision-making and smoother implementation. It is crucial to recognize the transformative power of passionate individuals within the representative assembly. Such individuals symbolize proactive engagement and serve as a driving force. As Beukel and Geuns (2019) suggest, genuine change within organizations often originates from passionate individuals who actively participate in meetings and demonstrate innovative commitment to the cooperative's values.

To prioritize internal work over media implies that the CEO should not necessarily be the front figure of the organization. Dealing with the media takes time, including photo sessions and responses to public criticism. During the interviews conducted by Asfaldo and Nilsson (2023), they encountered numerous stakeholders who expressed their discontent with the inadequate level of communication between the management and the members. The stakeholders perceived communication as one-sided, with management frequently appearing in the media without providing sufficient opportunities for members to engage in a dialogue rather than responding to journalists. There was a perception that CEO Siraj spent a considerable amount of time in the media, further exacerbating the disconnection between the organization's leadership and its stakeholders.

9.7 Assessment of Examination Maturity

Fraud examiners at KPMG (2021) concluded in their investigation report that neither executives at Obos nor the company Obos did anything wrong. They had been accused of wrongdoing by some cooperative members in the public. But investigators found no wrongdoing. One reason for their conclusion was the limited scope of their investigation. It was mainly a legal exercise to determine whether laws, rules, or guidelines were formally violated. According to the investigation report, they were not.

A broader and more relevant perspective would be the vision and mission of Obos as a provider of affordable housing for low-income residents of Oslo. Since World War II, Obos had received preferential treatment from state and municipal officials to support the social democratic movement's goal of providing all Oslo citizens with decent homes that they could own themselves. For example, when land areas were regulated for housing, Obos was an important stakeholder in the city of Oslo.

As emphasized by the critics, Siraj and his team had abandoned the basic idea of Obos as a social instrument in society. This, however, was not an issue within the mandate for the investigation. Fraud examiners were lawyers at KPMG (2021) who only looked at formal violations. While fraud examiners may not be blamed for a very limited mandate, it is nevertheless up to them to accept the assignment, reject the assignment, or request a revision of that mandate.

Based on this assessment, the investigation was assigned level 2 in the maturity model in Figure 9.2 as a problem-oriented investigation, where the problem was whether laws and regulations had been violated.

The formalism, rather than substance, is evidenced not only in the KPMG (2021) report. Before the report, two legal reviews were made public. One legal review was written by Harald Benestad Anderssen, a professor of law at BI Norwegian Business School in Oslo. Anderssen (2021: 1) wrote in his note of consideration:

> By telephone call and e-mail on April 21, 2021, I have been asked to assess the legality of certain aspects of a real estate transaction Obos has carried out at Ulven in Oslo. This document is a short version of the full report, also submitted today. This document is a short version of the full report, also submitted today. Assessments and statements in this

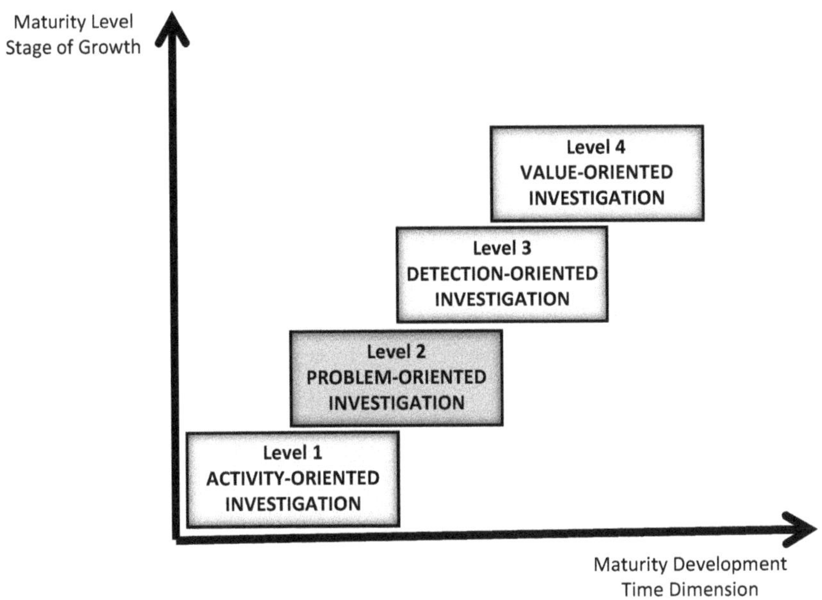

Figure 9.2. Maturity level for the KPMG (2021) investigation at Obos.

> document are short and incomplete. For the full assessments, referral is made to the complete note of consideration. My mandate is to make "a legal assessment of the legality of the transaction in relation to the statutes and the rules of the Housing Construction Act, and with a conclusion as to whether this is contrary to the statutes or not" (…) Based on the discussion above, I conclude as follows: (1) The agreement between Obos and QLR is not in conflict with the Housing Construction Act. (2) The agreement between Obos and QLR is not in conflict with Obos' statutes.

The complete note of consideration by the law professor was never made publicly available. Nevertheless, it is obvious that the assessment is limited to a narrow perspective on whether or not violations have occurred. There was no assessment of the Ulven transaction's alignment with the intentions of Obos' statutes. The other legal review by Knudsen and Arvnes (2021: 1) at KPMG was an assessment of the purpose provisions of the statutes:

> KPMG Law assists the board of Obos in connection with the investigation of allegations related to Obos' sale of a residential area on Ulven in Oslo to commercial rental business. As part of the mandate, KPMG shall "assess whether the purpose of the sale is in line with Obos' statutes and other relevant rules" (…) The sale of residential area B4 at Ulven in Oslo is in accordance with the statutory purpose of Obos.

While Knudsen and Arvnes (2021) do not find that the Ulven transaction is in line with the main purpose of Obos, they nevertheless conclude that the sale is not a violation. The primary purpose of Obos is to provide housing to its members. The transaction was contrary to the purpose by removing access to 182 apartments for members and transferring those apartments to an outside vendor of rental arrangements.

References

Agnew, R. (2014). Social concern and crime: Moving beyond the assumption of simple self-interest, *Criminology*, 52(1), 1–32.

Anderssen, H.B. (2021). *Betenkning, kortversjon (Note of Consideration, short version)*, available at www.obos.no, published May 21.

Asfaldo, D.B. and Nilsson, E.C. (2023). *Violations of the Social License to Operate: How can Management Regain the Social License?* Master of Science Thesis, BI Norwegian Business School, Oslo, Norway, July 2, 99 p.

Baba, S., Hemissi, O., Berrahou, Z. and Traiki, C. (2021). The spatiotemporal dimension of the social license to operate: The case of a landfill facility in Algeria, *Management International – Mi*, 25(4), 247–266.

Bell, E., Bryman, A. and Harley, B. (2022). *Business Research Methods*, Oxford University Press, Oxford, UK.

Berghoff, H. (2018). "Organized irresponsibility?" The Siemens corruption scandal of the 1990s and 2000s, *Business History*, 60(3), 423–445.

Beukel, J. and Geuns, L. (2019). Groningen gas: The loss of a social license to operate, *Hague Centre for Strategic Studies*, Netherlands, 22 p.

Biernacki, P. and Waldorf, D. (1981). Snowball sampling: Problems and techniques of chain referral sampling, *Sociological Methods & Research*, 10(2), 141–163.

Braun, V. and Clarke, V. (2012). Thematic analysis, in *APA Handbook of Research Methods in Psychology, Vol 2: Research designs: Quantitative, qualitative, neuropsychological, and biological*, pp. 57–71, American Psychological Association.

Brown, K., Grace, S. and Redman, S. (2025). Policing vulnerability: The care and control of sex workers through designated police officers, *British Journal of Criminology*, 65, 17–36.

Bryman, A. and Bell, E. (2022). *Business Research Methods* (5th edition), Oxford University Press, Oxford, UK.

Bundy, J. and Pfarrer, M.D. (2015). A burden of responsibility: The role of social approval at the onset of a crisis, *Academy of Management Review*, 40, 345–369.

Campbell, J.L. and Göritz, A.S. (2014). Culture corrupts! A qualitative study of organizational culture in corrupt organizations, *Journal of Business Ethics*, 120(3), 291–311.

Carnahan, S., Kryscynski, D. and Olson, D. (2017). When does corporate social responsibility reduce employee turnover? Evidence from attorneys before and after 9/11, *Academy of Management Journal*, 60(5), 1932–1962.

Chan, J., Logan, S. and Moses, L.B. (2022). Rules in information sharing for security, *Criminology & Criminal Justice*, 22(2), 304–322.

Cui, J., Jo, H. and Velasquez, M.G. (2016). Community religion, employees, and the social license to operate, *Journal of Business Ethics*, 136, 775–807.

Davidson, R.H., Dey, A. and Smith, A.J. (2019). CEO materialism and corporate social responsibility, *The Accounting Review*, 94(1), 101–126.

Davies, M.B. and Francis, P. (2018). *Researching With Interviews: A Guide for Doing Qualitative Research* (3rd edition), Routledge, London, UK.

Demuijnck, G. and Fasterling, B. (2016). The social license to operate, *Journal of Business Ethics*, 136, 675–685.

Desai, V.M. (2016). Under the radar: Regulatory collaborations and their selective use to facilitate organizational compliance, *Academy of Management Journal*, 59(2), 636–657.

Dodge, M. (2009). *Women and white-collar crime*, Prentice Hall, Saddle River, NJ.

Durand, R., Hawn, O. and Ioannou, I. (2019). Willing and able: A general model of organizational responses to normative pressures, *Academy of Management Review*, 44(2), 299–320.

Eberl, P., Geiger, D. and Assländer, M.S. (2015). Repairing trust in an organization after integrity violations. The ambivalence of organizational rule adjustments, *Organization Studies*, 36(9), 1205–1235.

Endrissat, N. and Lüthy, C. (2025). Moving with the trouble: How vulnerability and critical hope enable reckoning with complicity in entrepreneurial initiatives, *Human Relations*, published first online https://doi.org/10.1177/00187267241309792.

Fitzgibbon, W. and Lea, J. (2018). Privatization and coercion: The question of legitimacy, *Theoretical Criminology*, 22(4), 545–562.

Gardiner, S., Parry, J. and Robinson, S. (2017). Integrity and corruption debate in sport: Where is the integrity? *European Sport Management Quarterly*, 17(1), 6–23.

Gomulya, D. and Mishina, Y. (2017). Signaler credibility, signal susceptibility, and relative reliance on signals: How stakeholders change their evaluative processes after violation of expectations and rehabilitative efforts, *Academy of Management Journal*, 60(2), 554–583.

Gottschalk, P. and Benson, M.L. (2020). The evolution of corporate accounts of scandals from exposure to investigation, *British Journal of Criminology*, 60, 949–969.

Haack, P., Martignoni, D. and Schoeneborn, D. (2021). A bait-and-switch model of corporate social responsibility, *Academy of Management Review*, 46(3), 440–464.

Haines, F., Bice, S., Einfeld, C. and Sullivan, H. (2022). Countering corporate power through social control: What does a social license offer? *The British Journal of Criminology*, 62, 184–199.

Holm, E.D. (2021). Er Obos løsningen eller problemet? (Is Obos the solution or the problem?), daily Norwegian newspaper *Aftenposten*, www.aftenposten.no, published June 21.

Hurst, B., Johnston, K.A. and Lane, A.B. (2020). Engaging for a social license to operate, *Public Relations Review*, 46(4), 1–9.

Jacobsen, S. (2020). Har solgt 182 leiligheter for 936 millioner (Have sold 182 apartments for 936 million), daily Norwegian business newspaper *Finansavisen*, www.finansavisen.no, published December 3.

Jardine, M.R., Marti, E. and Durand, R. (2020). Why activist hedge funds target socially responsible firms: The reaction costs of signaling corporate social responsibility, *Academy of Management Journal*, 64(3), 851–872.
Johnsen, L.W. (2021). Obs! Obos Brenner (Attention! Obos is on fire), daily Norwegian newspaper *Dagsavisen*, www.dagsavisen.no, April 30.
Jonnergård, K., Stafsudd, A. and Elg, U. (2010). Performance evaluations as gender barriers in professional organizations: A study of auditing firms, *Gender, Work and Organization*, 17(6), 721–747.
Kakkar, H., Sivanathan, N., and Globel, M.S. (2020). Fall from grace: The role of dominance and prestige in punishment of high-status actors, *Academy of Management Journal*, 63(2), 530–553.
Kim, P.H., Dirks, K.T. and Cooper, C.D. (2009). The repair of trust: A dynamic bilateral perspective and multilevel conceptualization, *Academy of Management Review*, 34(3), 401–422.
Knudsen, T.H.R. and Arvnes, E. (2021). *Delrapport til styret i OBOS BBL, Vurdering av vedtektenes formålsbestemmelse, Sammendrag (Sub-report to the board at Obos, Assessment of the statutes' purpose regulation, Summary)*, law firm KPMG, Oslo, Norway, www.obos.no, published June 2.
Kourula, A., Moon, J., Salles-Djelic, M.L. and Wicker, C. (2019). New roles of government in the governance of business conduct: Implications for management and organizational research, *Organization Studies*, 40(8), 1101–1123.
KPMG (2021). *Ulven-transaksjonen – Granskingsrapport til styret i Obos (The Ulven transaction – Investigation report to the board at Obos)*, law firm KPMG, Oslo, Norway, 34 p.
Larsen, B.E. (2021). Noen betraktninger før Obos' generalforsamling 2021 (Some considerations before Obos' general assembly 2021), *Benjamin E. Larsen's blog*, www.benjaminlarsen.net, posted June 19.
Lorch-Falch, S. and Tomter, L. (2021). Slaget om Obos (The battle of Obos), public Norwegian broadcasting corporation *NRK*, www.nrk.no, published June 22.
Lorch-Falch, S., Tomter, L. and Engebretsen, D.K. (2021). Obos-opprøret tapte kamp om maktseter (The Obos uprising lost the battle for seats), Norwegian public broadcasting *NRK*, www.nrk.no, published June 22.
Loyens, K., Claringbould, I., Heres-van Rossem, L. and Eekeren, Frank van. (2022). The social construction of integrity: A qualitative case study in Dutch football, *Sports in Society*, 25(9), 1714–1733.
Lundgaard, H. and Sørgjeld, C. (2021). Milliardene renner inn i Obos-kassen. Men mer enn 80 prosent kommer ikke fra boligbygging (The billions are floating into the Obos cash register. But more than 80 percent do not come from housing construction), daily Norwegian newspaper *Aftenposten*, www.aftenposten.no, published June 21.

Maslow, A.H. (1943). A theory of human motivation, *Psychological Review*, 50(4), 370–396.

Mauno, H. (2017). Han er pinsevenn og BMW-eier. Men ikke si at han er fra Flekkefjord (He is a Pentecostal friend and BMW owner. But do not say that he is from Flekkefjord), daily Norwegian newspaper *Dagsavisen*, www.dagsavisen.no, published June 25.

McClean, E.J., Martin, S.R., Emich, K.J. and Woodruff, T. (2018). The social consequences of voice: An examination of voice type and gender on status and subsequent leader emergence, *Academy of Management Journal*, 61(5), 1869–1891.

Melé, D. and Armengou, J. (2016). Moral legitimacy in controversial projects and its relationships with social license to operate: A case study, *Journal of Business Ethics*, 136, 729–742.

Meyer, J.W. and Rowan, B. (1977). Institutionalized organizations: Formal structure as myth and ceremony, *American Journal of Sociology*, 83, 340–363.

Morrison, J. (2014). *The Social License to Operate. How to Keep Your Organization Legitimate*, Palgrave MacMillan, New York, NY.

Nardi, L. (2022). The corporate social responsibility price premium as an enabler of substantive CSR, *Academy of Management Review*, 47(2), 282–308.

Panda, S.S. and Sangle, S. (2019). An exploratory study to investigate the relationship between social license to operate and sustainable development strategies, *Sustainable Development*, 27, 1085–1095.

Paternoster, R., Jaynes, C.M. and Wilson, T. (2018). Rational choice theory and interest in the "fortune of others", *Journal of Research in Crime and Delinquency*, 54(6), 847–868.

Rooney, D., Leach, J. and Ashworth, P. (2014). Doing the social in social license, *Social Epistemology*, 28(3–4), 209–218.

Saenz, C. (2019). Building legitimacy and trust between a mining company and a community to earn social license to operate: A Peruvian case study, *Corporate Social Responsibility and Environmental Management*, 26(2), 296–306.

Sajko, M., Boone, C., and Buyl, T. (2021). CEO greed, corporate social responsibility, and organizational resilience to systemic shocks, *Journal of Management*, 47(4), 957–992.

Sale, H.A. (2021). The corporate purpose of social license, *Sothern California Law Review*, 94(4), 785–842.

Sanger, S.W., Duke, E.A., James, D.M. and Hernandez, E. (2017). *Independent Directors of the Board of Wells Fargo & Company: Sales Practices Investigation Report*, April 10, 113 p., https://www08.wellsfargomedia.com/assets/pdf/about/investor-relations/presentations/2017/board-report.pdf, downloaded September 7, 2018.

Skjerven, A. (2023). Dette er Oslos nye skamplett (This is Oslo's new disgrace), daily Norwegian newspaper *Aftenposten*, www.aftenposten.no, published January 6.

Sorour, M.K., Boadu, M. and Soobaroyen, T. (2021). The role of corporate social responsibility in organizational identity communication, co-creation and orientation, *Journal of Business Ethics*, 173, 89–108.

Stang, F. (2021). Obos saboterer sitt eget samfunnsoppdrag (Obos sabotages its own social mission), daily Norwegian newspaper *Aftenposten*, www.aftenposten.no, published June 21.

Stephansen, E. (2021). Nei, Obos – smarte tanker er ikke det samme som smarte triks (No, Obos – smart thoughts are not the same as smart tricks), web-based Norwegian newspaper *Nettavisen*, www.nettavisen.no, published May 3.

Sørgjeld, C. (2021). På utsiden demonstrerte Obos-opprøret. På innsiden ble de nedstemt (On the outside, the Obos demonstration revolted. On the inside, they were voted down), daily Norwegian newspaper *Aftenposten*, www.aftenposten.no, published June 22.

Thomson, L. and Boutilier, R.G. (2011). *Modeling and Measuring the Social License to Operate: Fruits of a Dialogue between Theory and Practice*, published at www.sociallicense.com.

Uygur, S.A. and Napier, C.J. (2023). Understanding fraud in the not-for-profit sector: A stakeholder perspective for charities, *Journal of Business Ethics*, published first online https://doi.org/10.1007/s10551-023-05373-5.

Welsh, D.T. and Ordonez, L.D. (2014). The dark side of consecutive high-performance goals: Linking goal setting, depletion, and unethical behavior, *Organizational Behavior and Human Decision Processes*, 123, 79–89.

Chapter 10

JFC Research Articles

When conducting this review of recently published articles in the *Journal of Financial Crime* (JFC) in 2024, it was found that the journal had published four issues with 69 research articles so far in that year. While only 12 articles focused on the motives of possibilities and threats, and only 6 articles focused on attitudes of deviant willingness, surprisingly many – 51 articles – focused on the opportunity structure of committing and concealing financial crime. This review is relevant, as it may illuminate both the important and unimportant aspects of understanding financial crime and explore propositions in convenience theory that warrant attention in future research, considering the convenience triangle's suggestions of motives, opportunities, and attitudes for financial criminals.

The theory of convenience for financial crime suggests that offenders have motives of possibilities and threats, opportunities to commit and conceal crime, and attitudes of willingness for deviant behavior driven by choice and innocence. Convenience theory suggests fourteen propositions regarding motives, opportunities, and attitudes. In this chapter, research articles from the JFC are reviewed from the perspective of convenience theory. Specifically, the chapter addresses the following research questions: **What propositions in convenience theory are supported by published articles in the journal? What aspects of crime convenience seem to be missing so far in research articles published in the journal?**

This chapter explores the extent of support found so far for the various propositions in articles published in the JFC from the beginning of 2024 until the month of August. The review is additionally relevant to adding substance to the theory of convenience, which emerged less than a decade ago and has since been developed and applied by various scholars. The review is also interesting from the perspective of understanding which aspects of crime convenience are implicitly and explicitly addressed in financial criminology research – specifically, whether motives, opportunities, or attitudes are primarily addressed in current economic crime research. Furthermore, the review responds to Lord and Levi's (2023: 1) call for "research into the nature, organization and control of serious crimes for economic gain [that] ought to begin from the perspective of how we can create integrative, collaborative or multi-dimensional accounts of these behaviors in order to better organize, and identify, the most plausible explanations and interventions". In this review, the response to the call takes the form of organizing research articles published in the journal into the dimensions of offender motives, opportunities, and attitudes, rather than the opposite approach of organizing conceptually for new theorizing based on the articles.

This chapter begins with a description of convenience theory, followed by a description of the research method for reviewing journal articles. More substance is added to convenience theory when presenting the reviewed journal articles along the model structure, as illustrated in Figure 10.1.

10.1 The Crime Convenience Triangle

The traditional fraud triangle consists of pressures, opportunities, and rationalizations (Cressey, 1972; Wells, 1997). Similarly, the convenience triangle consists of motives, opportunities, and attitudes (Braaten and Vaughn, 2021; Chan and Gibbs, 2022; Gottschalk, 2025; Lee, 2025). However, there are three distinct differences. First, convenience is a relative concept, indicating that offenders have the option of alternative actions to achieve their goals that do not represent illegitimate behavior. While the fraud triangle suggests that opportunities stimulate crime, the convenience triangle suggests that relative convenience in terms of time and effort, as well as strain and pain, will stimulate crime. Second, it is primarily in professional settings, where offenders have access to resources, that opportunity arises to commit and conceal crime. Third, an offender can influence the opportunity structure over time. Therefore, opportunity in convenience theory is a dynamic rather than a static condition. The convenience triangle suggests that motives, opportunities, and attitudes can reinforce each other to commit and conceal crime.

Possibilities and threats can be motives for individuals and units where greed is typical at the individual level (Sajko *et al.*, 2021) and goals are typical at the unit level of a group or organization (Welsh and Ordonez, 2014) for possibilities, while strain is typical at the individual level (Thaxton and Agnew, 2018) and failure is typical at the unit level (Pontell *et al.*, 2014) for threats, as illustrated in Figure 10.1.

The opportunity structure for economic crime consists of committing and concealing wrongdoing. The convenience of committing crime is based on the offender's status and resource access. Status is an individual's social rank within a formal or informal hierarchy or the person's

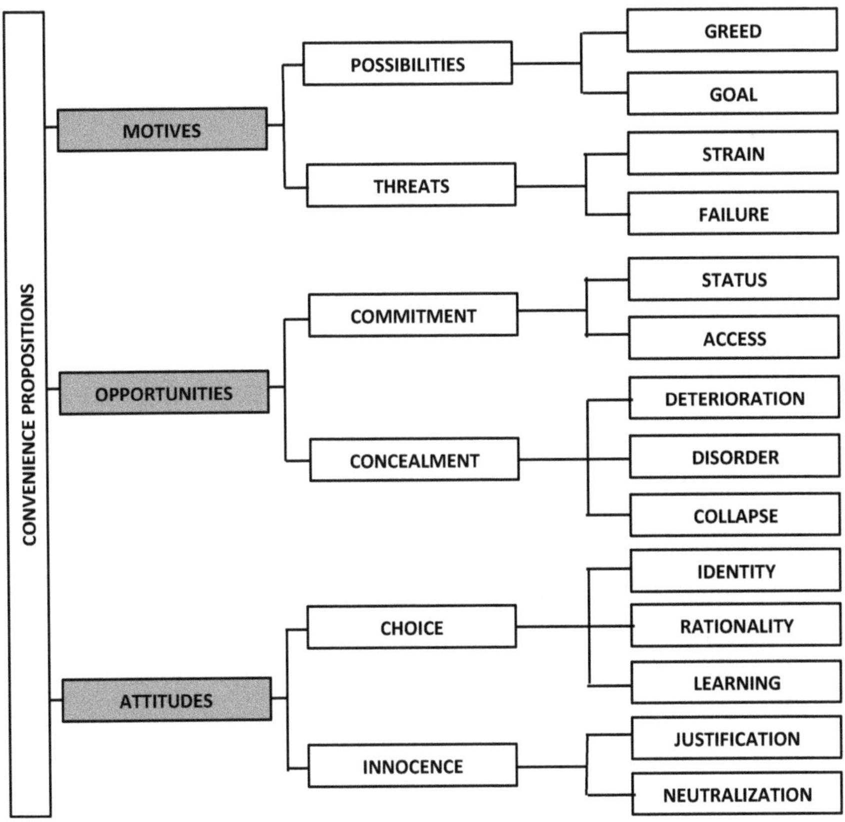

Figure 10.1 Structural model of convenience theory.

relative standing along a valued social dimension (Kakkar *et al.*, 2020). Status is the extent to which an individual is respected and admired by others, and status is the outcome of a subjective assessment process (McClean *et al.*, 2018). A resource is an enabler applied and used to satisfy human and organizational needs that the offender has access to (Huang and Knight, 2017; Williams *et al.*, 2019). The convenience of concealing crime is based on social deterioration (Karimi-Ghartemani *et al.*, 2022), a lack of guardianship, oversight, and control that causes disorder (Uygur and Napier, 2023), and criminal market forces, such as competition-avoiding cartels, leading to eventual business collapse (Goncharov and Peter, 2019; Huric-Larsen, 2023).

The willingness attitude is based on choice and innocence. Choice can derive from deviant identities (Crank, 2018), such as narcissistic identification with the unit (Galvin *et al.*, 2015). Choice can also derive from rationality, which is all about weighing up the pros and cons, as well as the advantages and disadvantages, of alternative courses of action in terms of incentives and disincentives for offending (McGloin *et al.*, 2021). Learning is the final choice proposition in Figure 9.1, where learning refers to differential association – suggesting that whether individuals engage in crime is largely based on their socialization, where they associate with those who agree with them and distance themselves from those who disagree (Hoffmann, 2002; Sutherland, 1983).

The perception of innocence is based on justification and neutralization. In a justification, the actor admits responsibility for the act in question while denying its pejorative and negative content (Schoen *et al.*, 2021: 730):

> People use justification mechanisms to protect their sense of self. People who sincerely believe that they are a specific kind of person but routinely demonstrate behaviors that indicate otherwise may avoid cognitive dissonance and maintain their sense of self by using justification mechanisms that allow them to "explain away" their behavior.

Silver and Garofalo (2024: 3) discussed the difference between an excuse and a justification:

> When confronting someone for acting wrongly, they may defend themselves by offering either a justification or an excuse. Scholars have

> disagreed about exactly how to capture this distinction both in the law and in morality, but a plausible and common way of understanding the distinction in the moral context is to say that an agent who is justified in performing some action has not acted wrongly, and an agent who is excused has acted wrongly but should not be blamed or punished.

Neutralization is similar to rationalization: a matter of denying guilt by application of various neutralization techniques (Sykes and Matza, 1957). Offenders deny responsibility, injury, and victimization. They condemn the condemners. They claim appeals to higher loyalties and the normality of action. They claim entitlement and argue the case of legal error. They find their own mistakes acceptable. They argue that a dilemma arose, resulting in a reasonable trade-off before committing the act (Jordanoska, 2018; Kaptein and Helvoort, 2019; Siponen and Vance, 2010). Such claims enable offenders to find crime convenient since they do not consider it criminal, and they do not feel guilty of wrongdoing (Cullen *et al.*, 2022).

10.2 Research Method for Reviewing Articles

Six volumes of the JFC are published annually. This review was conducted in August 2024, when the journal had published four issues containing 69 research articles that year. The sample is considered large enough to review focal concerns. The choice of the most recent research articles published in the JFC was made to identify the topics primarily covered recently.

Content analysis through archival study is the research method applied in this review. The search focused on potential motives, opportunities, and attitudes related to deviance as described in each research article. From each journal article, the theme that seemed to dominate was recorded and reported in the following. The reporting is visualized using bold font for each identified author and also bold font in the list of references.

Content analysis is a research method used to identify characteristics within texts attempting to make valid inferences (Braaten and Vaughn, 2021). Content analysis assumes that language reflects both how people understand their surroundings and their cognitive processes (Hsieh and Shannon, 2005). Cognition refers to what people think and how they think, as well as how cognitive processes affect the way in which people interpret and make sense of what is around them. Therefore, content analysis makes it possible to identify and determine relevant text within a context (McClelland *et al.*, 2010).

The presentation of research results follows the structural model of convenience theory, as illustrated in Figure 10.1, which lists 14 propositions. For some of the propositions, many articles in the JFC were found. For other propositions, no evidence of the convenience theme was found in journal articles.

10.3 Research Result: Crime Motives

Personal Greed by Individual Offenders
No evidence of this convenience proposition was found in the JFC articles.

Organizational Goal by Corporate Offenders
Corruption may improve business performance, according to the "grease the wheels" hypothesis (**Amoh** *et al.*, 2024; **Hope**, 2024; **Kalaj and Golemi**, 2024). Corruption can compensate for poorly functioning enterprises and for a variety of aspects of dysfunction in public and private organizations. The hypothesis implies that dishonesty is beneficial to business performance (**Adam** *et al.*, 2024: 782): "Firms consider paying bribes to state institutions or officials when the payment benefits their performance and growth, and when not paid, firms will lose capital and resources". Similarly, **Putra and Sihombing** (2024: 828) argued that "countries with weak legal systems and poor institutional governance will enhance the performance of corrupt public officials". However, at the national level, **Danlami** (2024: 922) found positive causality between control of corruption and economic growth, and vice versa:

> The result reveals the existence of bidirectional causality between control of corruption and economic growth. Similarly, in both the short run and long run, corruption can affect economic growth and economic growth can as well affect corruption.

Also at the national level, and again adopting a positive perspective on corruption, **Magableh** *et al.* (2024: 177) found that "corruption may be the glue that holds a country together, reducing the likelihood of conflict and thereby advancing economic growth".

Personal Strain by Individual Offenders

Perceptions of inequality and a lack of equity can create personal strain for individuals. Inequality refers to the situation where everyone is not given the same resources and opportunities, while a lack of equity means that resources are not distributed based on the needs of the recipients. As argued by **Gupta** *et al.* (2024: 856), "restoring the perception of equity and equality might (also) be a matter of responding to dehumanization, which is a feeling of being a tool or an instrument based on a perception of a treatment as lesser than or different from others".

Strain is linked to anomie, which refers to a sense of confusion without moral guidance (Benson and Simpson, 2018). Anomie is the lack of social or ethical norms, which places a strain on individuals. To the extent rules exist, anomie means a low commitment to those rules where the guiding power of normative standards is undermined (Schoepfer and Piquero, 2006). Instead, as individuals assume positions of power, influence, and trust, their participation in financial crime will increase. The foundational values of the American dream – achievement, individualism, universalism, and the importance of money – create pressure to achieve material success at the expense of a commitment to social and ethical norms (Benson *et al.*, 2021). Similarly, **Maulidiyah** (2024: 885) argued that "the tendency of individuals to commit crimes or fraud can increase when anomie conditions occur", where "individualism is negatively associated with financial crime".

Pressure as a determinant of financial crime by individuals in business organizations to benefit their corporations was emphasized by **Owusu** *et al.* (2024: 632), who noted that "individuals under such pressure tend to seek interim solutions to their problems, which include engaging in fraudulent activities as a possible option". A variety of pressures, or strains, increase the likelihood of engaging in crime (Holtfreter, 2015).

Generally, the strain perspective emphasizes strains and stressors that increase the likelihood of crime, the negative emotions (including anger) resulting from those strains that create pressure for corrective action, and the factors that influence or condition the likelihood of criminal coping (Thaxton and Agnew, 2018). Stress is a psychological state that arises from a mismatch between perceived demands and one's ability to meet those demands, given available resources (Linder *et al.*, 2021).

Organizational Failure by Corporate Offenders

Rahman and Jie (2024: 106) suggested that "a company with a high debt-to-asset ratio likely falsifies its financial statements", "a company with a low liquidity ratio likely falsifies its financial statements", "the lower the return on equity, the more likely that a company falsifies its financial statements", and "firms that are not audited by a big accounting firm have a high likelihood of fraud in their financial statements". "The different motives of companies cause different types of accounting fraud" (**Rahman** *et al.*, 2024: 558).

10.4 Research Result: Crime Opportunities

High-Status Offender

The opportunity structure for an offender consists of both committing wrongdoing and concealing it. According to the theory of convenience, high status and resource access enable wrongdoing within an organizational setting. Status is an individual's rank within a formal or informal hierarchy. "Status is a property that rests in the eyes of others and is conferred to individuals who are deemed to have a higher rank or social standing in a pecking order based on a mutually valued set of social attributes" (Kakkar *et al.*, 2020: 532). High-status offenders, such as top executives, may, for example, "modify the financial statements to deceive investors into investing in the company with false data and information" (**Xuan** *et al.*, 2024: 558) in their "financial statements fraud" (**Ahmadi** *et al.*, 2024) that "results in the greatest monetary loss" (**Toit**, 2024: 311).

High status may enable access to money mules who "permit the use of their own banking account as intermediary to launder ill-gotten funds at the behest of the criminal" where "the dirty funds are acquired from illegal activities which could trigger an alarm to the authority if they are directly siphoned into the criminal accounts" (**Rani** *et al.*, 2024: 347). An example of a money mule is an attorney who uses the attorney-client privilege of secrecy to help clients transfer money through law firm accounts (Gottschalk and Hamerton, 2023).

Legitimate Resource Access

Privileged offenders have legitimate access to resources such as lawyers, accountants, and other financial intermediaries to commit and conceal financial crimes. As exemplified by Chan and Gibbs (2022: 321) in their article "When guardians become offenders", some of these professionals change their roles from guardians to offenders, where "top management directly charged with implementing guardianship procedures and protocols were able to leverage their positions/roles to circumvent controls as they acquire motivation to offend". Similarly, **Goldbarsht and Benson** (2024) exemplified avoidance of compliance by means of experts in the legal profession in money laundering activities, while **Ordower** (2024) exemplified tax evasion by the help of tax advisors in tax planning, and **Kemsley** *et al.* (2024) exemplified tax evasion by not reporting income from overseas.

Some offenders have legitimate access to financial transaction systems, such as digital peer-to-peer (P2P) lending platforms, which facilitate money laundering. As argued by **Teichmann** *et al.* (2024c: 994), "these platforms have also attracted the interest of financial criminals who want to exploit anti-money laundering (AML) vulnerabilities to launder and finance terrorist activities through P2P lending platforms. Similarly, some offenders have legitimate access to arbitration by arbitrators where "the arbitration procedure is misused to launder illicit assets" (**Teichmann** *et al.*, 2024b: 760), and yet other offenders have access to resources to hide their real identities (**Pavlidis**, 2024). Furthermore, "because the FinTech sector as a whole moves quickly, lenders have little time to carefully consider the applications of their clients, which makes it easier for fraudsters to carry out their crimes" (**Saluja**, 2024: 155).

Given the high social offender status and legitimate access to resources, "the white collar criminal tries to make his actions appear legal, even in the assumption of discovering the crime and arrest by forging documents and recording, hiding, using financial experts and well-known and influential lawyers in the judiciary" (**Kamaei** *et al.*, 2024: 252).

Singh (2024: 260) claimed that "London is the preferred Laundromat for Russian ill-gotten gains, and therefore, financial institutions are seen to be particularly vulnerable". Access to financial institutions to launder money from crime by Russian oligarchs and organized criminals also serves the purpose of circumventing and evading sanctions (Montenarh and Marsden, 2024).

An example of a resource is access to a trust, as discussed by **Dubber** *et al.* (2024). Trusts can be used to conceal and protect assets. During insolvency proceedings, assets can remain hidden in trusts. Transferring assets to defraud creditors during insolvency is a form of fraud known as asset concealment. By transferring values to the trust, the offender isolates the property of trust from personal or organizational assets, thereby protecting the property from external parties.

Social Deterioration

When a financial criminal is detected and brought to justice, the proceeds of the offense should be recovered to ensure the criminal does not benefit from the offender after release from prison. However, law enforcement in many jurisdictions is often reluctant to invest resources in asset recovery efforts resulting from crime. Therefore, an element of convenience is the social deterioration in society due to criminals not having to "pay back the money" because of failures in "asset forfeiture" in society (**Curlewis**, 2024: 772). Also, **Tan** (2024: 864) addressed asset recovery by stating that "the indictment of corrupt officials raises an interesting question as to how authorities can recover the assets (e.g., monies and property) stolen by such officials". As an example of institutional failure, Körtl and Chbib (2024: 1) found that "illicit enrichment in Germany" is still possible since their "evaluation of the reformed asset recovery regime's ability to confiscate proceeds of crime" highlighted several shortcomings. Crime convenience increases at low-level political institutions that are characterized by weak democratic institutions, high government bureaucracy, and a dependent judiciary (**Tee and Teoh**, 2024: 44).

Another element of convenience when committing financial crimes is that individuals who notice the wrongdoing do not report it. They remain bystanders. Bystanders are conformers who are passive (Thoroughgood *et al.*, 2012). A bystander is a person present at a situation or event but not involved. They observe deviance but are reluctant to intervene. A bystander has the choice to speak up but decides to do nothing (Fulbrook, 2023). The research by **Garg and Aggarwal** (2024: 908) supports the idea that failing to report when handling counterfeit currency is common: "The result shows that in approximately 38% of cases, bank staff returns the fake notes to the customer without reporting, and approximately 57%–58% are unaware of the fake currency notes". Generally, as argued by **Menz** (2024: 302), "it is best to say nothing at all" when there is suspicious activity in the financial services sector.

During the COVID-19 pandemic, social deterioration occurred when offenders disrupted the public distribution of palliatives that relieved symptoms and treated the disease. Offenders profited through corruption, with those paying the most for the medicine, rather than those most in need, receiving the palliative care. The purpose of **Olujobi and Yebisi's** (2024: 490) study was to "examine the corruption prevalent in the distribution of COVID-19 palliatives during the lockdown and movement restrictions in the country". They found that "corruption, bribery and diversion of these palliatives tainted the distribution process".

Credit card fraudsters benefit from the convenience of credit card companies' reluctance to investigate reports from cardholders. Credit card companies deny responsibility because they were "refusing to conduct an investigation" and they "passed on the responsibility of proving fraud to the complainant by asking the complainant to present third-party evidence (such as receipts or testimony from a vendor) that the transaction was not authorized by the cardholder" (**Estelami and Liu**, 2024: 623).

Social deterioration can occur within the criminal justice system. For example, when the defense lawyer is successful in absolving the guilty accused of criminal responsibility, "the accused is acquitted by the court" (**Agbor**, 2024: 434).

Lack of Guardianship

To stimulate global trade, governments introduced "free trade liberalization across countries" (**Beebeejaun**, 2024a: 362) and "gave an impetus to the growth of offshore finance" (**Scott**, 2024: 548):

> These policies focused on liberalizing global trade, deregulating global economies and privatizing state-owned assets. They emphasized fiscal competition between nation-states for business investment and did not prioritize information-sharing arrangements to facilitate revenue collection and tax enforcement.

There are hindrances and obstructions to controlling activities that contribute to the convenience of concealing crime. **Nortje and Myburgh** (2024: 810) discussed "impediments during the execution of a search and seizure warrant for digital information by forensic investigators in South Africa". For example, if investigators find information on computers that does not relate to the initial purpose of the search, they are not allowed to access or use that information. Also, the more a search intrudes on a person's privacy, the more restrictive the guidelines for investigators.

Lack of regulation prevents guardianship against cyber fraud in the banking industry (**Akinbowale** *et al.*, 2024b, 2024c) and *et al.* against fraud in the capital markets (**Nwatu** *et al.*, 2024), while Mahadew (2024) reported a lack of corporate criminal liability. Lack of regulation makes compliance irrelevant since compliance is a matter of being consistent with regulations (**Teichmann and Wittmann**, 2024a). Regulatory rollback schemes improve the convenience of convicting crime, for example, the rollback scheme promoted in the United States by the Trump administration (Friedrichs and Rothe, 2020). Lack of regulation was also exemplified by **Sudarwanto** *et al.* (2024) when discussing Islamic crowdfunding and Shariah compliance in countries such as Indonesia and Malaysia. **Feridun** (2024) found that financial crime is particularly convenient within jurisdictions characterized by evasion of regulation, political instability, and regulatory ambiguity. Adding to the lack of regulation is sometimes "the lack of adequate legal responsibility" for combatting financial crime (**Bondarenko and Utkina**, 2024: 63).

The lack of regulation for cryptocurrency makes it convenient to use this currency for various frauds, such as Ponzi schemes, since "the digital age has provided fraudsters with an opportunity to 'reheat an old scheme with a new sauce'" (**Heyman**, 2024: 711). The use of digital currencies in financial crime expands "due to factors such as anonymity, low cost and low barriers to entry" (**Smith and Tiwari**, 2024: 237). See (2024: 416) argued that "there remains a gap for criminals to launder money through Bitcoin mixing services as known methods would unlikely be able to trace a tainted transaction that goes through a decentralized mixer that uses off-chain communication techniques to coordinate the mixing and charges randomized mixing fees". In the virtual world, sometimes labeled the "metaverse", "users can interact with each other and engage in various activities, such as socializing, gaming and commerce" (**Pandey and Gilmour**, 2024: 211). Generally, in cyberspace, , which refers to "the universe beyond the physical and real world", "the emergence of the metaverse ecosystem brings various risks related to legislation, property, control, fraud, private threats, ethics, accountability and security issues inherent in any transaction in the metaverse environment" (**Smaili and**

Rancourt-Raymond, 2024: 192), representing a convenient opportunity structure for financial criminals.

Organizations attempt to mitigate cyber fraud by various anti-fraud technologies such as "filtering software, firewalls, continuous auditing, virus protection software, encryption, digital analysis, financial ratios, data mining and discovery sample", yet "cyber fraud incidents were still reported" (**Akinbowale** *et al.*, 2024a: 222), thereby raising questions about whether antifraud technologies work as intended or whether the convenience for offenders remains unchanged.

Trust is an important contributor to the convenience of economic crime. Trust is the intention to accept (Sala and Pratt, 2023) or the actual acceptance of vulnerability to another's actions (Baer *et al.*, 2021). Trust sometimes replaces guardianship when trust involves making oneself vulnerable to another's behavior. A typical example is romance fraud (**Kassem and Carter**, 2024: 976):

> While trust is crucial to all fraudulent schemes, in romance fraud, "relationships are established explicitly by perpetrators to defraud the victim. Romance fraudsters use the façade of the romantic relationship to cultivate trust and rapport with victims, allowing them to manipulate their targets into sending money. They take advantage of the victims' genuine quest for a romantic relationship to deceive their victims through false pretense, impersonation, counterfeiting, forgery, and other fraudulent representations of facts.

Another example of a trust violation is investors trusting fraudulent stockbrokers (**Kandukuri**, 2024: 1037): "Stockbrokers' frauds in India frequently occur, causing investors significant financial loss", where "investors who invest in the stock market repose confidence and trust in the stockbrokers and make investment decisions based on their advice". The study found that fraudulent stockbrokers abuse clients' money to raise funds for their own self-interests. A third example of trust violation is "cyber financial scams", which "aim to steal sensitive information like usernames, passwords and credit card details by masquerading as trustworthy entities" (**Ridho**, 2024: 749). **Nguyen** *et al.* (2024: 160) found that "trust has a positive impact on Vietnamese people's fraud susceptibility to cryptocurrency Ponzi schemes", where "the trust factors are strictly related to the subjective norm of the theory of planned behavior which is understood as the impact of an important person or group of people on individuals' motivation and behavior in society".

An example of guardianship avoidance in financial transactions is crowdfunding, which makes money laundering more convenient (**Teichmann** *et al.*, 2024a: 575):

> Crowdfunding is a method of funding usually via the internet, allowing individual founders of for-profit projects to solicit funding from multiple people, often in exchange for future products or actions. Online crowd-funding platforms (CFPs) facilitate the exchange of money, services or goods between funders and fundraisers.

Crowdfunding was also addressed by **Beebeejaun** (2024b) as a convenient enabler of tax evasion and money laundering since "it will be difficult for the tax authority of a particular jurisdiction to assess if the money lent through the crowdfunding platform has been declared initially and if any revenue stream from this platform has been properly disclosed for tax purposes".

People who are financially stressed may lack relevant guardianship against fraud and thus become convenient targets for offenders. Financial stress refers to a person's unpleasant feeling of not being able to meet financial obligations. **Kasim** *et al.* (2024) found that such persons might become convenient targets for investment scams, where victims are promised considerable returns on their investments.

The work of accountants and auditors is intended to function as control mechanisms against financial crime. However, when such control agents do not take personal responsibility for preventing and detecting wrongdoing, the control lacks efficiency. "Personal responsibility represents the cognitive process that assumes the complaint as a behavior" that "stems from the individual's prescribed responsibility for reporting a suspicious act" (**Sallaberry *et al.*,** 2024: 671). Even more convenient is the situation for an offender when auditors slide over to the wrong side of the law. For example, Mohliver (2019: 310) found that some auditors prioritize their clients' interests over their legal obligations by recommending client malfeasance, for example, in terms of illegal stock option backdating. Combined with disintegrated or lacking governance within the organization, risk mismanagement and failing audits increase the convenience of financial crime (**Siahaan** *et al.*, 2024).

Lack of control mechanisms was exemplified by **Putri** *et al.* (2024: 466) regarding village governance in Indonesia, where they identified "weak internal control implementation", "absence of accounting standards and conflicts among current governance regulations", and "poor information technology development".

The reluctance of whistleblowers to blow the whistle and report observations of wrongdoing contributes to the lack of guardianship, oversight, and control. As argued by Keil *et al.* (2010), perceived costs tend to exceed perceived benefits for individual whistleblowers. In addition, as argued by Bussmann *et al.* (2018), employees in societies characterized by collectivist values are reluctant to blow the whistle on others. An example of reported high collectivism was presented by **Prabowo** (2024: 1) for Indonesia, where "multiple cultural and behavioral factors have created and shaped an environment where fraudsters can exploit people's behavioral loopholes for their fraudulent schemes".

The lack of whistleblowing in Europe has been explained by governments' refusal "to proactively recruit whistleblowers" as compared to the United States (**Karpacheva and Hock**, 2024: 9).

Criminal Market Collapse

Sanctions and blacklisting create criminal market structures that make illicit financial flows more convenient (Gottschalk, 2024; Mgadmi *et al.*, 2023; Montenarh and Marsden, 2024). As argued by **Yeo** *et al.* (2024) when studying blacklisted developing countries, "rather than altering illicit inflows in blacklisted countries, financial restrictions have produced the inverse, causing a boomerang effect on financial crime activities".

10.5 Research Result: Willingness Attitudes

Deviant Personal Identity

Machiavellian personality "is associated with manipulation, cynicism, and amorality" (Karandikar and Jones, 2023: 1). "Machiavelli asserted that wise leaders want to be liked and feared by people" (Dion, 2020: 1032). Machiavellian individuals might commit complex kinds of financial crime, such as antitrust violations (Karandikar and Jones, 2023). "Machiavellian personality leads to unethical behavior carried out based on self-interest, using deception and manipulation to achieve goals" (**Wijayanti** *et al.*, 2024: 120).

Rational Choice of Crime

"Offender-search theory assumes that criminals are at least somewhat rational and select targets based on the perceived reward, risk and effort involved compared to perceived available alternatives" (**Vanhee and McNealey**, 2024: 595). The economic model of rational self-interest is all about weighing up the pros and cons of alternative courses of action in terms of incentives and disincentives for, as well as advantages and disadvantages of, offending (McGloin *et al.*, 2021). An advantage is the low probability of detection and the low punishment costs associated with it (**Chaiwat and Yomnak**, 2024; Gottschalk and Gunnesdal, 2018) since financial crime is generally not considered as serious as physical crime (Alcadipani and Medeiros, 2020). Guebert *et al.* (2024: 131) found that the media tend to present crime as "intelligible", that is, understandable, and thus somehow defendable.

Learning by Association

Learning refers to differential association, suggesting that whether individuals engage in crime is largely based on their socialization, where they might associate with peers and others who share deviant behaviors, while simultaneously distancing themselves from those who disagree (Hoffmann, 2002; Sutherland, 1983; Velásquez-Giraldo *et al.*, 2023). "Humans have a cognitive tendency to follow the behavior of others", especially when confronted by an uncertain situation (**Teichmann and Wittmann**, 2024b: 408).

Innocence from Justification

In a justification, the actor admits responsibility for the act in question while denying its pejorative and negative content (Schoen *et al.*, 2021: 730):

> People use justification mechanisms to protect their sense of self. People who sincerely believe that they are a specific kind of person but routinely demonstrate behaviors that indicate otherwise may avoid cognitive dissonance and maintain their sense of self by using justification mechanisms that allow them to "explain away" their behavior.

The convenience of committing financial crimes is dependent on perceptions of seriousness (Simpson *et al.*, 2023). When committing financial crime is considered understandable (**Gottschalk and Kamaei**, 2024) and perceived as irresponsibility rather than misconduct or crime (Alcadipani and Medeiros, 2020), the feeling of guilt is reduced and may be eliminated among offenders when justification is provided.

Innocence from Neutralization

A neutralization technique applied by some offenders is claiming the normalcy of their actions – everyone else does and would do the same. The offender argues that it is so common to commit the offense, so that one can hardly define it as an offense at all. The offense is no deviant behavior since most people do it or would do it in the same situation. The offender might even suggest that what may constitute deviant behavior is when people in the same situation obey the law. The claim of normality depends on the perceived frequency of crime. When **Asomah** *et al.* (2024: 524) asked different groups about their corruption perceptions in Canada, they got varying answers:

> First, people accessing corruption news from the traditional news media are less likely than those receiving information from the new media to perceive the state (in this case, Canada) as corrupt. Second, people who have less confidence in public institutions are more likely to perceive a country as corrupt. Third, people who participate in electoral and non-electoral forms of political participation are more likely to perceive the state and its public officials as corrupt. Fourth, regardless of which political party is in power, individuals who lean right politically are more likely than those on the left to perceive the state as corrupt. Finally, immigrants are less likely than those born in Canada to perceive the state as corrupt.

10.6 Future Research on Offender Perspectives

A distinction is often made between the offender-based perspective and the offense-based perspective when discussing criminals and crime. The offender-based perspective emphasizes characteristics of actors, such as social and occupational status, respectability, and power (Dodge, 2009; Friedrichs *et al.*, 2018; Piquero and Schoepfer, 2010; Pontell *et al.*, 2014; Stadler *et al.*, 2013; Sutherland, 1983; Uhl, 2023). This offender-based definition emphasizes some combination of the actors' high social status, power, and respectability as the key features of financial crime (Benson, 2021). The offense-based definition, on the other hand, focuses on the acts of financial crime, where distinctions can be made between crime groups such as fraud, theft, manipulation, and corruption, with a number of subgroups. Offense-based approaches to financial crime emphasize the actions and nature of the illegal acts as the defining agent (Galvin *et al.*, 2018; Piquero, 2018). For example, financial crime is considered a non-violent offense (Berghoff and Spiekermann, 2018; Logan *et al.*, 2022).

When determining whether propositions in convenience theory have primarily offender-based or offense-based perspectives, it seems that attitudes of choice and innocence can be classified as the former. Furthermore, opportunities based on status can also be classified as offender-based perspectives. Remaining convenience propositions can be classified as offense-based perspectives. Given this classification, of the 69 research articles, only 10 (14%) present offender-based perspectives, while 59 (86%) present offense-based perspectives. One suggestion for future research might thus be to focus on the offender-based perspective by discussing characteristics of individuals and entities that commit and conceal financial crime. Simply stated, you cannot fight someone you do not understand. Therefore, more insights into offender characteristics are needed.

One convenience proposition does not appear to be fully covered in the JFC this year. It focuses on the personal greed of individual offenders. A second suggestion for future research is thus to stimulate further research into individuals who attempt to climb the hierarchy of human needs through illegitimate means (Maslow, 1943). The offender seeks to climb higher in the pyramid toward characteristics such as self-realization, admiration by others, fame and improved reputation, recognition, and wealth (Cleff *et al.*, 2013; Hirschi and Gottfredson, 1987). To the extent the offender has a strong motive when illegitimate financial resources can help climbing, while legitimate means are inconvenient, then financial crime may be a convenient option (Pillay and Kluvers, 2014; Welsh *et al.*, 2014).

When conducting this review of recently published articles in the JFC in 2024, the journal had published four issues with 69 research articles so far that year. While only 12 articles focused on the motives, possibilities, and threats, and only six articles focused on attitudes of deviant willingness, surprisingly many –51 articles – focused on the opportunity structure of committing and concealing financial crime. The convenience triangle of motives, opportunities, and attitudes is thus far dominated by the opportunity corner of the triangle in the journal. A third suggestion for future research is therefore to focus more on motive and attitudes and less on opportunities to commit and conceal crime.

A fourth important suggestion for future research concerns the convenience proposition of learning by association. This issue lies at the core of white-collar and corporate crime research tradition. Sutherland (1983) has emphasized the focus on learning by differential association, suggesting that whether individuals engage in crime is largely based on their socialization, where they might associate with peers and others who share deviant behaviors, while simultaneously distancing themselves from those who disagree (Hoffmann, 2002). The limited coverage to date – specifically only one research article – in the journal examining the learning issue by differential association and threats to corporate existence, while covering a number of seemingly peripheral issues in published research articles, motivates a fifth and final suggestion relevant for future research, that is, to focus on core issues in financial crime.

The substance added to the theory of convenience from this review is primarily perspectives from non-Western studies, such as corruption potentially having the positive effect of adding grease (Amoh *et al.*, 2024; Hope, 2024; Kalaj and Golemi, 2024), where dishonesty may be advantageous to business performance (Adam *et al.*, 2024; Magableh *et al.*, 2024; Putra and Sihombing, 2024).

In conclusion, this study reviewed 69 research articles published to date in the JFC. The review focused on identifying the focal concerns of motives, opportunities, or attitudes. Surprisingly, many of the reviewed articles (86%) had a focal concern of opportunities to commit and conceal crime. There was little attention to motives of personal greed by individual offenders or organizational failure by corporate offenders. Surprisingly, many articles were concerned with regulation that potentially could enable somewhat better guardianship, oversight, and control. Criminal market mechanisms such as cartel activities were not addressed. Deviant personalities were hardly discussed, which indicates a lack of awareness regarding the offender's perspective when studying financial crime. Generally, it seems that many of the published articles address the periphery of financial crime issues rather than their core, as defined by key scholars in recent decades. Research should prioritize crime motives and willingness attitudes toward deviance, considering an offender-based perspective.

References

Adam, B.M., Sarpong-Kumankoma, E. and Fiador, V. (2024). Economic freedom, corruption and bank stability: Evidence from sub-Saharan Africa, *Journal of Financial Crime*, 31(4), 781–794.

Agbor, A.A. (2024). Sentencing for the offence of misappropriation of public funds: The flawed and problematic approach of Cameroon's special criminal court, *Journal of Financial Crime*, 31(2), 427–445.

Ahmadi, Z., Salehi, M. and Rahmani, M. (2024). The effect of economic complexities and green economy on financial statements fraud, *Journal of Financial Crime*, 31(2), 267–286.

Akinbowale, O.E., Klingelhöfer, H.E. and Zerihun, M.F. (2024a). Investigating the level of effectiveness of the anti-fraud technologies employed by the South African banking industry for cyberfraud mitigation, *Journal of Financial Crime*, 31(1), 201–225.

Akinbowale, C.E., Klingenhöfer, H.E. and Zerihun, M.F. (2024b). The assessment of the impact of cyberfraud in the South African banking industry, *Journal of Financial Crime*, 31(2), 287–301.

Akinbowale, C.E., Mashigo, P. and Zerihun, M.F. (2024c). Analysis of cyberfraud in the South African banking industry: A multiple regression approach, *Journal of Financial Crime*, 31(4), 952–973.

Alcadipani, R. and Medeiros, C.R.O. (2020). When corporations cause harm: A critical view of corporate social irresponsibility and corporate crimes, *Journal of Business Ethics*, 167, 285–297.

Amoh, J.K., Abdul-Mumuni, A., Nsor-Ambala, R. and Amenyitor, E.A. (2024). The corruption-foreign direct investment nexus in sub-Saharan Africa. Fresh evidence from a panel threshold regression approach, *Journal of Financial Crime*, 31(3), 681–697.

Asomah, J.Y., Dim, E.E., Li, Y. and Cheng, H. (2024). What factors are associated with public corruption perception? Evidence from Canada, *Journal of Financial Crime*, 31(3), 524–544.

Baer, M.D., Frank, E.L., Matta, F.K., Luciano, M.M. and Wellman, N. (2021). Untrusted, overtrusted, or just right? The fairness of (in)congruence between trust wanted and trust received, *Academy of Management Journal*, 64(1), 180–206.

Beebeejaun, A. (2024a). Insider trading laws to counter financial crime: A comparative study of Mauritius, UK and US laws, *Journal of Financial Crime*, 31(2), 362–375.

Beebeejaun, A. (2024b). Tax evasion and money laundering through crowdfunding: A comparative study of the laws of Mauritius, UK and UK, *Journal of Financial Crime*, 31(3), 698–710.

Benson, M.L. (2021). Theoretical and empirical advances in the study and control of white-collar offenders, *Justice Evaluation Journal*, 4(1), 1–20.

Benson, M.L. and Simpson, S.S. (2018). *White-Collar Crime: An Opportunity Perspective*, Third Edition, Routledge, New York, NY.

Benson, M.L., Feldmeyer, B., Gabbidon, S.L. and Chio, H.L. (2021). Race, ethnicity, and social change: The democratization of middle-class crime, *Criminology*, 59(1), 10–41.

Berghoff, H. and Spiekermann, U. (2018). Shady business: On the history of white-collar crime, *Business History*, 60(3), 289–304.

Bondarenko, O. and Utkina, M. (2024). Martial law and smuggling of goods: The search for the optimal model of legal liability, *Journal of Financial Crime*, 31(1), 63–75.

Braaten, C.N. and Vaughn, M.S. (2021). Convenience theory of cryptocurrency crime: A content analysis of U.S. federal court decisions, *Deviant Behavior*, 42(8), 958–978.

Bussmann, K.D., Niemeczek, A. and Vockrodt, M. (2018). Company culture and prevention of corruption in Germany, China and Russia, *European Journal of Criminology*, 15(3), 255–277.

Chaiwat, T. and Yomnak, T. (2024). Criminal behavior on detection and penalty: An experimental evidence from drug market game, *Journal of Financial Crime*, 31(1), 135–145.

Chan, F. and Gibbs, C. (2022). When guardians become offenders: Understanding guardian capability through the lens of corporate crime, *Criminology*, 60, 321–341.

Cleff, T., Naderer, G., and Volkert, J. (2013). Motives behind white-collar crime: Results of a quantitative study in Germany, *Society and Business Review*, 8(2), 145–159.

Crank, B.R. (2018). Accepting deviant identities: The impact of self-labeling on intentions to desist from crime, *Journal of Crime and Justice*, 41(2), 155–172.

Cressey, D. (1972). *Criminal Organization: Its Elementary Forms*, Harper and Row, New York, NY.

Cullen, F.T., Graham, A., Jonson, C.L., PIckett, J.T., Sloan, M.M. and Haner, M. (2022). The denier in chief: Faith in Trump and techniques of neutralization in a pandemic, *Deviant Behavior*, 43(7), 829–851.

Curlewis, L.G. (2024). "Pay back the money" – a paper on criminal and civil asset forfeiture within South Africa and suggestions for reform, *Journal of Financial Crime*, 31(4), 772–780.

Danlami, I.A. (2024). Corruption and economic growth in Nigeria: Dynamic causality and asymmetric relationships, *Journal of Financial Crime*, 31(4), 922–937.

Dion, M. (2020). Bribery, extortion and "morally ambiguous" leadership in organizations, *Journal of Financial Crime*, 27(4), 1027–1046.

Dodge, M. (2009). *Women and White-Collar Crime*, Prentice Hall, Saddle River, NJ.

Dubber, A., Graan, C.V. and Groenewald, A. (2024). The abuse of the beneficial ownership of trusts to conceal assets in insolvency and divorce proceedings: A South African study, *Journal of Financial Crime*, 31(1), 76–87.

Estelami, H. and Liu, K. (2024). Content analysis of American consumers' credit card fraud complaints filed with the Consumer Financial Protection Bureau, *Journal of Financial Crime*, 31(3), 618–628.

Feridun, M. (2024). Cross-jurisdictional financial crime risks: What can we learn from the UK regulatory data? *Journal of Financial Crime*, 31(3), 608–617.

Friedrichs, D.O. and Rothe, D.L. (2020). Regulatory rollback and white-collar crime in the era of Trump: The challenges of perspective, *Journal of White Collar and Corporate Crime*, 1(2), 95–102.

Friedrichs, D.O., Schoultz, I. and Jordanoska, A. (2018). *Edwin H. Sutherland, Routledge Key Thinkers in Criminology*, Routledge, UK: London.

Fulbrook, M. (2023). *Bystander Society: Conformity and Complicity in Nazi Germany and the Holocaust*, Oxford University Press, UK: Oxford.

Garg, S. and Aggarwal, R. (2024). Is the counterfeit currency mechanism strictly enforced by banks and regulatory authorities? *Journal of Financial Crime*, 31(4), 908–921.

Galvin, B.M., Lange, D. and Ashforth, B.E. (2015). Narcissistic organizational identification: Seeing oneself as central to the organization's identity, *Academy of Management Review*, 40(2), 163–181.

Galvin, M.A., Loughran, T.A., Simpson, S.S. and Cohen, M.A. (2018). Victim compensation policy and white-collar crime: Public preferences in a national willingness-to-pay survey, *Criminology & Public Policy*, 17, 553–594.

Goldbarsht, D. and Benson, K. (2024). From later to sooner: Exploring compliance with the global regime of anti-money laundering and counter-terrorist financing in the legal profession, *Journal of Financial Crime*, 31(4), 795–809.

Goncharov, I. and Peter, C.D. (2019). Does reporting transparency affect industry coordination? Evidence from the duration of international cartels, *The Accounting Review*, 94(3), 149–175.

Gottschalk, P. (2024). How convenient is deviance to circumvent and evasion sanctions against Russia? The case of alleged economic crime in a Norwegian seafood company, *Journal of Economic Criminology*, 4, published first online https://doi.org/10.1016/j.jeconc.2024.100045.

Gottschalk, P. (2025). Trusted chief executives in convenient white-collar crime, *Crime & Delinquency*, 7(8), 2845–2873.

Gottschalk, P. and Gunnesdal, L. (2018). *White-Collar Crime in the Shadow Economy: Lack of Detection, Investigation, and Conviction compared to Social Security Fraud*, Palgrave Macmillan, UK: London.

Gottschalk, P. and Hamerton, C. (2023). *Lawyer Roles in Knowledge Work: Defender, Enabler, Investigator*, Intersentia, UK: Cambridge.

Gottschalk, P. and Kamaei, M. (2024). Understanding business offending: Survey research in Iran, *Journal of Financial Crime*, 31(2), 446–454.

Guebert, K., Bittle, S. and Frauley, J. (2024). Corruption in the news: Complicity in Canadian newspaper claims making, *Journal of White Collar and Corporate Crime*, 5(2), 122–134.

Gupta, C.M., Gottschalk, P. and Kamaei, M. (2024). Role of gender in white-collar crime: An examination of the emancipation and focal concerns hypothesis, *Journal of Financial Crime*, 31(4), 849–863.

Heyman, C.E. (2024). A red flag checklist for cryptocurrency Ponzi schemes, *Journal of Financial Crime*, 31(3), 711–747.

Hirschi, T. and Gottfredson, M. (1987). Causes of white-collar crime, *Criminology*, 25(4), 949–974.

Hoffmann, J.P. (2002). A contextual analysis of differential association, social control, and strain theories of delinquency, *Social Forces*, 81(3), 753–785.

Holtfreter, K. (2015). General theory, gender-specific theory, and white-collar crime, *Journal of Financial Crime*, 22(4), 422–431.

Hope, K.R. (2024). The corruption and sustainable development nexus in Africa: A contemporary review and analysis, *Journal of Financial Crime*, 31(2), 331–346.

Hsieh, H. and Shannon, S.E. (2005). Three approaches to qualitative content analysis, *Qualitative Health Research*, 15(9), 1277–1288.

Huang, L. and Knight, A.P. (2017). Resources and relationships in entrepreneurship: An exchange theory of the development and effects of the entrepreneur-investor relationship, *Academy of Management Review*, 42(1), 80–102.

Huric-Larsen, J.F. (2023). Cartel formation and the business cycle, *European Competition Journal*, published first online https://doi.org/10.1080/17441056.2023.2234233.

Jordanoska, A. (2018). The social ecology of white-collar crime: Applying situational action theory to white-collar offending, *Deviant Behavior*, 39(11), 1427–1449.

Kakkar, H., Sivanathan, N., and Globel, M.S. (2020). Fall from grace: The role of dominance and prestige in punishment of high-status actors, *Academy of Management Journal*, 63(2), 530–553.

Kalaj, E. and Golemi, E. (2024). A comparative analysis of the nexus between corruption and firm performance for a selection of Western Balkan countries, *Journal of Financial Crime*, 31(3), 583–593.

Kamaei, M., Abolhasani, S. and Farhood, N. (2024). A comparative analysis of the role of gender in the commission of white-collar crimes: A review in Norway, America, Portugal, India and Iran, *Journal of Financial Crime*, 31(2), 249–258.

Kandukuri, R. (2024). An analysis of stockbroking frauds and regulatory action in India, *Journal of Financial Crime*, 31(4), 1037–1046.

Kaptein, M. and Helvoort, M. (2019). A model of neutralization techniques, *Deviant Behavior*, 40(10), 1260–1285.

Karandikar, S. and Jones, D.N. (2023). From embezzlement to antitrust: White collar crime preferences of the dark triad, *Journal of White Collar and Corporate Crime*, published first online https://doi.org/10.1177/26311309X231210846.

Karimi-Ghartemani, S., Khani, N. and Isfahani, A.N. (2022). Designing a conceptual model for organizational stupidity using a combination of grounded theory and interpretive structural modeling, *Iranian Journal of Management Studies*, 15(3), 549–568.

Karpacheva, E. and Hock, B. (2024). Foreign whistleblowing: The impact of US extraterritorial enforcement on anti-corruption laws in Europe, *Journal of Financial Crime*, 31(1), 1–13.

Kasim, E.S., Awalludin, N.R., Zainal, N., Ismail, A. and Shukri, N.H.A. (2024). The effect of financial literacy, financial behavior and financial stress on awareness of investment scams among retirees, *Journal of Financial Crime*, 31(3), 652–666.

Kassem, R. and Carter, E. (2024). Mapping romance fraud research – A systematic review, *Journal of Financial Crime*, 31(4), 974–992.

Keil, M., Tiwana, A., Sainsbury, R. and Sneha, S. (2010). Toward a theory of whistleblowing intentions: A benefit-cost differential perspective, *Decision Sciences*, 41(4), 787–812.

Kemsley, D., Kemsley, S.A. and Morgan, F.T. (2024). Tax evasion on lawful income: Is it a form of money laundering, *Journal of Financial Crime*, 31(1), 33–43.

Körtl, C. and Chbib, I. (2024). Illicit enrichment in Germany: An evaluation of the reformed asset recovery regime's ability to confiscate proceeds of crime, *International Review of Law and Economics*, published first online https://doi.org/10.1016/j.irle.2024.106230.

Lee, J.Y. (2025). Unveiling insider threats in South Korean companies: Causes and countermeasures through convenience theory and perceived punishment, *Deviant Behavior*, published first online https://doi.org/10.1080/01639625.2025.2545442.

Linder, S., Leca, B., Zicari, A. and Casarin, V. (2021). Designing ethical management control: Overcoming the harmful effect of management control systems on job-related stress, *Journal of Business Ethics*, 172, 747–764.

Logan, M.W., Morgan, M.A., Long, J.S. and Hazelwood, A. (2022). More similar than different? Examining prison infractions and recidivism among female and male white-collar offenders, *Journal of Criminal Justice*, 82, September–October, 8 p.

Lord, N. and Levi, M. (2023). Economic crime, economic criminology, and serious crimes for economic gain: On the conceptual and disciplinary (dis)order of the object of study, *Journal of Economic Criminology*, 1(1), published first online https://doi.org/10.1016/j.jeconc.2023.100014.

Magableh, S., Hailat, M., Al-qalawi, U. and Qudah, A.A. (2024). Corruption suppression and domestic investment of emerging economies: BRICS and CIVERTS groups – panel ARDL approach, *Journal of Financial Crime*, 31(1), 174–187.

Mahadew, B. (2024). The need for a robust legal framework on corporate criminal liability in Mauritius: Lessons from the French model, *Journal of Financial Crime*, 31(1), 88–100.

Maslow, A.H. (1943). A theory of human motivation, *Psychological Review*, 50(4), 370–396.

Maulidiyah, D.N. (2024). Consensus on the role of culture in restraining financial crime: A systematic literature review, *Journal of Financial Crime*, 31(4), 883–897.

McClean, E.J., Martin, S.R., Emich, K.J. and Woodruff, T. (2018). The social consequences of voice: An examination of voice type and gender on status and subsequent leader emergence, *Academy of Management Journal*, 61(5), 1869–1891.

McClelland, P.L., Liang, X. and Barker, V.L. (2010). CEO commitment to the status quo: Replication and extension using content analysis, *Journal of Management*, 36(5), 1251–1277.

McGloin, J.M., Thomas, K.J. and Rowan, Z.R. (2021). Can the group disincentivize offending? Considering opt-out thresholds and decision reversals, *Criminology*, 59, 738–765.

Menz, M. (2024). It is best to say nothing at all – Suspicious activity reporting in the financial services sector, *Journal of Financial Crime*, 31(2), 302–310.

Mgadmi, N., Sadraoui, T., Alkaabi, W. and Abidi, A. (2023). The interconnectedness of stock indices and cryptocurrencies during the Russia-Ukraine war, *Journal of Economic Criminology*, 2, published first online https://doi.org/10.10016/j.jeconc.2023.100039.

Mohliver, A. (2019). How misconduct spreads: Auditors' role in the diffusion of stock-option backdating, *Administrative Science Quarterly*, 64(2), 310–336.

Montenarh, J. and Marsden, S. (2024). Unmasking the oligarchs – Using open source data to detect sanctions violations, *Journal of Economic Criminology*, 3, published first online https://doi.org/10.1016/j.jeconc.2024.100055.

Nguyen, N.T., Nguyen, A.T., To, H.T.N. and Le, T.T.H. (2024). Why are Vietnamese people susceptible to cryptocurrency Ponzi schemes? Findings from using the PLS-SEM approach, *Journal of Financial Crime*, 31(1), 158–173.

Nortje, J.G.J. and Myburgh, D.C. (2024). Impediments during the execution of a search and seizure warrant for digital information by forensic investigators in South Africa, *Journal of Financial Crime*, 31(4), 810–822.

Nwatu, S.I., Arum, E.C. and Chime, I.P. (2024). Securities regulation and capital market development in Nigeria: Recurring challenges and prospect for solution, *Journal of Financial Crime*, 31(4), 938–951.

Olujobi, O.J. and Yebisi, T.E. (2024). Tacking corruption in the distribution of Covid-19 palliatives and public health facilities in Nigeria: Legal insights and strategic blueprint for future emergencies, *Journal of Financial Crime*, 31(3), 489–523.

Ordower, H. (2024). Is aggressive tax planning a failure of tax adviser integrity? *Journal of Financial Crime*, 31(4), 837–848.

Owusu, G.M.Y., Koomson, T.A.A. and Donkor, G.N.A. (2024). A scientometric analysis of the structure and trends in corporate fraud research: A 66-year review, *Journal of Financial Crime*, 31(3), 629–651.

Pandey, D. and Gilmour, P. (2024). Accounting meets metaverse: Navigating the intersection between the real and virtual worlds, *Journal of Financial Reporting and Accounting*, 22(2), 211–226.

Pavlidis, G. (2024). The birth of the new anti-money laundering authority: Harnessing the power of EU-wide supervision, *Journal of Financial Crime*, 31(2), 322–330.

Pillay, S. and Kluvers, R. (2014). An institutional theory perspective on corruption: The case of a developing democracy, *Financial Accountability & Management*, 30(1), 95–119.

Piquero, N.L. (2018). White-collar crime is crime: Victims hurt just the same, *Criminology & Public Policy*, 17(3), 595–600.

Piquero N.L. and Schoepfer A. (2010). Theories of white-collar crime and public policy, in Barlow H.D. and Decker S.H. (editors), *Criminology and Public Policy: Putting Theory to Work*, Temple University Press, Philadelphia.

Pontell, H.N., Black, W.K. and Geis, G. (2014). Too big to fail, too powerful to jail? On the absence of criminal prosecutions after the 2008 financial meltdown, *Crime, Law and Social Change*, 61(1), 1–13.

Prabowo, H.Y. (2024). When gullibility becomes us: Exploring the cultural roots of Indonesians' susceptibility to investment fraud, *Journal of Financial Crime*, 31(1), 14–32.

Putra, I.P.M.J.S. and Sihombing, R.P. (2024). The potential of corruption based on Hofstede cultural dimensions and institutional quality: An international evidence, *Journal of Financial Crime*, 31(4), 823–836.

Putri, C.M., Argilés-Bosch, J.M. and Ravenda, D. (2024). Creating good village governance: An effort to prevent village corruption in Indonesia, *Journal of Financial Crime*, 31(2), 455–468.

Rahman, M.J. and Jie, X. (2024). Fraud detection using fraud triangle theory: Evidence from China, *Journal of Financial Crime*, 31(1), 101–118.

Rahman, M.J., Xuan, J., Zhu, H. and Hossain, M.M. (2024). Accounting fraud and corporate sustainability: Chinese listed companies, *Journal of Financial Crime*, 31(3), 558–574.

Rani, M.I.A., Nazri, S.N.F.S.M. and Zolkaflil, S. (2024). A systematic literature review of money mule: Its roles, recruitment and awareness, *Journal of Financial Crime*, 31(2), 347–361.

Ridho, W.F. (2024). Unmasking online fake job group financial scams: A thematic examination of victim exploitation from perspective of financial behavior, *Journal of Financial Crime*, 31(3), 748–758.

Sala, G.R. and Pratt, M.G. (2023) How organizations influence interpersonal trust repair: The case of a French antiterrorist unit, *Academy of Management Journal*, 66(4), 1263–1293.

Sajko, M., Boone, C., and Buyl, T. (2021). CEO greed, corporate social responsibility, and organizational resilience to systemic shocks, *Journal of Management*, 47(4), 957–992.

Sallaberry, J.D., Venturini, L.D.B., Martinez-Conesa, I. and Flach, L. (2024). Personal responsibility and knowledge about money laundering: A study with Brazilian accountants, *Journal of Financial Crime*, 31(3), 667–680.

Saluja, S. (2024). Identity theft fraud – Major loophole for FinTech industry in India, *Journal of Financial Crime*, 31(1), 146–157.

Schoen, J.L., DeSimone, J.A., Meyer, R.D., Schnure, K.A. and LeBreton, J.M. (2021). Identifying, defining, and measuring justification mechanisms: The implicit biases underlying individual differences, *Journal of Management*, 47(3), 716–744.

Schoepfer, A. and Piquero, N.L. (2006). Exploring white-collar crime and the American dream: A partial test of institutional anomie theory, *Journal of Criminal Justice*, 34(3), 227–235.

Scott, B. (2024). "Everyone freaks out when the leaks are made": Data leaks, investigative journalism and intelligence practice, *Journal of Financial Crime*, 31(3), 545–557.

See, K. (2024). The Satoshi Laundromat: A review on the money laundering open door of Bitcoin mixers, *Journal of Financial Crime*, 31(2), 416–426.

Siahaan, M., Suharman, H., Fitrijanti, T. and Umar, H. (2024). When internal organizational factors improve detecting corruption in state-owned companies, *Journal of Financial Crime*, 31(2), 376–407.

Silver, K. and Garofalo, P. (2024). Excusing corporate wrongdoing and the state of nature, *Academy of Management Review*, published first online https://doi.org/10.5465/amr.2020.0236, 1–23.

Simpson, S.S., Galvin, M.A., Loughran, T.A. and Cohen, M.A. (2023). Perceptions of white-collar crime seriousness: Unpacking and translating attitudes into policy preferences, *Journal of Research in Crime and Delinquency*, 60(5), 582–622.

Singh, C. (2024). Artificial intelligence and deep learning: Considerations for financial institutions for compliance with the regulatory burden in the United Kingdom, *Journal of Financial Crime*, 31(2), 259–266.

Siponen, M. and Vance, A. (2010). Neutralization: New insights into the problem of employee information security policy violations, *MIS Quarterly*, 34(3), 487–502.

Smaili, N. and Rancourt-Raymond, A. (2024). Metaverse: Welcome to the new fraud marketplace, *Journal of Financial Crime*, 31(1), 188–200.

Smith, M. and Tiwari, M. (2024). The implications of national blockchain infrastructure for financial crime, *Journal of Financial Crime*, 31(2), 236–248.

Stadler, W.A., Benson, M.L., and Cullen. F.T. (2013). Revisiting the special sensitivity hypothesis: The prison experience of white-collar inmates, *Justice Quarterly*, 30(6), 1090–1114.

Sudarwanto, A.S., Kharisma, D.B. and Cahyaningsih, D.T. (2024). Islamic crowdfunding and Shariah compliance regulation: Problems and oversight, *Journal of Financial Crime*, 31(4), 1022–1036.

Sutherland, E.H. (1983). *White Collar Crime – The Uncut Version*, Yale University Press, New Haven, CT.

Sykes, G. and Matza, D. (1957). Techniques of neutralization: A theory of delinquency, *American Sociological Review*, 22(6), 664–670.

Tan, V. (2024). Belt and road initiative: Legal mechanisms to recover stolen assets, *Journal of Financial Crime*, 31(4), 864–882.

Tee. C.M. and Teoh, T.T.M. (2024). The cost of debt and political institutions, *Journal of Financial Crime*, 31(1), 44–62.

Teichmann, F.M.J. and Wittmann, C. (2024a). Compliance cultures and the role of financial incentives, *Journal of Financial Crime*, 31(1), 226–232.

Teichmann, F.M.J. and Wittmann, C. (2024b). Psychology and white collar crime – Compliance recommendations based on the social and psychological reality dictating perception, *Journal of Financial Crime*, 31(2), 408–415.

Teichmann, F.M.J., Boticiu, S.R. and Sergi, B.S. (2024a). Compliance risk for crowdfunding: A neglected aspect off money laundering, terrorist financing, and fraud, *Journal of Financial Crime*, 31(3), 575–582.

Teichmann, F.M.J., Boticiu, S.R. and Sergi, B.S. (2024b). Compliance issues in arbitration proceedings – Bribery, money laundering and other abuses, *Journal of Financial Crime*, 31(3), 759–767.

Teichmann, F.M.J., Boticiu, S.R. and Sergi, B.S. (2024c). Compliance concerns in sustainable finance: An analysis of peer-to-peer (P2P) lending platforms and sustainability, *Journal of Financial Crime*, 31(4), 993–1001.

Thaxton, S. and Agnew, R. (2018). When criminal coping is likely: An examination of conditioning effects in general strain theory, *Journal of Quantitative Criminology*, 34, 887–920.

Thoroughgood, C.N., Padilla, A., Hunter, S.T. and Tate, B.W. (2012). The susceptible circle: A taxonomy of followers associated with destructive leadership, *The Leadership Quarterly*, 23, 897–917.

Toit, E. (2024). The red flags of financial statement fraud: A case study, *Journal of Financial Crime*, 31(2), 311–321.

Uhl, A. (2023). Carceral experiences of white-collar offenders: Qualitative research design utilizing the offender-based definition and Pierre Bourdieu's capital theory, *Crime, Law and Social Change*, 79, 129–151.

Uygur, S.A. and Napier, C.J. (2023). Understanding fraud in the not-for-profit sector: A stakeholder perspective for charities, *Journal of Business Ethics*, published first online https://doi.org/10.1007/s10551-023-05373-5.

Vanhee, A.J. and McNealey, R. (2024). Individual residence and identity theft: How residential characteristics shape exposure and risk of offline and online identity theft victimization, *Journal of Financial Crime*, 31(3), 594–607.

Velásquez-Giraldo, M. Canavire-Bacarreza, G. and Lundberg, A. (2023). Crime variability, peer effects, and economic inequality in social networks, *Journal of Economic Criminology*, 1, published first online https://doi.org/10.1016/j.jeconc.2024.100011.

Wells, J.T. (1997). *Occupational Fraud and Abuse*, Obsidian Publishing Company, Texas: Austin.

Welsh, D.T. and Ordonez, L.D. (2014). The dark side of consecutive high performance goals: Linking goal setting, depletion, and unethical behavior, *Organizational Behavior and Human Decision Processes*, 123, 79–89.

Welsh, D.T., Ordonez, L.D., Snyder, D.G. and Christian, M.S. (2014). The slippery slope: How small ethical transgressions pave the way for larger future transgressions, *Journal of Applied Psychology*, 100(1), 114–127.

Wijayanti, D.M., Senjani, Y.P. and Farah, W. (2024). The role of Machiavellian personality, altruistic personality, religiosity, whistleblowing system, and accounting firm size in mitigating fraud intention, *Journal of Financial Crime*, 31(1), 119–134.

Williams, M.L., Levi, M., Burnap, P. and Gundur, R.V. (2019). Under the corporate radar: Examining insider business cybercrime victimization through an application of routine activities theory, *Deviant Behavior*, 40(9), 1119–1131.

Xuan, M.J.R., Zhu, H. and Hossain, M.M. (2024). Accounting fraud and corporate sustainability: Chinese listed companies, *Journal of Financial Crime*, 31(3), 558–574.

Yeo, N., Ahizi, D.A. and Coulibaly, S.K. (2024). Does blacklisting cause a boomerang effect in combating illicit financial flows? Evidence from developing countries, *Journal of Financial Crime*, 31(4), 1002–1021.

Chapter 11

Deviant Behavior Willingness

Three academic journals primarily publish research articles on crime for profit: the *Journal of Economic Criminology* (JEC), the *Journal of White Collar and Corporate Crime* (JWCCC), and the *Journal of Financial Crime* (JFC). Research articles in these journals are reviewed in this chapter to identify offender attitudes that contribute to a willingness for deviant behavior when committing and concealing economic crimes. The theory of convenience is applied, which suggests five willingness propositions addressing choice (personal identity, rational choice, and learning from others) as well as innocence (justification and neutralization). Deviant personal identity is exemplified by psychopathic and narcissistic traits, as well as Machiavellian personality traits. Rational choice is exemplified by the lack of perceived deterrence. Learning from others is exemplified by differential association. Justification is exemplified by a lack of crime seriousness, while neutralization is exemplified by romance fraudsters in Ghana who cause no perceived harm, as victims in Western countries have access to safety nets such as social welfare and other benefits.

In crime-for-profit research, the fraud triangle is traditionally used as a model to study incidents. While the traditional fraud triangle consists of pressures, opportunities, and rationalizations (Cressey, 1972; Wells, 1997), the more recent convenience triangle consists of motives, opportunities, and attitudes (Braaten and Vaughn, 2021; Chan and Gibbs, 2022; Gottschalk, 2025; Lee, 2025). Convenience theory is applied in this study to review crime-for-profit research articles in three academic journals that primarily publish research on crime for profit: the JEC, the JWCCC, and the JFC. The review concentrates on the attitudes causing the choice of crime and the perception of innocence.

This literature review is important, as it identifies propositions for deviant behavior willingness among crime-for-profit offenders. The review thus addresses the following research question: *What convenience propositions for deviant behavior willingness can be identified in journals on economic crime, white-collar and corporate crime, and financial crime?*

The theory of convenience suggests that offenders possess motives of possibilities and threats, opportunities to commit and conceal crime, and attitudes of willingness for deviant behavior stemming from choice and innocence. Convenience theory suggests 14 propositions regarding motives, opportunities, and attitudes. In this chapter, the review focuses on five propositions that address attitudes to answer the research question.

This review is relevant, as it may identify both important and unimportant factors in understanding offenses and offenders, and it may also highlight propositions in the theory of convenience that warrant further attention in future criminology research.

This chapter begins with a description of convenience theory, followed by a description of the research method for reviewing the journal articles. More substance is added to convenience theory when presenting the reviewed journal articles along the model structure, as illustrated in Figure 10.1.

Neutralization is similar to rationalization: a matter of denying guilt by application of various neutralization techniques (Sykes and Matza, 1957). Offenders deny responsibility, injury, and victimization. They condemn the condemners. They claim appeals to higher loyalties and the normality of action. They claim entitlement and argue the case of legal error. They find their own mistakes acceptable. They argue that a dilemma arose, resulting in a reasonable trade-off before committing the act (Jordanoska, 2018; Kaptein and Helvoort, 2019; Siponen and Vance, 2010). Such claims enable offenders to find crime convenient since they do not consider it criminal, and they do not feel guilty of wrongdoing (Cullen *et al.*, 2022).

11.1 Research Method for Reviewing Articles

The first volume with research articles in the JEC was published in September 2023. This review was conducted in August 2024, when the journal had published 61 articles labeled "research article". Some other articles were not marked "research article", and some of the research articles addressed convenience theory directly. These articles were removed from the review, making the sample for review consist of 61 articles.

The first volume featuring research articles in the JWCCC was published in January 2020. This review was conducted in August 2024, when the journal had published 51 articles labeled "research article".

Six volumes of the JFC are published annually. This review was conducted in August 2024, when the journal had published four issues with 69 research articles that year. The sample is considered large enough to review focal concerns. The choice of the most recent research articles published in the JFC was made to identify the topics primarily covered recently.

A total of 181 articles (61 + 51 + 69) were reviewed in terms of their emphasis on motives, opportunities, and attitudes. The majority of articles focused on opportunities to commit and conceal crimes. The number of articles relevant for this review addressing attitudes was 7 (12%) in the JEC, 9 (18%) in the JWCCC, and 6 (9%) in the JFC. The final sample of articles for this research is thus 7 + 9 + 6 = 22 articles.

Content analysis through archival study is the research method applied in this review. The search focused on potential motives, opportunities, and attitudes related to deviance as described in each research article. From each journal article, the theme that seemed to dominate was recorded and reported in the following. The reporting is visualized using bold font for each identified author and also bold font in the list of references.

Content analysis is a research method used to identify characteristics within texts attempting to make valid inferences (Braaten and Vaughn, 2021). Content analysis assumes that language reflects both how people understand their surroundings and their cognitive processes (Hsieh and Shannon, 2005). Cognition refers to what people think and how they think, as well as how cognitive processes affect the way in which people interpret and make sense of what is around them. Therefore, content analysis makes it possible to identify and determine relevant text within a context (McClelland *et al.*, 2010).

The presentation of research results follows the structural model of convenience theory, where 14 propositions are listed and five are relevant to this research.

11.2 Research Result: Attitudes in JEC Articles

Deviant Personal Identity

Boddy *et al.* (2024) argued that psychopathy is a personality trait of many economic crime offenders. Identity is generally how an individual sees themselves in relation to others (Ingram, 2023). While age is usually not viewed as a personal identity characteristic, it is nevertheless interesting to note the research by **Vincent *et al.*** (2023: 8) that age matters in tax non-compliance in terms of "the insensitivity of the age group 18–35 years to tax compliance".

Rational Choice of Crime

The rational choice of crime addresses pros and cons, advantages and disadvantages, and incentives versus disincentives (McGloin *et al.*, 2021). A key element of rational choice decision is the extent to which deterrence – a process of discouraging criminal acts through threatened or actual sanctions – is applied. Deterrence refers to discouraging and preventing someone from doing something wrong and discouraging and terminating wrongdoing by someone who is doing something undesirable (Fang and Yang, 2024). **Torres *et al.*** (2024: 3) discussed "marginal deterrence effect stemming from a punishment scale that progressively increased with more harmful acts". Similarly, when discussing foreign exchange offenses, **Ramanambonona** (2024: 1) argued that "a rational offender is expected to be able to compare the cost-benefit before undertaking activities that generate exchange infractions". Similarly, **Tiwari *et al.*** (2023: 9) argued that "the rational decision making of a money launderer can be substantiated through the concepts in systems theory, such as structural coupling that acknowledges the codependency between factors in a system in this context, the factors influencing the choice of laundering technique". **Kabra and Gori** (2023: 1) applied rational choice theory to explain offenders in drug trafficking on crypto markets, where offenders "make a rational choice of dealing drugs online as the benefits attached to drug trafficking on crypto markets outweigh the potential costs, such as getting arrested".

Learning by Association

Learning refers to differential association, suggesting that whether individuals engage in crime is largely based on their socialization, where they might associate with peers and others who share deviant attitudes and behaviors, while simultaneously distancing themselves from those who disagree (Hoffmann, 2002; Sutherland, 1983). **Velásquez-Giraldo *et al.*** (2023: 1) applied this perspective of differential association and found "each assumption around these peer effects upon the nine principles of differential association, which form the most famous explanation of criminal influence".

Innocence from Justification

No research article was identified.

Innocence from Neutralization

Some offenders refuse to acknowledge damage from harm, claiming that there is no visible harm resulting from the action (Sims and Barreto, 2022). This neutralization technique might also be applied by romance fraudsters on the internet, as suggested by **Lazarus *et al.*** (2023b: 5) when reviewing research on online romance fraud using empirical evidence from Ghana and other poor countries:

> The studies suggest that cybercriminals underestimate the financial harm inflicted on victims from Western countries: they assume that these victims have access to safety nets, such as social welfare and benefits, available in Western societies.

11.3 Research Result: Attitudes in JWCCC Articles

Deviant Personal Identity

Identity is how an individual sees themselves in relation to others, influenced by personality traits (Ingram, 2023). For example, narcissistic identification is a special type of narcissism in which the offender sees little or no difference between oneself and the corporation (Galvin *et al.*, 2015). The three personality traits of Machiavellianism, narcissism, and psychopathy are sometimes called the "dark triad" (Karandikar and Jones, 2023: 1):

> Machiavellianism is associated with manipulation, cynicism, and amorality. Machiavellian individuals are strategically focused on selfish instrumental gain with a longer-term focus. In contrast, narcissism is

> associated with entitlement, grandiosity, and self-enhancement tendency. Narcissistic individuals are typically ego driven, constantly searching for social reinforcement. Finally, psychopathy is associated with impulsivity, recklessness, and overt antisocial tendencies. Psychopathic individuals seek immediate gratification and fail to temper their antisocial behavior in the face of risk.

Potential offenders with the personality traits of the dark triad generally seem to have a more positive attitude and a stronger belief in committing and concealing white-collar crime. (WCC). Specifically, **Amos *et al.*** (2024: 58) found "significant relationships between subclinical psychopathy (disinhibition and meanness), narcissism, and attitudes and beliefs towards WCC", yet "subcomponents of the dark triad do not have the same predictive powers".

Karandikar and Jones (2023) studied the effects of the dark triad on white-collar offending. They found that individuals high on the three personality traits have different preferences for categories of financial crime based on their complexity. For example, Machiavellian individuals might commit complex WCCs such as antitrust violations. Psychopathic individuals may commit simple kinds of WCCs such as embezzlement. Narcissistic individuals showed no specific preference for particular kinds of WCC.

Also, **Peixoto *et al.*** (2023) studied the effects of the dark triad on white-collar offending. They found tolerance of unethical behavior to be positively linked to the extent of a personality characterized by dark triad traits. They referred to previous research that found positive and moderate correlations between every aspect of the triad, namely Machiavellianism, narcissism, and psychopathy. At the same time, they found that entrepreneurs displayed higher scores on dark triad personality traits compared to non-entrepreneurs, where entrepreneurship is considered a positive factor in creating new jobs through innovation.

Rational Choice of Crime

The convenience of committing crime depends on perceptions of its seriousness (Simpson *et al.*, 2023). At the lower end of seriousness, as mentioned above, Alcadipani and Medeiros (2020) found that white-collar and corporate crime tends to be perceived as and treated as corporate irresponsibility, rather than misconduct, wrongdoing, offense, or law violations. Similarly, **Guebert *et al.*** (2024: 131) found that the media tend to present crime as "intelligible", that is, understandable and thus somehow defendable. In a rational choice perspective of pros and cons, as well as advantages and disadvantages, the disadvantage of committing crime is reduced when white-collar and corporate crime is portrayed as less serious.

The convenience of participating in corruption may be a rational choice when corruption is part of a business culture (Artello and Albanese, 2022). For example, the Brazilian corruption scheme involving the oil company Petrobras had corrupt participants in 61 countries (**Alencar and Jackson-Green**, 2023).

Learning by Association

No research article was identified.

Innocence from Justification

No research article was identified.

Innocence from Neutralization

A common neutralization technique applied by offenders to avoid guilt perceptions is to deny that the crime has a victim – nobody is suffering from the action. A version of this technique involves claiming that the alleged victim is unworthy of concern (Sims and Barreto, 2022). **Hagan** (2024) discussed such a distinction between victims who seem worthy of concern and others who do not seem worthy. Similarly, **Dodge** (2020) argued that WCC victimization receives little attention.

Another common neutralization technique is to deny that the action caused any harm. In the case study presented by **Budó** (2021: 90), corporations denied risks, hazards, and harms associated with the use of asbestos:

> This empirical study aimed to contribute to the literature about the alliances between science and industry by providing insights on the ways in which the disputes for truth on asbestos risks to human health have taken a path that diverts studies from the route of specific engagement with medical topics, to find other languages: economic, legal and political ones. The shared representations about the consequences of these disputes resonate with what we already know about the massive harms, victimization, and impunity associated with the crimes of the powerful.

A slightly less common neutralization technique is the slippery slope argument, which can make the offender feel innocent because they did not realize they would end up on the wrong side of the law (Theoharakis *et al.*, 2021). **Marques and Tavares** (2023) applied the slippery slope perspective when studying tax evasion, where tax compliance is a desirable outcome following tax inspections by state tax authorities.

Innocence from neutralization was reported by **Schoultz and Flyghed** (2021: 24) when presenting the case of three former executives in Sweden who denied responsibility:

> In 2018, three former executives from the global telecommunication company Telia were put on trial in Sweden in a bribery case involving the eldest daughter of the late Uzbek President Islam Karimov (...) Telia's initially denial eventually changed into a partial acknowledgment in combination with a scapegoating discourse. While Telia hardly defended itself at all in the Swedish court, the company's former executives employed a defense of legality, denial of knowledge, of deviance, and of responsibility as well as a claim of being scapegoated.

11.4 Research Result: Attitudes in JFC Articles

Deviant Personal Identity

Machiavellian personality "is associated with manipulation, cynicism, and amorality" (Karandikar and Jones, 2023: 1). "Machiavelli asserted that wise leaders want to be liked and feared by people" (Dion, 2020: 1032). Machiavellian individuals might commit complex kinds of financial crime, such as antitrust violations (Karandikar and Jones, 2023). "Machiavellian personality leads to unethical behavior carried out based on self-interest using deception and manipulation to achieve goals" (**Wijayanti *et al.***, 2024: 120).

Rational Choice of Crime

"Offender-search theory assumes that criminals are at least somewhat rational and select targets based on the perceived reward, risk and effort involved compared to perceived available alternatives" (**Vanhee and McNealey**, 2024: 595). The economic model of rational self-interest is all about weighing up the pros and cons of different courses of action in terms of incentives and disincentives for and the advantages and disadvantages of offending (McGloin *et al.*, 2021). An advantage is the low probability of detection and the low punishment costs associated with it

(**Chaiwat and Yomnak**, 2024; Gottschalk and Gunnesdal, 2018) since financial crime is generally not considered as serious as physical crime (Alcadipani and Medeiros, 2020). Guebert *et al.* (2024: 131) found that the media tend to present crime as "intelligible", that is, understandable, and thus somehow defendable.

Learning by Association

"Humans have a cognitive tendency to follow the behavior of others", especially when confronted by an uncertain situation (**Teichmann and Wittmann**, 2024: 408).

Innocence from Justification

In a justification, the actor admits responsibility for the act in question while denying its pejorative and negative content (Schoen *et al.*, 2021: 730):

> People use justification mechanisms to protect their sense of self. People who sincerely believe that they are a specific kind of person but routinely demonstrate behaviors that indicate otherwise may avoid cognitive dissonance and maintain their sense of self by using justification mechanisms that allow them to "explain away" their behavior.

The convenience of committing financial crimes is dependent on perceptions of seriousness (Simpson *et al.*, 2023). When committing financial crime is considered understandable (**Gottschalk and Kamaei**, 2024) and perceived as irresponsibility rather than misconduct or crime (Alcadipani and Medeiros, 2020), the feeling of guilt is reduced and possibly removed among offenders when justification is enabled.

Innocence from Neutralization

A neutralization technique applied by some offenders is claiming the normalcy of their actions – everyone else does and would do the same. The offender argues that it is so common to commit the offense, so that one can hardly define it as an offense at all. The offense is no deviant behavior since most people do it or would do it in the same situation. The offender might even suggest that what may constitute deviant behavior is when people in the same situation obey the law. The claim of normality depends on the perceived frequency of crime. When **Asomah *et al.*** (2024: 524) asked different groups about their corruption perceptions in Canada, they got varying answers:

> First, people accessing corruption news from the traditional news media are less likely than those receiving information from the news media to perceive the state (in this case, Canada) as corrupt. Second, people who have less confidence in public institutions are more likely to perceive a country as corrupt. Third, people who participate in electoral and non-electoral forms of political participation are more likely to perceive the state and its public officials as corrupt. Fourth, regardless of which political party is in power, individuals who lean right politically are more likely than those on the left to perceive the state as corrupt. Finally, immigrants are less likely than those born in Canada to perceive the state as corrupt.

11.5 Future Research on Crime Justification

In this review of research articles in three journals oriented toward crime-for-profit, the first deviant behavior willingness derives from personal identity. Individuals with deviant personality traits, such as psychopathic or narcissistic traits, may feel entitled to commit crime (Amos *et al.*, 2024; Boddy *et al.*, 2024; Peixoto *et al.*, 2023). A Machiavellian personality, associated with manipulation, cynicism, and amorality, may also cause a perception of entitlement among potential and actual offenders (Wijayanti *et al.*, 2024).

The second deviant behavior willingness derives from rational choice, where incentives for crime are stronger than disincentives, pros are stronger than cons, advantages are stronger than disadvantages, and the benefits of crime exceed the costs (Ramanambonona, 2024; Vanhee and McNealey, 2024). Factors entering such assessments include deterrence from potential punishment (Chaiwat and Yomnak, 2024; Kabra and Gori, 2023; Tiwari *et al.*, 2023; Torres *et al.*, 2024) and the general perception of crime seriousness (Guebert *et al.*, 2024) and its spread (Alencar and Jackson-Green, 2023).

The third deviant behavior willingness derives from learning from others through differential association. Velásquez-Giraldo *et al.* (2023) argued that differential association, as suggested by Sutherland (1983), forms the most famous explanation of criminal influence. Similarly, Teichmann and Wittmann (2024) argued that humans have a cognitive tendency to follow others, as differential association suggests that humans associate with those in agreement and distance themselves from those in disagreement.

The fourth deviant behavior willingness derives from innocence by justification. However, this convenience proposition was only addressed by Gottschalk and Kamaei (2024), who suggested that people might find financial crime understandable.

The fifth and final deviant behavior willingness derives from innocence by neutralization. One potential neutralization technique implicit in the research by Asomah *et al.* (2024) is that people often do not perceive financial crime as serious, with offenders claiming normality of action and asserting no real harm (Budó, 2021; Lazarus *et al.*, 2023b). A common neutralization technique is denial of responsibility (Schoultz and Flyghed, 2021). A third technique discussed in the reviewed literature is the slippery slope argument, where offenders may claim to not realize that they had slid over to the wrong side of the law (Marques and Tavares, 2023). A fourth technique is to claim that victims are not worthy of concern (Hagan, 2024) or are not worthy of attention (Dodge, 2020).

Some reviewed research articles present new insights, as they originated outside the traditional Western hemisphere. An example is the research by Lazarus *et al.* (2023a, 2023b), who presented empirical research from Africa suggesting other reasons for deviant behavior willingness. Online fraudsters may aspire to a higher offender status by idolizing music heroes, as discussed by Lazarus *et al.* (2023a: 13):

> Thus, we argue that glorifying wealthy and prominent individuals who acquired their riches through illicit means in Nigerian music predated the digitalization of fraud and music and the subsequent glamorization of online fraudsters. This is evident in jùjú and high-life genres, songs predating the digitalization of fraud, and music also glamorize criminal actors.

Online fraudsters claim no harm, as their victims in Western countries are wealthy (Lazarus *et al.*, 2023b: 5):

> The studies suggest that cybercriminals underestimate the financial harm inflicted on victims from Western countries: they assume that these victims have access to safety nets, such as social welfare and benefits, available in Western societies.

Some offenders refuse to acknowledge damage from harm, claiming that there is no visible harm resulting from the action (Sims and Barreto, 2022). This neutralization technique might also be applied by romance fraudsters on the internet, as suggested by Lazarus *et al.* (2023b) in the quote above, when the research reviewed online romance fraud studies with empirical evidence from Ghana and other low-income countries.

The review presented in this paper included 61 articles from the JEC, 51 articles from the JWCCC, and 69 articles from the JFC. The dominant propositions in most articles addressed opportunities to commit and conceal crime. From our perspective of attitudes, only seven articles (12%) addressed willingness in JEC, nine articles (18%) addressed willingness in JWCCC, and six articles (9%) addressed willingness in JFC. Therefore, we have a sample of 7 + 9 + 6 = 22 articles covering the five convenience propositions for willingness. The distribution here is five articles about deviant personal identity, seven articles about rational choice of crime, two articles about learning by association, one article about innocence by justification, and seven articles about innocence by neutralization. Just like the dominance of opportunity articles at the detriment of motive and willingness articles seems unfortunate, the dominance of rationality and neutralization themes seems unfortunate. Therefore, a suggestion for future research is to revisit common attempts by individual and corporate offenders to justify their wrongdoing.

In previous research on justification, Silver and Garofalo (2024: 3) discussed the difference between an excuse and a justification:

> When confronting someone for acting wrongly, they may defend themselves by offering either a justification or an excuse. Scholars have disagreed about exactly how to capture this distinction both in the law and in morality, but a plausible and common way of understanding the distinction in the moral context is to say that an agent who is justified in performing some action has not acted wrongly, and an agent who is excused has acted wrongly but should not be blamed or punished.

Innocent justifications can occur, for example, when an offender feels entitled to financial crime following negative life events (Engdahl, 2015). The perspective of negative life events suggests that events such as divorce, accidents, lack of promotion, and financial problems can cause potential offenders to consider financial crime a convenient solution.

Schnatterly *et al.* (2018) found that offenders might explain their acts of wrongdoing as morally justifiable. They found that deviant chief executive officers refer to pressures and other circumstances that justify their financial wrongdoing.

References

Alcadipani, R. and Medeiros, C.R.O. (2020). When corporations cause harm: A critical view of corporate social irresponsibility and corporate crimes, *Journal of Business Ethics*, 167, 285–297.

Alencar, E.C.N. and Jackson-Green, B. (2023). Applying synthetic control method to estimate the impact of the Lava Jata Operation on the worldwide governance indicators in Brazil, *Journal of White Collar and Corporate Crime*, 4(1), 38–55.

Amos, B., Longpré, N. and Roos, M. (2024). The dark triad of personality: Attitudes and beliefs towards white-collar crime, *Journal of White Collar and Corporate Crime*, 5(1), 58–73.

Artello, K. and Albanese, J.S. (2022). Culture of corruption: Prosecutions, persistence, and desistence, *Public Integrity*, 24, 142–161.

Asomah, J.Y., Dim, E.E., Li, Y. and Cheng, H. (2024). What factors are associated with public corruption perception? Evidence from Canada, *Journal of Financial Crime*, 31(3), 524–544.

Boddy, C.R., Freeman, C. and Karpacheva-Hock, E. (2024). Fraud and corporate psychopaths: The proposition for reintroducing personality traits of the economic crime offender, *Journal of Economic Criminology*, 5, published first online https://doi.org/10.1016/j.jeconc.2024.100081.

Braaten, C.N. and Vaughn, M.S. (2021). Convenience theory of cryptocurrency crime: A content analysis of U.S. federal court decisions, *Deviant Behavior*, 42(8), 958–978.

Budó, M.N. (2021). Corporate crime and the use of science in the case of asbestos: Producing harm through discursive shields, *Journal of White Collar and Corporate Crime*, 2(2), 81–96.

Chaiwat, T. and Yomnak, T. (2024). Criminal behavior on detection and penalty: Experimental evidence from drug market game, *Journal of Financial Crime*, 31(1), 135–145.

Chan, F. and Gibbs, C. (2022). When guardians become offenders: Understanding guardian capability through the lens of corporate crime, *Criminology*, 60, 321–341.

Crank, B.R. (2018). Accepting deviant identities: The impact of self-labeling on intentions to desist from crime, *Journal of Crime and Justice*, 41(2), 155–172.

Cressey, D. (1972). *Criminal Organization: Its Elementary Forms*, Harper and Row, New York, NY.

Cullen, F.T., Graham, A., Jonson, C.L., PIckett, J.T., Sloan, M.M. and Haner, M. (2022). The denier in chief: Faith in Trump and techniques of neutralization in a pandemic, *Deviant Behavior*, 43(7), 829–851.

Dion, M. (2020). Bribery, extortion and "morally ambiguous" leadership in organizations, *Journal of Financial Crime*, 27(4), 1027–1046.

Dodge, M. (2020). A black box warning: The marginalization of white-collar crime victimization, *Journal of White Collar and Corporate Crime*, 1(1), 24–33.

Engdahl, O. (2015). White-collar crime and first-time adult-onset offending: Explorations in the concept of negative life events as turning points, *International Journal of Law, Crime and Justice*, 43(1), 1–16.

Fang, L. and Yang, N. (2024). Measuring deterrence motives in dynamic oligopoly games, *Management Science*, 70(6), 3527–3565.

Galvin, B.M., Lange, D. and Ashforth, B.E. (2015). Narcissistic organizational identification: Seeing oneself as central to the organization's identity, *Academy of Management Review*, 40(2), 163–181.

Goncharov, I. and Peter, C.D. (2019). Does reporting transparency affect industry coordination? Evidence from the duration of international cartels, *The Accounting Review*, 94(3), 149–175.

Gottschalk, P. (2025). Trusted chief executives in convenient white-collar crime, *Crime & Delinquency*, 7(8), 2845–2873.

Gottschalk, P. and Gunnesdal, L. (2018). *White-Collar Crime in the Shadow Economy: Lack of Detection, Investigation, and Conviction Compared to Social Security Fraud*, Palgrave Macmillan, UK: London.

Gottschalk, P. and Kamaei, M. (2024). Understanding business offending: Survey research in Iran, *Journal of Financial Crime*, 31(2), 446–454.

Guebert, K., Bittle, S. and Frauley, J. (2024). Corruption in the news: Complicity in Canadian newspaper claims making, *Journal of White Collar and Corporate Crime*, 5(2), 122–134.

Hagan, J. (2024). Banking on genocide: The racial disparities and patriotic politics of a massive international corruption case, *Journal of White Collar and Corporate Crime*, 5(1), 4–14.

Hoffmann, J.P. (2002). A contextual analysis of differential association, social control, and strain theories of delinquency, *Social Forces*, 81(3), 753–785.

Hsieh, H. and Shannon, S.E. (2005). Three approaches to qualitative content analysis, *Qualitative Health Research*, 15(9), 1277–1288.

Huang, L. and Knight, A.P. (2017). Resources and relationships in entrepreneurship: An exchange theory of the development and effects of the entrepreneur-investor relationship, *Academy of Management Review*, 42(1), 80–102.

Huric-Larsen, J.F. (2023). Cartel formation and the business cycle, *European Competition Journal*, published first online https://doi.org/10.1080/17441056.2023.2234233.

Ingram, P. (2023). Identity multiplicity and the formation of professional network ties, *Academy of Management Journal*, 66(3), 720–743.

Jordanoska, A. (2018). The social ecology of white-collar crime: Applying situational action theory to white-collar offending, *Deviant Behavior*, 39(11), 1427–1449.

Kabra, S. and Gori, S. (2023). Drug trafficking on crypto markets and the role of organized crime groups, *Journal of Economic Criminology*, 2, published first online https://doi.org/10.1016/j.jeconc.2023.100026.

Kakkar, H., Sivanathan, N., and Globel, M.S. (2020). Fall from grace: The role of dominance and prestige in punishment of high-status actors, *Academy of Management Journal*, 63(2), 530–553.

Kaptein, M. and Helvoort, M. (2019). A model of neutralization techniques, *Deviant Behavior*, 40(10), 1260–1285.

Karandikar, S. and Jones, D.N. (2023). From embezzlement to antitrust: White collar crime preferences of the dark triad, *Journal of White Collar and Corporate Crime*, published first online https://doi.org/10.1177/26311309X231210846.

Karimi-Ghartemani, S., Khani, N. and Isfahani, A.N. (2022). Designing a conceptual model for organizational stupidity using a combination of grounded theory and interpretive structural modeling, *Iranian Journal of Management Studies*, 15(3), 549–568.

Lazarus, S., Olaigbe, O., Adeduntan, A. and Dibiana, E.T. (2023a). Cheques or dating scams? Online fraud themes in hip-hop songs across popular music apps, *Journal of Economic Criminology*, 2, published first online https://doi.org/10.1016/j.jeconc.2023.100033.

Lazarus, S., Whittaker, J.M., McGuire, M.R. and Platt, L. (2023b). What do we know about online romance fraud studies? A systematic review of the empirical literature (2000 to 2021), *Journal of Economic Criminology*, 2, published first online https://doi.org/10.1016/j.jeconc.2024.100013.

Lee, J.Y. (2025). Unveiling insider threats in South Korean companies: Causes and countermeasures through convenience theory and perceived punishment, *Deviant Behavior*, published first online https://doi.org/10.1080/01639625.2025.2545442.

Marques, J.A. and Tavares, A.H. (2023). Responsive regulation and tax investigations: The tax investigation diamond model assumptions, *Journal of White Collar and Corporate Crime*, 4(1), 14–23.

McClean, E.J., Martin, S.R., Emich, K.J. and Woodruff, T. (2018). The social consequences of voice: An examination of voice type and gender on status and subsequent leader emergence, *Academy of Management Journal*, 61(5), 1869–1891.

McClelland, P.L., Liang, X. and Barker, V.L. (2010). CEO commitment to the status quo: Replication and extension using content analysis, *Journal of Management*, 36(5), 1251–1277.

McGloin, J.M., Thomas, K.J. and Rowan, Z.R. (2021). Can the group disincentivize offending? Considering opt-out thresholds and decision reversals, *Criminology*, 59, 738–765.

Peixoto, A., Gouveia, T., Sousa, P., Faria, R. and Almeida, P.R. (2023). Dark personality traits and tolerance towards unethical behaviors on entrepreneurship: A comparison between entrepreneurs and non-entrepreneurs, *Journal of White Collar and Corporate Crime*, 4(1), 5–13.

Pontell, H.N., Black, W.K. and Geis, G. (2014). Too big to fail, too powerful to jail? On the absence of criminal prosecutions after the 2008 financial meltdown, *Crime, Law and Social Change*, 61(1), 1–13.

Ramanambonona, A. (2024). An economic approach to deterring foreign exchange offenses: Evidence from Madagascar, *Journal of Economic Criminology*, 3, published first online https://doi.org/10.1016/j.jeconc.2024.100049.

Sajko, M., Boone, C., and Buyl, T. (2021). CEO greed, corporate social responsibility, and organizational resilience to systemic shocks, *Journal of Management*, 47(4), 957–992.

Schnatterly, K., Gangloff, K.A. and Tuschke, A. (2018). CEO wrongdoing: A review of pressure, opportunity, and rationalization, *Journal of Management*, 44(6), 2405–2432.

Schoen, J.L., DeSimone, J.A., Meyer, R.D., Schnure, K.A. and LeBreton, J.M. (2021). Identifying, defining, and measuring justification mechanisms: The implicit biases underlying individual differences, *Journal of Management*, 47(3), 716–744.

Schoultz, I. and Flyghed, J. (2021). "We have been thrown under the bus": Corporate versus individual defense mechanisms against transnational corporate bribery charges, *Journal of White Collar and Corporate Crime*, 2(1), 24–35.

Silver, K. and Garofalo, P. (2024). Excusing corporate wrongdoing and the state of nature, *Academy of Management Review*, published first online https://doi.org/10.5465/amr.2020.0236, 1–23.

Simpson, S.S., Galvin, M.A., Loughran, T.A. and Cohen, M.A. (2023). Perceptions of white-collar crime seriousness: Unpacking and translating attitudes into policy preferences, *Journal of Research in Crime and Delinquency*, 60(5), 582–622.

Sims, R.L. and Barreto, T.S. (2022). In defense of leader misconduct: The use of neutralization techniques by ingroup members, *The Journal of Social Psychology*, 162(5), 621–639.

Siponen, M. and Vance, A. (2010). Neutralization: New insights into the problem of employee information security policy violations, *MIS Quarterly*, 34(3), 487–502.

Sutherland, E.H. (1983). *White Collar Crime – The Uncut Version*, Yale University Press, New Haven, CT.

Sykes, G. and Matza, D. (1957). Techniques of neutralization: A theory of delinquency, *American Sociological Review*, 22(6), 664–670.

Teichmann, F.M.J. and Wittmann, C. (2024). Psychology and white-collar crime – Compliance recommendations based on the social and psychological reality dictating perception, *Journal of Financial Crime*, 31(2), 408–415.

Thaxton, S. and Agnew, R. (2018). When criminal coping is likely: An examination of conditioning effects in general strain theory, *Journal of Quantitative Criminology*, 34, 887–920.

Theoharakis, V., Voliotis, S. and Pollack, J.M. (2021). Going down the slippery slope of legitimacy lies in early-stage ventures: The role of moral disengagement, *Journal of Business Ethics*, 172, 673–690.

Tiwari, M., Ferrill, J., Gepp, A. and Kumar, K. (2023). Factors influencing the choice of technique to launder funds: The APPT framework, *Journal of Economic Criminology*, published first online https://doi.org/10.1016/j.jeconc.2024.100006.

Torres, C.E., D'Alessio, S.J. and Stolzenberg, L. (2024). Marginal deterrence: The effect of illicit incentive on robbery escalation, *Journal of Economic Criminology*, 4, published first online https://doi.org/10.1016/j.jeconc.2024.100062.

Uygur, S.A. and Napier, C.J. (2023). Understanding fraud in the not-for-profit sector: A stakeholder perspective for charities, *Journal of Business Ethics*, published first online https://doi.org/10.1007/s10551-023-05373-5.

Vanhee, A.J. and McNealey, R. (2024). Individual residence and identity theft: How residential characteristics shape exposure and risk of offline and online identity theft victimization, *Journal of Financial Crime*, 31(3), 594–607.

Velásquez-Giraldo, M. Canavire-Bacarreza, G. and Lundberg, A. (2023). Crime variability, peer effects, and economic inequality in social networks, *Journal of Economic Criminology*, 1, published first online https://doi.org/10.1016/j.jeconc.2024.100011.

Vincent, O., Stevenson, A. and Owolabi, A. (2023). Do socio-demographic characteristics of SME entrepreneurs influence their tax (non)compliance behavior? *Journal of Economic Criminology*, 1, published first online https://doi.org/10.1016/j.jeconc.2024.100008.

Wells, J.T. (1997). *Occupational Fraud and Abuse*, Obsidian Publishing Company, Texas: Austin.

Welsh, D.T. and Ordonez, L.D. (2014). The dark side of consecutive high-performance goals: Linking goal setting, depletion, and unethical behavior, *Organizational Behavior and Human Decision Processes*, 123, 79–89.

Wijayanti, D.M., Senjani, Y.P. and Farah, W. (2024). The role of Machiavellian personality, altruistic personality, religiosity, whistleblowing system, and accounting firm size in mitigating fraud intention, *Journal of Financial Crime*, 31(1), 119–134.

Williams, M.L., Levi, M., Burnap, P. and Gundur, R.V. (2019). Under the corporate radar: Examining insider business cybercrime victimization through an application of routine activities theory, *Deviant Behavior*, 40(9), 1119–1131.

Conclusion

Before concluding, it is relevant to reiterate what this book has been all about. For a long time, crime was mainly referred to as violations of laws and regulations. This book takes a criminological rather than a legal view of criminal liability. In a moral sense, an action can be labeled a crime if it satisfies two requirements: (1) people think it is wrong to do and (2) people think it should be punished. Crime is then wrongdoing that requires punishment, while law constitutes statutory principles, which may or may not cover the specific wrongdoing. One reason for the choice of the criminological rather than the legal reference to crime is the variations among jurisdictions. Another reason for the choice is the liability consequences of compliance violations versus conformity violations, where the latter tend to have more serious, sudden, and unpredictable consequences for corporate performance. An important objective of the book is to demonstrate the consequences of conformance violations through a number of case studies.

As argued in this book, responding to conformance pressures regarding norms, values, and ethical issues through adaptation is markedly different from and more successful than responding through strategy. Responding through adaptation is a matter of knowledge readiness, where knowledge is applied in improvisation. Knowledge depth and breadth are important in improvisation, as knowledge represents the fuel that feeds the engine of creative idea generation when communicating with stakeholders. Restoring the social license to operate by conformance needs entrepreneurship based on creative ideas, where entrepreneurs discover, create, or actualize opportunities. Top managers are not necessarily entrepreneurs, as they sometimes are committed to the status quo. Instead, "change champions" in the organization take on the role of entrepreneurs. Change champions apply bottom-up approaches to recovery that typically derive from their own experience. The bottom-up approach to corporate conformance focuses on organizational measures to make deviance less attractive. Bottom-up control refers to the manner in which organizational members can use different types of control mechanisms – such as whistle-blowing, transparency, resource constraints, and organizational culture – to monitor, measure, and evaluate executives' avoidance of deviant behaviors and influence them toward corporate conformance in efficient, effective, and socially acceptable ways. Bottom-up approaches can be informal and flexible systems based on social influence.

Chapter 1 addressed management alignment for the legal license to operate by compliance and organizational alignment for the social license to operate by conformity. Compliance is alignment to avoid violations of legally binding statutes and is typically pursued through formal controls. Conformity is alignment to avoid violations of norms and values among stakeholders and in society in general. Legitimacy stems from the alignment of values and actions with those of a company's stakeholders and society. Business activities are then considered legitimate in the eyes of society. In recent years, conformity rather than compliance has gained attention in executive suites. While compliance with laws, regulations, statutes, and other formal legal frameworks for corporate activity has been on the agenda for decades, conformity with norms, values, ethics, and guidelines expected by stakeholders and others in society has recently become the top priority of executive agendas. An important reason for this shift in focus from compliance to conformity is the speed and severity of damage and harm resulting from breaches and violations of the social license to operate, as compared to violations of the legal license to operate. While a legal process in the criminal justice system addressing corporate wrongdoing tends to last for years before a final outcome is reached, a social process in society addressing corporate misconduct tends to have serious consequences in just a few days after disclosure, exposure, and condemnation. An example is boycotts of companies quickly mobilizing in social and traditional media as a reaction to corporate misconduct.

Chapter 2 addressed corruption in sports as a research topic that has received increased attention and interest in recent years. One of the reasons is the rapidly growing flow of money in sports. Both public and commercial television stations, as well as advertising agencies with their sponsors, are willing to pay much more to broadcast and be visible at popular sporting events. The price to pay for such actors depends on the popularity of each sport based on television viewers and spectators. When popularity grows, so does the price to broadcast, as well as the price to be visible at sporting events. More money involved increases the temptation of corruption, both among potential actors seeking to bribe others to achieve what they want and among potential actors seeking to be bribed to achieve what they desire. There are many causes of corruption in sports. The selection presented in the chapter was based on a literature review examining sport corruption in general, reflecting the situation at the International Biathlon Union (IBU). Seven causes presented there included the rapidly increasing amounts of money involved in sports, the rapidly increasing prestige and fame in hosting major sporting events, the rapidly rising gambling and betting industry aligned with the modern sports industry, the lack of recognition and organizational inclusion of diversity, the lack of compensation for people in leadership positions, the potential for narcissistic leadership styles, and an organizational culture dominated by competition rather than cooperation and secrecy rather than transparency.

Chapter 3 presented a case study of a former president at the IBU. Anders Besseberg was IBU president from 1992 until he was laid off in 2018 based on accusations of wrongdoing. During those years, the sport of biathlon evolved from being a sport for people who were particularly interested in it to becoming one of the most popular winter sports on television. Besseberg is considered the architect of the various successful forms of competition in biathlon, such as the hunting start, joint start, and mixed relays. He elevated the sport of biathlon to new heights during his tenure as president. Having served as president for such a long time, he became a powerful individual with great influence internationally. There were no restrictions on being the union president or how many terms he could serve in such a central position without being replaced. Besseberg has been a central figure in shaping the business, culture, ethics, structure, and compliance of right and wrong at IBU as an organization. The suspected fraud involved the president receiving favors and bribes from Russian biathlon union officials.

Chapter 4 discussed the role of stakeholders in compliance and conformance pressures. It has been argued that sponsors will reconsider their support and possibly withdraw their financial support when the supported entity and events become subject to allegations of economic crime.

The IBU and its world cups and championships have, for a decade, been accused of corruption, and the former president of the union is being prosecuted in court. Yet, the German car manufacturer BMW did not change its position as the main sponsor. In the email exchange presented in that chapter, the compliance officer at BMW responded, "We confirm that BMW AG is the official title sponsor of the BMW IBU World Cup Biathlon". The case study presented in the chapter is interesting, as it illustrates limited stakeholder concerns as long as the sponsor perceives sufficient benefits from the sponsorship. However, the case study also illustrates that the company has some interest in addressing compliance while demonstrating no apparent interest in addressing conformity. In many jurisdictions globally, both the bribed and the briber are considered criminals in a corruption relationship. While the bribed has committed the offense of accepting an improper and undue advantage, the briber has committed the offense of providing such an advantage. There is no necessarily legal requirement that the briber was able to or even successful in influencing the bribed, as legislation varies among jurisdictions. In the current case study of the former IBU president prosecuted in Norway, there was no such requirement. He had at home a BMW X5 car free of charge for his private and exclusive use from 2011 to 2018. In the Norwegian district court, he was convicted of corruption due to the car and other illegitimate benefits he had received. Besseberg appealed the verdict in 2025.

Chapter 5 presented a case study from Norway that supplements previous research in other jurisdictions, such as Australia, Canada, the Netherlands, and the United Kingdom, regarding a lack of justice when corporate investigators conduct internal examinations in client organizations. A university violated its social license to operate due to a lack of conformity when handling personnel issues involving a faculty member. The case is concerned with a university researcher who was investigated after allegations of violating the National Labor Relations Act. Investigators applied a likelihood of fifty percent rather than the criterion of beyond reasonable doubt. There was no real contradiction offered, and many more deviances from a fair process occurred when compared to the public criminal justice system. The presented maturity model, with four stages, is applied to illustrate the low level of investigative performance in the case. This research does not, in any way, claim that the presented case is representative of work by corporate investigators conducting internal examinations in client organizations.

Nevertheless, this research is important, as it illustrates the lack of justice caused by the absence of regulation of the private investigation industry as performed by law firms, audit firms, consulting firms, and others.

Chapter 6 discussed the fraud investigation business. Some corporate investigators hide their work behind the client-attorney privilege. They prevent transparency by claiming secrecy based on that privilege. Yet, corporate examination work has little or nothing to do with legal work. It is detective work to reconstruct past events and sequences of events. It is knowledge work to assess collected information. Corporate investigators should never assess information in terms of evidence to draw conclusions about criminal liability. They should always stop their assessment before drawing any conclusions regarding criminal codes. Therefore, two conformity issues arise related to the client-attorney privilege: The first is the norm violation of hiding work behind the privilege, preventing transparency in society, and the other is crossing the line between their role and the criminal justice system within the jurisdiction. Of course, some investigations and their resulting investigation reports need to be prevented from disclosure for various reasons. However, the attorney-client privilege is not such an acceptable reason for secrecy. Sensitive personal information about individuals, sensitive business secrets within the client organization, and the requirements of the criminal justice system to protect police and prosecution work are some acceptable reasons for maintaining secrecy and preventing investigation disclosure.

Chapter 7 discussed sanctions against Russia from the perspective of compliance and conformity. Russia attacked and invaded Ukraine in the winter of 2022. Countries such as the United States, the United Kingdom, and Canada, as well as multinational organizations such as the European Union, quickly introduced sanctions against Russia, which should represent a penalty for disobeying international law. Western companies that were affected by the sanction regime had to modify or terminate their business activities in and with Russia. This was a matter of compliance. However, many voiced criticisms of companies that continued their business activities without violating their legal licenses to operate. For example, the Yale School of Management in the United States updated, on a daily basis, a list of companies that had terminated their business in Russia, as well as those that remained. The two lists were updated every hour for a while by Professor Jeffrey Sonnenfeld and his research team at the Yale Chief Executive Leadership Institute to reflect new announcements from companies in real time. Some companies on the wrong list quickly informed Yale about their termination of business activities in Russia. This was a matter of conformity.

Chapter 8 discussed sanctions against Myanmar from the perspective of compliance and conformity. The Danish garment producer Bestseller did not violate the legal license to operate, as its manufacturing activities were not subject to sanctions against the military junta in Myanmar. An investigative report by a law firm concluded that the company was indeed compliant. However, negative reactions continued against the company. Eventually, Bestseller withdrew from Myanmar to demonstrate conformity in order to regain and maintain the company's social license to operate. This case study applies the perspective of social license to operate. This perspective suggests that legal and social obligations and expectations represent separate but interacting issues for assessing how business conduct aligns with community norms. While each business enterprise serves a number of purposes in the community, such as employment and goods and services, business conduct has to meet both legal and social requirements to operate. The community does not exist to serve the business enterprise. Rather, each corporate entity exists to serve the community with benefits without violating the legal and social licenses. The social license to operate can be part of a bottom-up as well as an outside-in effort to enhance social control of business activity. Business enterprises attempt to respond to indicate that their activities are not only legally legitimate but also socially legitimate. The expression is often used when a company's activities may face disapproval – especially when such disapproval could result in resistance that might harm its business interests.

Chapter 9 presented the case of a social housing company in Norway, which did not violate its legal license when it entered the luxury and rental markets. However, the norm of building and managing ordinary housing for ordinary people had been violated. A member revolt in the cooperative organization of the company led to the termination of luxury and rental apartments in the future. The termination was necessary to regain the social license to operate by conformity. This aligns with the two perspectives of compliance and conformity, where compliance refers to legal issues and conformity refers to social issues. Economic crime can occur even when no law is violated as long as people perceive it as bad and believe it should be punished. People in this setting include everyone, however, with an emphasis on those who are influenced by or influence the situation. Those being influenced by the actor and those influencing the actor are labeled "stakeholders". Stakeholders have a special role related to conformity. If they believe that an observed action constitutes wrongdoing and that the wrongdoing should be punished, then the action qualifies as a crime. Daniel Kjørberg Siraj was appointed chief executive officer (CEO) at Obos in 2017. His predecessor, Martin Mæland, held the CEO position for 34 years since 1983. He was a social democrat who had a loyal approach to the vision and mission of Obos as a construction cooperative, building ordinary homes for ordinary people. Lars Buer, who held the board chair position, was a trade unionist also committed to the social democracy of Obos, as a member organization for ordinary people.

Chapter 10 reviewed recently published articles in the *Journal of Financial Crime* in 2024, when the journal had published four issues with 69 research articles until the time of writing. While only 12 articles focused on the motives, possibilities, and threats, and only 6 articles focused on attitudes of deviant willingness, surprisingly many – 51 articles – focused on the opportunity structure of committing and concealing financial crime. The review is relevant, as it may illuminate both what seems important and unimportant in understanding management violations of compliance and conformance, and it explores propositions in convenience theory that might deserve attention in future research, considering the convenience triangle's suggestion of motives, opportunities, and attitudes for financial criminals. The theory of convenience for financial crime suggests that offenders have motives of possibilities and threats, opportunities to commit and conceal crime, and attitudes of willingness for deviant behavior driven by choice and innocence. Convenience theory suggests 14 propositions regarding motives, opportunities, and attitudes. In this chapter, research articles from the *Journal of Financial Crime* are reviewed from the perspective of convenience theory. Specifically, the chapter addresses the following research questions: What propositions in convenience theory are supported by published articles in the journal? What aspects of criminal convenience seem to be missing so far in research articles published in the journal?

Chapter 11 combined three academic journals that primarily publish research articles on crime for profit: the *Journal of Economic Criminology*, the *Journal of White Collar and Corporate Crime*, and the *Journal of Financial Crime*. Research articles in these journals are reviewed in this chapter to identify offender attitudes that contribute to a willingness for deviant behavior when committing and concealing economic crimes. The theory of convenience is applied, suggesting five willingness propositions addressing choice (personal identity, rational choice, and learning from others) as well as innocence (justification and neutralization). Deviant personal identity is exemplified by psychopathic and narcissistic traits, as well as Machiavellian personality traits. Rational choice is exemplified by the lack of perceived deterrence. Learning from others is exemplified by differential association. Justification is exemplified by a lack of crime seriousness, while neutralization is exemplified by romance fraudsters in Ghana who cause no perceived harm, as victims in Western countries have access to safety nets such as social welfare and other benefits.

In conclusion, during challenging times of scandals and crises, organizational resilience may contribute to maintaining compliance and conformity. Resilience refers to "the maintenance or quick recovery of mental health during and after stressor exposure" (Ahrens *et al.*, 2024: 1076). Resilience is related to the ability to navigate successfully during disruptive events, where there is "an ability to absorb change and disturbance" and still maintain and uphold a sense of self (Hernes *et al.*, 2025: 74). Corporate conformance in practice is needed to maintain the social license to operate, as discussed in this book. Upon detecting conformance violations, measures are needed to restore conformance and regain the social license to operate. Required measures have to align with the expectations, values, and norms of stakeholders. Successful measures tend to be the result of communication with stakeholders based on creative ideas regarding opportunities for change. Therefore, creativity is an important element when a violation has occurred. Creative ideas are characterized by novelty and usefulness (Choi *et al.*, 2023: 430):

> Novelty describes ideas that are unique and rare; usefulness describes ideas that are appropriate, feasible, and effective. As such, to generate creative ideas, an individual needs to think differently from others to make unique and unusual associations, while also understanding what others will view as appropriate and practical.

As argued in this book, responding to conformance pressures regarding norms, values, and ethical issues through adaptation is markedly different from and more successful than responding through strategy. Responding through adaptation is a matter of knowledge readiness, where knowledge is applied in improvisation. Knowledge depth and breadth are important in improvisation, where knowledge represents the fuel that feeds the engine of creative idea generation when communicating with stakeholders (Mannucci and Yong, 2018; Mannucci *et al.*, 2021).

Restoring the social license to operate by conformance needs entrepreneurship based on creative ideas, where entrepreneurs discover, create, or actualize opportunities (Ramoglou and Tsang, 2016). Top managers are not necessarily entrepreneurs, as they sometimes are committed to the status quo (Behr and Fehre, 2019), "particularly to their organization's current strategy and leadership profile" (Hambrick *et al.*, 1993: 401). Instead, "change champions" in the organization take on the role of entrepreneurs. Change champions apply bottom-up approaches to recovery that typically derive from their own experience. The bottom-up approach to corporate conformance focuses on organizational measures to make deviance less attractive. Bottom-up control refers to the manner in which organizational members can use different types of control mechanisms – such as whistleblowing, transparency, resource constraints, and organizational culture – to monitor, measure, and evaluate executives' avoidance of deviant behaviors and influence them toward corporate conformance in efficient, effective, and socially acceptable ways (Zhong and Robinson, 2021). Bottom-up approaches can be informal and flexible systems based on social influence (Haines *et al.*, 2022).

References

Ahrens, K.F., Schenk, C., Kollmann, B., Puhlmann, L.M.C., Neumann, R.J., Schäfer, S.K. and Reis, D. (2024). Resilience to major life events: Advancing trajectory modeling and resilience factor identification by controlling for background stressor exposure, *American Psychologist*, 79(8), 1076–1091.

Behr, H. and Fehre, K. (2019). CEO succession and the CEO's commitment to the status quo, *Business Research*, 12(2), 355–381.

Choi, Y., Ingram, P. and Han, S.W. (2023). Cultural breath and embeddedness: The individual adoption of organizational culture as a determinant of creativity, *Administrative Science Quarterly*, 68(2), 429–464.

Haines, F., Bice, S., Einfeld, C. and Sullivan, H. (2022). Countering corporate power through social control: What does a social license offer? *The British Journal of Criminology*, 62, 184–199.

Hambrick, D.C., Geletkanycz, M.A. and Fredrickson, J.W. (1993). Top executive commitment to status quo: Some tests of its determinants, *Strategic Management Journal*, 14(6), 401–418.

Hernes, T., Blagoev, B., Kunisch, S. and Schultz, M. (2025). From bouncing back to bouncing forward: A temporal trajectory model of organizational resilience, *Academy of Management Review*, 50(1), 72–92.

Mannucci, P.V. and Yong, K. (2018). The differential impact of knowledge depth and knowledge breadth on creativity over individual careers, *Academy of Management Journal*, 61(5), 1741–1763.

Mannucci, P.V., Orazi, D.C. and Valck, K. (2021). Developing improvisation skills: The influence of individual orientations, *Administrative Science Quarterly*, 66(3), 612–658.

Ramoglou, S. and Tsang, E.W.K. (2016). A realist perspective of entrepreneurship: Opportunities as propensities, *Academy of Management Review*, 41, 410–434.

Zhong, R. and Robinson, S.L. (2021). What happens to bad actors in organizations? A review of actor-centric outcomes of negative behavior, *Journal of Management*, 47(6), 1430–1467.

Index

A

acceptance of business operations, 12
accountability, 6, 41
Aftenposten, 148
Aggarwal, R., 218
Agnew, R., 166, 196
Alon, A., 7
Alstadheim, K.B., 152, 155
Amos, B., 244
Anderssen, Harald Benestad, 201
Andreassen, Gunn Margit, 62
anti-bribery, 70
Antonsen, H.H., 10
Arikan, G., 83
Armengou, J., 22
Arvnes, E., 202
Asfaldo, D.B., 174, 178–180, 199–200
Asomah, Y.J., 225, 247–249
asset concealment, 218
Association of Certified Fraud Examiners (ACFE), 117
athletes, 36
attorney-client privilege, 140
Aung San Suu Kyi, 166
Australia, 135, 137
Azerbaijan, 82

B

Baba, S., 199
Baer, M.H., 3
Baumann, Arne, 196
Beebeejaun, A., 222
Benjaminsen, Arne, 122
Benson, K., 217
Benson, M.L., 182
Berg, Fredrik, 52–53
Berger, Anastasia, 77
Bergh, H., 72
Besseberg, Anders, xi–xiii, 51, 53–55, 57, 61–62, 79, 81, 84, 88, 134, 259
Bestseller, 164–170, 262
Beukel, J., 200
Biathlon sponsor, 84–89
blacklisted companies, 148–151
Blatter, Philippe, 61
BMW, 45, 59, 61, 67–89, 260
Boddy, C.R., 242
Bonnesen, Birgitte, 2, 134
Borgarting Court of Appeal, xiii
Borgen, Thomas, 2, 134
Borrell, Joseph, 153
Borrows, Gavin, 136
bottom-up control, 265

Boutilier, R.G., 178, 180, 184
boycotted companies, 148–151
Bradshaw, Stephen, 63
Brooks, G., 135
Brother Elephants, 35–36
Budó, M.N., 245
Bundy, J., 181, 199
business integrity, 183
business legitimacy, 21–24
Button, M., 135, 137

C

Canada, 147, 261
Carlos, W.C., 12–13
Cattani, G., 13
Chadwick, S., 69, 73
Chan, F., 139
change champions, 258, 265
charade, 133
Chen, H., 8
Cheong, C., 68–74
chief executive officer (CEO), 8, 85, 166, 192, 263
Chinese Professional Baseball League (CPBL), 35
choice, 212
Christoffersen, J., 169
client organization, 140
CMS Kluge report, 99–111, 114–115, 119, 122–125, 140
cognition, 241
cognitive legitimacy, 23
committees, 189
compliance, xi, xiv, xvii, 1–10, 41, 81–83, 138–139, 154–158, 182, 258–259
compliance audits, 5
compliance officer, 74–81
compliance risk assessment, 5
conformance, 10–11, 139, 257
conformance pressures, 259
conformance violations, xvii
conformity, xiv, 1, 20, 81–83, 135, 139, 151–158, 258
conformity deviance, 174–176
conformity violation, 15
consequential legitimacy, 22
content analysis, 213–214, 241
contradiction, 103
convenience, 8–9
convenience themes, 164–167
convenience theory, xviii, 18, 209, 227, 239–240, 263
convenience triangle, 18–19
Coop, 149, 152, 155
corporate compliance, 3, 7
corporate conformity, 20
corporate deviance, 12
corporate investigators, 133–141, 261
corporate offenders, 214–216
corporate social responsibility (CSR), 19–20, 167
corruption, 33–39, 45–43, 133, 138, 258–259
corruption legislation, 57
Cowen, A.P., 9
credibility, 20, 41, 178, 180, 186
credit card, 219
Crepaz, M., 83
crime, xi, 173, 216–224, 242, 246–247, 257
crime convenience triangle, 210–213
crime justification, 248–251
crime motives, 214–216
crime-for-profit research, 239
criminal conformity deviance, 174–176
criminal investigation, 60
criminal justice system, 1, 62–63, 141, 261
criminal law, 13
criminal market collapse, 223
criminology, 173

crowdfunding, 222
cryptocurrency, 220
culture, 37
cumulative pyramid model, 178, 180
cyber fraud, 221
cyberspace, 220

D
Dahl, Maria Bache, xv
Dahlin, Olle, 77
Dahlkamp, J., 78
Danish Ministry of Foreign Affairs, 162
Danlami, I.A., 214
dark triad, 243–244
de facto transparency, 83
defense lawyers at appeal, 52–54
Demuijnck, G., 175, 185
Denmark, xvii
Der Spiegel, 78
deterrence, 242
deviance, 12
deviant behavior willingness, 239–265
deviant personal identity, xviii, 223, 239, 242–246
DiBari, D.D., 134
digital peer-to-peer (P2P) lending platforms, 217
diversity, 36–37
Djupvik, Morten, 86
Dodge, M., 245
Dubber, A., 218
due process, 102
Durand, R., 2, 12, 17, 181–182

E
economic crime, 53, 173, 211, 262
emotional concerns, 71
empirical education, 137–138
enforcement, 70
Engdahl, O., 8
enthusiasm, 106
European Union, 153, 162, 261
examination maturity assessment, 200–202
external compliance, 8

F
Facebook, 177
Færø, Magnus Johan, 120, 123
Fasterling, B., 175, 185
feedback, 106
Feridun, M., 220
FIFA World Cup, 34, 73
Fiss, P.C., 21
Flyghed, J., 246
Fotaki, M., 4, 6–7
fraud investigation business, 133–141
fraud investigation report, 167–169
fraud triangle, 239
Freia, 148–149, 155

G
gambling, 35–36
Gardiner, S., 41
Garg, S., 218
Garofalo, P., 39, 212, 250
German, 74
Germany, 72, 82
Geuns, L., 200
Gibbs, C., 139
Gimse, Mikkel Toft, 52–53, 56
Goldbarsht, D., 217
Gori, S., 242
Gottschalk, P., 60, 78, 125, 134, 162, 182
Gözen, Irep, 118, 120
gray zones, xi
Greece, 153
guardianship, 219–223
Guebert, K., 224, 244
Gupta, C.M., 215

H
Hagan, J., 245
Haines, F., 182–183
Hamerton, C., 78, 125
harassment accusations, 95–126
Harvard University, 98
Helgaker, Eivind, 85
Hersel, M.C., 2
high-status offender, 216
Hjejle, Bruun, 134
Hjort, Christian B., 52–53, 56
Holch Povlsen, Anders, 165
Holch Povlsen, Troels, 165
homogeneity, 14–15
homogenization, 17
housing, 173–202
Hovda, Kjell, 53
Hungary, 153

I
Ice Communications, 58, 84–89
inclusion, 36–37
individual offenders, 215–216
Industrial Workers Federation of Myanmar (IWEM), 169
IndustryALL Global Union, 169
Infront Sport & Media, 61
Ingebo, Kari Aasen, 56
innocence, 212, 243
institutional theory, 18, 182
integrity, 40–41, 55, 133, 139
internal investigation outcome, 192–193
International Biathlon Union (IBU), xi–xii, 33–34, 37, 42–43, 51, 54–55, 60–61, 67, 133, 259
International War Sponsors, 156
investigation compliance, 138–139
investigation conformity, 139–141
Iqbal, F., 71

J
Jennings, A., 73
Jeong, S., 14
Jie, X., 216
Jones, D.N., 244
Journal of Economic Criminology (JEC), 239–240, 242–243, 246–248, 263
Journal of Financial Crime (JFC), 209–227, 239, 263
Journal of White Collar and Corporate Crime (JWCCC), 239–241, 243–246, 263
justice, 107
justification, 38–39, 212, 224–225, 245, 247

K
Kabra, S., 242
Kapend, R., 135–137, 139
Karandikar, S., 244
Kasim, E.S., 222
Keil, M., 223
Kemsley, D., 217
Kielland, Jacob Christie, 176
King, M., 134, 137
Knudsen, T.H.R., 202
Koenigstorfer, J., 42, 59, 72–73, 88
Kofod, Jeppe, 163
Koller, G., 5
Kourula, A., 69
KPMG, 140, 181, 192–193, 201–202
Kraus, Stefan, 60
Kulczycki, W., 42, 59, 72–73, 88
Kushchenko, Sergey, xii
Kvikk Lunsj, 148, 150–151

L
Lange, D., 69
Latsch, G., 78
law violations, xvi, 102
Lazarus, S., 249–250

learning, 224, 243, 247
legal license, 258
legislation, 3
legitimacy, xvi, 1, 178, 185–186, 258
legitimate resource access, 217–218
Lehman, D.W., 3
Levi, M., 210
Lewis, B.W., 12–13
Lilli, Marco, 96, 99–100, 102, 105, 107–108, 124, 134, 140
Lindqvist, H., 126
Liu, X., 38
Lord, N., 210
Lumineau, F., 24
Lund, Jacob, 89

M
Machiavellian personality, 43, 223, 248
Machiavellianism, 243
Madsen, Ø., 10
Mæland, Martin, 263
Magableh, S., 214
Mahadew, B., 220
Maher, R., 4
Mangold, F., 24
Margit, Gunn, 62
Marques, J.A., 246
Martinsen, K.D., 154
Maslow, A.H., 195
match-fixing, 35–36
maturity assessment, 100–116
Maulidiyah, D.N., 215
McDonald, Jacqueline, 136
McLaren, R.H., 55
Meerts, C.A., 134
mega-sport event syndrome, 59, 88
Melé, D., 22
member revolt, 173–202
Menz, M., 219
Meyer, J.W., 21
Mikkelsen, M.S., 169
miscarriage of justice, 63
Moe, Hedvig, 157
Mohliver, A., 139, 222
Mondelez International, 147
moral concerns, 71
moral disengagement, 38
moral legitimacy, 22
Morrison, J., 176
Murvold, Jan, 124
Myanmar, 161–170, 262
Myanmar Economic Holdings Limited (MEHL), 163
Myburgh, D.C., 219

N
Napier, C.J., 13
narrative, 118
National Investigation Committee, 120
National Labor Relations Act, 95, 260
Neuberger, I., 21
neutralization, 213, 225, 239–240, 243, 245, 247–248
Nguyen, N.T., 221
Nilsson, E.C., 174, 178–180, 199–200
Nortje, J.G.J., 219
Norway, xiv, 57, 74, 84, 95, 97–99, 102, 108, 135, 189, 260, 262
Norwegian Biathlon Union, 58
Norwegian Broadcasting Corporation, 179
Norwegian Center for Molecular Medicine, 98–99
Norwegian Central Bank, 156
Norwegian Labor Inspection Authority, 101
Norwegian law, 118
Norwegian Ministry of Foreign Affairs, 155
Norwegian Oil Fund, 151, 156

Norwegian Supreme Court, xiii
Norwegian Working Environment Act, 102

O
Oberhauser, M., 21
Obos, 174, 176–181, 188–190, 193–195, 263
offender convenience assessment, 193–200
offender-search theory, 224, 246
offense-based approaches, 226
Olujobi, O.J., 219
Omega, xii
Ondrackova, A., 71
online fraudsters, 249
Opøien, Ingvild, 120, 125
Ordonez, M., 6
organizational compliance, 2
organizational conformity, xvii, 10–21
organizational deviance, 14
organizational integrity, 40
Orskaug, Oliver, 52–53
Oslo Court Trial, 118–126
Owusu, G.M.Y., 215

P
Paternoster, R., 166
Pedersen, E.R.G., 15
Peixoto, A., 244
perceptions, 2
personal legitimacy, 22
personal responsibility, 222
Pfarrer, M.D., 182, 199
Philippou, C., 69–70
Pilgaard, M.S., 134, 140
Pontell, H.N., 4
Prabowo, H.Y., 223
pragmatic legitimacy, 22
Pratt, M.G., 24
pressure, 215
problematic internal investigation, 116–118
procedural legitimacy, 22
professionalization, 16
prostitution, xiv
psychopathic individuals, 244
Punch, M., 59, 89
Putra, I.P.M.J.S., 214
Putri, C.M., 223

Q
Quality Living Residential (QLR), 192

R
Rahman, M.J., 216
Ramanambonona, A., 242
rational choice theory, xviii, 38, 264
rational concerns, 71
rationalization, 213, 240
regulatory rollback schemes, 220
reliability, 111
Resch, Nicole, 59
research article, 241
Research Ethics Committee, 120
resilience, 264
resources, 20
risk assessment, 5
Roberts, S., 83
Rodchenkov, Grigory, 55
Rooney, D., 181
Rose, Alison, 2
rotten apple metaphor, 58–63
Rowan, B., 21
rule complexity, 3
Russia, 147–158, 261
Russian Biathlon Federation, xii
Ruyter, Knut W., 97

S
Saarela, Janna, 123
Saenz, C., 170, 181, 184

Sala, G.R., 24
Sale, H.A, 170, 184, 187
Samherji, 9–10
sanctions, 161–170
Sanden, Gunnar Andre, 56
Sandlie, Irene, 122
Scandinavian Airlines System (SAS), 148, 155–156
Scherer, A.G., 4
Schilke, O., 24
Schmid, Volker, 60, 77
Schnatterly, K., 251
Schneider, A., 4
Schoultz, I., 246
self-identify, 18
self-regulatory processes, 38
Sihombing, R.P., 214
Silver, K., 39, 212, 250
Singh, C., 217
Skjelbreid, Liv Grete, 62
Smestad, Marthe Stømner, 56
social conflict theory, 61
social conformity pressure, 12–13
social contract theory, 175
social control agents, 13
social deterioration, 218–219
social license, 139, 163–164, 169–170, 175, 177, 183
social license recovery measures, 181–187
social responsibility, 19
socialization, 16–17
Solbakk, Jan Helge, 123
Soltes, E., 8
Sonnenfeld, Jeffrey, 147
sponsors, 42, 45, 68–74, 83
sport, 33–39, 45–43, 51–63
sportswashing, 82–83
stakeholder, 12, 17–18, 42, 68–74, 174, 187–192, 259
Stang, F., 194
status, 211–212
Stephansen, E., 180
Stepien, B., 20
Stiernstedt, P., 135
stockbrokers, 221
Stokke, O.M., 154
Strandli, Martin, 176
structural legitimacy, 22
substance, 20
substantive conformity, 182
substantive CSR, 20
Sudarwanto, A.S., 220
Sunde, L., 96, 99–100, 102, 105, 107–108, 134, 140
Sutherland, E.H., 227, 248
Svarstad, J., 120
symbolic conformity, 16, 182
symbolic CSR, 19
symbolic responses, 2
symbolism, 16
system strategy, 109

T

Tan, V., 218
Tavares, A.H., 246
Taylor, J., xiii–xiv, 34, 55, 62, 133–134
Teekay Offshore, xv
Teichmann, F.M.J., 217, 248
thematic analysis, 110, 187
Thomson, L., 178, 180, 184
Tiwari, M., 242
Toftøy-Lohne, Vidar, 56
Tolstedt, Carrie, 2
Tønnessen, Ingebjørg, 124
Torres, C.E, 242
transparency, 70, 81–83
Trautendorfer, J., 83
trust, 186

U

Ukraine, 148, 152–153, 156
UN Human Rights Council, 163

United Kingdom (UK), 147, 261
United Nations (UN), 162, 167
United States (US), 7, 43, 147, 261
University of Oslo (UiO), 97, 107–108, 112, 118, 120, 150
Uygur, S.A., 13

V

Vaagan, Anne-Marte Brevig, 124
validity, 111
Veggeland, Andreas, 85
Velásquez-Giraldo, M., 243, 248
Verschuuren, P., 71
Vincent, O., 242
vulnerability, 186

W

Waterson, J., 139
Weber, P.M., 20
whistleblowing, 42, 71, 223
white-collar crime (WCC), 8, 244
willingness, 182
willingness attitudes, 223–225
Witold Banka, 51
Wittmann, C., 248
workplace deviance, 7
World Anti-Doping Agency (WADA), 51, 58
World War II, 200

X

Xiaomi Corporation, 149

Y

Yale Chief Executive Leadership Institute, 147, 261
Yale School of Management, 147
Yebisi, T.E., 219

Z

Zajac, E.J., 21

www.ingramcontent.com/pod-product-compliance
Lightning Source LLC
LaVergne TN
LVHW051052210926
848486LV00002B/80
9781800619500